DICK LEONARD is an historian, journalist and author and a former Labour MP. A former Assistant Editor of *The Economist*, he has also worked for the *Observer*, the BBC, the Centre for European Policy Studies, the universities of Essex and Brussels (ULB) and the Fabian Society. His many books include, notably, *The Great Rivalry: Gladstone and Disraeli* and *A History of British Prime Ministers: Walpole to Cameron*.

MARK GARNETT is Senior Lecturer in Politics at Lancaster University. Among numerous publications, he is the author of *From Anger to Apathy: The British Experience Since 1975*, and co-author of *Keith Joseph: A Life* (with Andrew Denham), and *Splendid! Splendid! The Authorized Biography of Willie Whitelaw* (with Ian Aitken).

Titans

Fox vs. Pitt

DICK LEONARD
&
MARK GARNETT

I.B. TAURIS

LONDON · NEW YORK

Published in 2019 by
I.B.Tauris & Co. Ltd
London • New York
www.ibtauris.com

ISBN: 978 1 78453 369 4
eISBN: 978 1 78672 577 6
ePDF: 978 1 78673 577 5

A full CIP record for this book is available from the British Library
A full CIP record is available from the Library of Congress

Library of Congress Catalog Card Number: available

Text design and typesetting by Tetragon, London
Printed and bound in Great Britain

For Irène,
always an inspiration

Contents

CONTENTS

List of Illustrations

Preface

CHARLES James Fox and William Pitt the Younger died more than two hundred years ago – in 1806, within a few months of each other – but in important respects their rivalry has never ended. Most obviously, they personify the timeless theme of government versus opposition. Pitt, after all, held office for almost the whole of his adult life, and over the same years Fox was chiefly occupied by the struggle to displace him. If Pitt is rightly judged to be one of Britain's greatest prime ministers, Fox undoubtedly ranks very high among leaders of the Opposition. For those who think that politics is about accepting responsibility for decisions which are often difficult, Pitt is a natural hero; but Fox's memory will be equally dear to anyone who understands the importance of a viable 'government-in-waiting', to prevent office holders from abusing their position.

Yet the enduring relevance of the Pitt/Fox rivalry goes far beyond the contest between 'ins' and 'outs', which after all takes place to some extent in all political systems. The two men are also widely regarded as embodiments of crucial principles. If Fox was doomed to spend most of his career in opposition, his supporters argue, this was largely because he was the unflinching champion of the underdog – the patron saint of just causes whose time was yet to come. One of these causes, the abolition of the slave trade, was coming close to realisation at the time of his death, thanks in large part to his passionate support. He had been a doughty defender of civil rights, even at the risk of his own freedom, at a time when they seemed in grave danger. He denounced a corrupt electoral system, and continued to argue in favour of a wider franchise while others were abandoning the case for reform because it was equated with support for the principles of the French Revolution. Above all, he was an eloquent advocate of peaceful negotiation when others were succumbing to war fever.

For many lovers of British political history, this record is far more glorious than any number of election victories – particularly since the elections in question were rigged in favour of the established order. This, indeed, has been the orthodox verdict of historians for most of the period since Fox's death. By contrast, Pitt is usually portrayed as being on the wrong side of all these controversies; even worse, he is said to have flirted with some of them when it suited him to do so, before giving them up when they became inconvenient. Of course, this means that Pitt played a crucial role in building Fox's legend, as a kind of anti-Fox, standing in the way of progress. Understandably, though, he has received very little credit for that. All too often, Pitt's defenders have had to take refuge in hypothetical scenarios, insisting that the implementation of Fox's ideas would have plunged Britain into revolution or condemned it to defeat at the hands of the French.

Perhaps the biggest problem for the Pitt camp is that their hero, while not lacking in charisma, was up against one of the most lovable figures in British political history. Even Fox's opponents had to acknowledge his personal charm, which meant that some followers who lost faith in his judgement found it very difficult to desert him. In sharp contrast, Pitt alienated some powerful supporters by failing to treat them with common courtesy. While Fox's big-hearted personality was in tune with the cultural products of the Romantic age, Pitt could seem like a cold fish even to his contemporaries.

Of course, the real story of these two parliamentary titans was more complicated than these generalisations suggest. For example, Fox was prepared to compromise to some extent in order to realise his ambition of holding high office, and Pitt never entirely abandoned his original hope of making Britain a fairer, freer and better-governed nation. In fact, on close examination the similarities between the two rivals were more striking than the contrasts. At the most basic level, both were superlative orators who, from their veneration of Greek and Roman exemplars, believed that audiences could be swayed by argument (even when they knew that most of the votes had been decided in advance of the parliamentary contest). In their different ways, both had been earmarked for political stardom by their doting parents. Both were natural leaders who were reluctant to take direction from any colleague, however eminent. This, of course, explains why they were always rivals, rather than allies. But on some issues – particularly the slave trade – they were able to join forces, providing tantalising glimpses of what might have been.

Thus the story of Pitt and Fox is worth retelling for its own sake, since by any reckoning these were extraordinary individuals. Since their careers coincided, they are obvious candidates for a 'dual biography'. The main difficulty, ironically, is their ability to evoke strong feelings so many years after the close of their careers. Even if the real Charles Fox was not entirely preoccupied by principle, and Pitt the Younger thought that politics was more than just 'the art of the possible', there is enough truth in these stereotyped views to regard their rivalry as a litmus test of political attitudes. As a result, historians as well as readers find it natural to identify themselves as 'Pittites' or 'Foxites', making it difficult to be fair to each of the protagonists in a single volume. Though valuable in many respects, the previous book-length attempt to chart the rivalry over two generations (first published in 1946) is unashamedly 'Foxite'.[1] More recently, John Campbell included a vivid and typically insightful account, but this represents just one chapter in a more general survey of political rivalries.[2]

Campbell's account is particularly noteworthy for its emphasis on the contemporary relevance of the parliamentary duel between Pitt and Fox. Yet his book appeared a few years after a BBC survey of 'Great Britons' which suggested that both of the protagonists had faded into obscurity. Neither of them appeared in the top 100. Admittedly, they were in good company: Gladstone and Disraeli were also overlooked, along with Pitt's father, the Earl of Chatham, who in 1912 had been ranked by the historian Sir George Trevelyan as possibly 'the greatest of Englishmen' and one of the outstanding individuals in the whole of world history.[3] But if Pitt and Fox had been available to comment on the survey, they would have been more surprised by the *inclusions*. Pitt would have been glad to see Lord Nelson in a prominent place, and overjoyed that his close friend William Wilberforce was in the top 30. His feelings about the popularity of the radical Thomas Paine (number 34, six places behind Wilberforce) would have been distinctly mixed, though Fox would not have minded much. Yet both of the rivals would have been puzzled (if not offended) by the tendency of the British public to commemorate individuals who are associated with specific causes, rather than the political leaders who either championed or obstructed them. The Wilberforce example is particularly instructive here. He was, of course, an MP himself, but he depended crucially on more senior politicians. If Fox proved more effective than Pitt in his practical support for the abolition of slavery, it was Pitt who suggested to Wilberforce that this campaign would be a suitable outlet for his energies. And while slavery was important to both Pitt and Fox, they were far more than single-issue crusaders. Pitt, for example, would have been entitled to protest that although Lord Nelson deserved most of the credit for his victories, he would never have achieved immortality without the prime minister's support, not least in the matter of ensuring an adequate supply of ships.

Like everything else, historical figures pass in and out of fashion. Pitt once said that no one could understand Fox's success as an orator without witnessing one of his speeches and falling under the spell cast by 'the magician's wand'.[4] Neither of these parliamentary magicians can perform to a modern audience – even the written record of their speeches is imperfect, because of the reporting restrictions of the time. Nevertheless, even the inadequate texts which have survived testify to the sheer brilliance of the rivals, who could outperform any other MPs even when they arrived at the House of Commons after a night of gambling (Fox) or the worse for wear for liquor (certainly true of Pitt on occasion, and probably applicable to Fox now and again). But these were not mere windbags; in their various ways they left constructive legacies and inspired future generations of politicians beyond the parties which cherished their memories (Pitt for the Conservatives, Fox for the Liberals).

Obviously *we* think that Pitt and Fox both deserved to be included in the BBC survey, which (for understandable reasons) featured a number of people who are unlikely to attract many votes in future polls. The present book was inspired by a belief that the importance of the rivalry between Pitt and Fox can only be appreciated when their careers are considered in a single volume. We cannot claim to have escaped from the tendency to take sides in the duel, but by working in collaboration we hope that we have kept our preferences within acceptable limits. We cannot – alas! – make the shades of Fox and Pitt shake hands across the centuries, but at least we can hope to persuade their contemporary partisans to approach the subject with a little more sympathetic understanding.

Authors' Note

T HE authors, each of whom has contributed almost exactly 50 per cent of the text, are grateful to a number of friends and colleagues who have helped to make it possible. These include Dr John Leonard and Professor David Denver, who kindly read several chapters and made valuable suggestions for improving the book, our copy-editor, Sarah Terry, who could not have been more diligent and creative in putting the book into an acceptable state, Alex Billington and his excellent team of typesetters at Tetragon, and our editor at I.B.Tauris, Jo Godfrey, who was unfailingly encouraging and showed exemplary patience in waiting for the receipt of the MS, which was seriously overdue. Any errors or misjudgements which have survived their scrutiny are entirely the responsibility of the authors.

Warm thanks are also due to the galleries who generously granted permission to reproduce pictures of which they own the copyright. Eighteen of them come from the National Portrait Gallery, and one each from the National Gallery of Ireland and a private collection.

The Grenville and Pitt Families

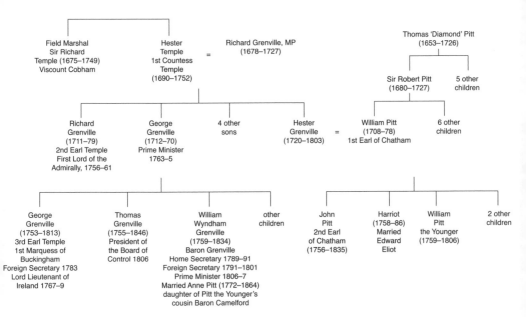

Field Marshal
Sir Richard
Temple (1675–1749)
Viscount Cobham

Hester
Temple
1st Countess
Temple
(1690–1752)
=
Richard Grenville, MP
(1678–1727)

Thomas 'Diamond' Pitt
(1653–1726)

Sir Robert Pitt
(1680–1727)

5 other
children

Richard
Grenville
(1711–79)
2nd Earl Temple
First Lord of the
Admirally, 1756–61

George
Grenville
(1712–70)
Prime Minister
1763–5

4 other
sons

Hester
Grenville
(1720–1803)
=
William Pitt
(1708–78)
1st Earl of Chatham

6 other
children

George
Grenville
(1753–1813)
3rd Earl Temple
1st Marquess of
Buckingham
Foreign Secretary 1783
Lord Lieutenant of
Ireland 1767–9

Thomas
Grenville
(1755–1846)
President of
the Board of
Control 1806

William
Wyndham
Grenville
(1759–1834)
Baron Grenville
Home Secretary 1789–91
Foreign Secretary 1791–1801
Prime Minister 1806–7
Married Anne Pitt (1772–1864)
daughter of Pitt the Younger's
cousin Baron Camelford

other
children

John
Pitt
2nd Earl
of Chatham
(1756–1835)

Harriot
(1758–86)
Married
Edward
Eliot

William
Pitt
the Younger
(1759–1806)

2 other
children

The Fox and Lennox Families

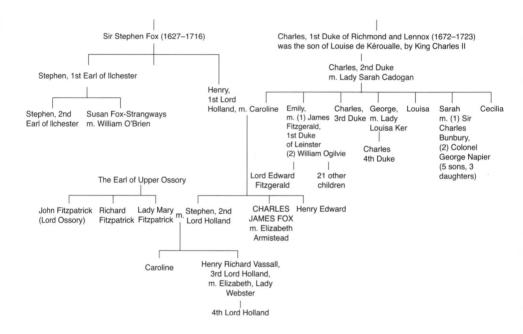

Sir Stephen Fox (1627–1716)

Charles, 1st Duke of Richmond and Lennox (1672–1723) was the son of Louise de Kéroualle, by King Charles II

Stephen, 1st Earl of Ilchester

Charles, 2nd Duke m. Lady Sarah Cadogan

Henry, 1st Lord Holland, m. Caroline

Stephen, 2nd Earl of Ilchester

Susan Fox-Strangways m. William O'Brien

Emily, m. (1) James Fitzgerald, 1st Duke of Leinster (2) William Ogilvie

Charles, 3rd Duke

George, m. Lady Louisa Ker

Louisa

Sarah m. (1) Sir Charles Bunbury, (2) Colonel George Napier (5 sons, 3 daughters)

Cecilia

Charles 4th Duke

Lord Edward Fitzgerald

21 other children

The Earl of Upper Ossory

John Fitzpatrick (Lord Ossory)

Richard Fitzpatrick

Lady Mary Fitzpatrick

m.

Stephen, 2nd Lord Holland

CHARLES JAMES FOX m. Elizabeth Armistead

Henry Edward

Caroline

Henry Richard Vassall, 3rd Lord Holland, m. Elizabeth, Lady Webster

4th Lord Holland

xviii

The House of Hanover

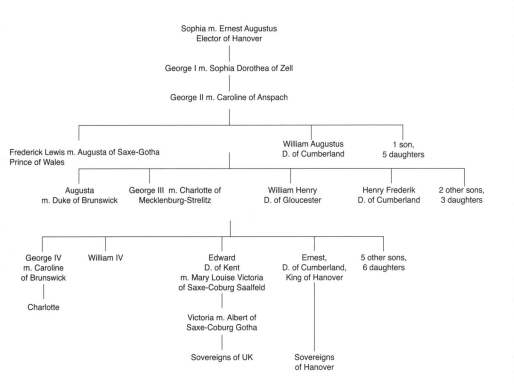

Sophia m. Ernest Augustus
Elector of Hanover

George I m. Sophia Dorothea of Zell

George II m. Caroline of Anspach

Frederick Lewis m. Augusta of Saxe-Gotha
Prince of Wales

William Augustus
D. of Cumberland

1 son,
5 daughters

Augusta
m. Duke of Brunswick

George III m. Charlotte of
Mecklenburg-Strelitz

William Henry
D. of Gloucester

Henry Frederik
D. of Cumberland

2 other sons,
3 daughters

George IV
m. Caroline
of Brunswick

William IV

Edward
D. of Kent
m. Mary Louise Victoria
of Saxe-Coburg Saalfeld

Ernest,
D. of Cumberland,
King of Hanover

5 other sons,
6 daughters

Charlotte

Victoria m. Albert of
Saxe-Coburg Gotha

Sovereigns of UK

Sovereigns
of Hanover

1

The Parliamentary Cockpit

THE best-known and longest-running rivalry in British political history was undoubtedly that between William Ewart Gladstone and Benjamin Disraeli, which dominated British politics for several decades in the nineteenth century.[1] But running it a close second was that between Charles James Fox and William Pitt the Younger, some eighty to a hundred years earlier. If you take into account the earlier feud between their respective fathers, Henry Fox (Lord Holland) and the elder Pitt (Earl Chatham), of which this was to some extent effectively a continuation, this went on far longer and arguably had an even greater influence on British politics. Much more so than between Gladstone and Disraeli, it was entirely a parliamentary contest, and the cockpit in which they fought was the House of Commons. In this pre-railway age it was not practical to criss-cross the country holding rallies and mass meetings to put political arguments directly to citizens; in fact, Charles James Fox was reported to have spoken to his first ever public meeting on 27 January 1780, 12 years after his first election to Parliament.[2]

What sort of body was the House of Commons in the mid-to-late eighteenth century, and who were its members? The answers to these questions are contained in Lewis Namier's groundbreaking book, *The Structure of Politics at the Accession of George III*, first published in 1929 but still a key text for all students of eighteenth-century politics. Namier described an assembly whose formal structure had scarcely changed since the reign of Henry VI in the mid-fifteenth century, despite the political upheavals of the seventeenth century and the arrival of the Hanoverian dynasty in 1714. Formally, the powers of the Commons were no greater than those of the House of Lords, although since the days of Charles I the informal balance had undoubtedly shifted in favour of the 'Lower Chamber'.

In 1760, when George III mounted the throne, the House of Commons had 558 members, representing 314 constituencies. Of these MPs, 489 represented English constituencies, 34 Welsh constituencies and 45 Scottish. All but a handful of the English constituencies returned two members, those in Wales and Scotland only one. The two universities of Oxford and Cambridge each had two members, elected by their graduates whether or not they were resident in those two cities.

The basis of membership had not changed from that of the very first Parliaments summoned by Simon de Montfort in 1264–5, which were attended by knights (originally four) to represent each of the counties and two burgesses chosen from the boroughs. There were relatively few of these at the time, but each succeeding monarch granted borough status to more and more towns until the total number was nearly 200 by the time of Henry VI's reign, when the representation was frozen. During the next 300 years the distribution of the population radically changed, with many once flourishing boroughs declining sharply – particularly in sea ports and in the county of Cornwall – while major new cities such as Birmingham, Leeds and Sheffield had no separate representation. Despite being restricted to two representatives, all of the counties had significant numbers of voters, ranging from 800 in Rutland to 20,000 in Yorkshire. This was because the property qualification for voters was relatively wide in the counties, being allotted to 'forty-shilling freeholders', that is, owners of freehold properties with an annual rental value of £2. That was a considerable sum in 1430, when Parliament set the limit, but over 300 years of inflation it meant that many more people were now qualified to vote. This was not the case in borough constituencies, where the rules were set according to monarchical whim and local custom. According to Namier,

> broadly speaking they can be divided into five types. There were boroughs: (1) with what practically amounted to universal [male] franchise;

(2) where the franchise was in those paying scot and lot [local taxes]; (3) where the vote was in the freemen; (4) where the franchise was limited to the corporation; (5) where the franchise was attached to certain houses or plots of ground called burgages.[3]

In the eighteenth century there were only about a dozen borough constituencies in category 1 and around 40 in category 2, where the franchise was quite wide. Only three borough constituencies, however, boasted more than 3,000 voters – Westminster (12,000), London (7,000) and Bristol (5,000). The vast majority of constituencies in the other three categories had fewer than 1,000 electors, and a large number less than 100. The most extreme examples were Gatton, with two voters, and Old Sarum, once represented by Pitt the Elder, which had an electorate of seven even though its last inhabitants seem to have left in the fifteenth century.[4] Both of these constituencies returned two MPs, the same number as Yorkshire, which had 20,000 qualified voters!

It was among these constituencies with a minuscule electorate that 'rotten' and 'pocket' boroughs were found. The former were those whose electorate had fallen so far that the bribing of only a few citizens was sufficient to win a place in Parliament. The latter were those where a single person, probably a local landowner, was able to determine who would be elected by various forms of persuasion. In 1793, no fewer than 308 out of 513 English constituencies fell into one or other of these categories, according to the reformist Society of the Friends of the People.[5] The figures for other elections in the mid-to-late eighteenth century are unlikely to be very different. Half or more of the 'proprietors' of these seats were members of the House of Lords, who typically nominated their sons or other relatives as candidates. Others quite blatantly put their seats up for sale; the going price for being elected for a single term was around £3,000 in 1780. Many of these MPs never set foot in their constituencies, including Pitt the Younger, who 'represented' Appleby between 1781 and 1784. Often the proprietors insisted that their nominees steered clear of their constituents, as they did not wish 'their' MPs to build up personal loyalties. Some proprietors controlled (or 'influenced') the representation of multiple seats. A legendary example was the Duke of Newcastle

(1693–1768), who at the peak of his influence nominated no fewer than 14 MPs. Another famous 'boroughmonger', who controlled almost as many seats in the north of England (including Appleby), was James Lowther (1757–1844), whose reward for making some of his seats available to the government was the earldom of Lonsdale. Edward Eliot (1727–1804), who acquired a barony by the same means, controlled six seats in Cornwall, including Liskeard, which the historian Edward Gibbon represented for just one term in the 1780s. Gibbon made little mark as an MP, but was remembered for a single bon mot in which he asked, 'What has a fat man in common with a Cornish borough?', answering, 'He never sees his own member.'[6]

About thirty seats were controlled by the government, being described either as Treasury or Admiralty boroughs. MPs elected for rotten or pocket boroughs were often seen as lacking in legitimacy, and as the more ambitious of them became better known they sought, not always successfully, to transfer to a more open and thus more 'respectable' constituency. Thus Pitt the Younger switched to represent the University of Cambridge, Charles Fox to Westminster, and Edmund Burke from the pocket borough of Wendover to Bristol.

In the opening chapter of his book Namier offered a variety of reasons to explain why rich men sought a seat in the House of Commons despite their numerous distractions. Of the four motives advanced by Namier, the first two were the most common. Number one was the enormous social *cachet* attached to being a Member of Parliament – the next best thing to having a peerage in the eyes of the country gentry, and often the first step to acquiring one. Second was the hope of material gain – the prospect of being offered a pension or a well-paid sinecure for oneself, or for relatives, friends or constituents, as a reward for consistently supporting the government in parliamentary votes. Third was the hope of building a ministerial career. Lagging behind in last place was a burning desire to promote a moral cause, or to improve the efficiency of government procedures. Although this would be condemned by twenty-first-century standards, it was not considered to be inherently corrupt at the time. MPs received no salaries, and those who enjoyed independent means would have been affronted by the suggestion that they should be recompensed for their service; but it was widely accepted that less affluent MPs should be the recipients of 'perks' of various kinds. Only those who too blatantly gave or received monetary bribes were disapproved of, and the same was true of the individuals who were chosen to serve as government ministers. Thus the Grenville family, which accumulated an excessive number of sinecures, was widely seen as avaricious, as was Henry Fox, who acquired a very large fortune from the eight years he spent in office as Paymaster General.

It was Sir Robert Walpole, the first prime minister, who devised the system of using secret service funds to ensure that the government was never defeated in a parliamentary vote, but the system was perfected by the Duke of Newcastle (Thomas Pelham-Holles), who was prime minister for nearly eight years and a senior Cabinet minister for more than forty. He kept a scrupulous account of how much was expended and to whom, which he submitted to the King every month. In a lengthy appendix to his book, Namier published a complete list of secret service disbursements from March 1754 to May 1762. Typical examples are the payments made during the month of May 1759:

			£
MAY	2d	To Mr. Martin towards Camelford election	300
	8th	To Mr. Medlycott for one year	600
	11th	To Lord Saye and Sele, one year to Lady Day	600
		To Mr. Hamilton, the late Duke of Hamilton's relation, ½ a year due at Lady Day	100
		To Mr. Henry Fane, for Lyme as usual	100
	17th	To Sir Francis Poole, one year due at Christmas	300
	18th	To Mr. Dodd, one year	500
	25th	Retained to myself by Your Majesty's special command, one quarter	1050
		To Lord Malpas, remainder	300
	29th	To Orford, ½ a year due at Midsummer last	100
		To Mr. Offley, ½ a year to Christmas	200[7]

The monarch at the time was George II, and his grandson and successor, George III, expressed strong disgust at the system in accordance with his stated desire to be a virtuous ruler. However, when he succeeded to the throne George had no compunction in employing the same methods. The payments were made mostly to MPs or to the 'proprietors' of pocket boroughs, and were mostly intended to meet their election expenses. This was one reason why no government ever lost a general election during the whole of the eighteenth century. Governments fell not because of electoral defeat but because they had lost the confidence of the monarch.

The great majority of MPs were, at least nominally, members of two political parties. These were the Whigs and the Tories, reflecting a division which dated from the previous century, in the reign of Charles II, and the attempt to exclude the King's younger brother, the Catholic James, Duke of York, from the succession. The opposition to James was led by the first Earl of Shaftesbury, whose Exclusion Bill failed to carry in 1680. His supporters were christened 'Whigs' by their opponents, after the Whiggamores, Scottish Presbyterian rebels who had opposed Charles I in 1648. The Whigs themselves happily accepted this appellation, claiming that Whig was an acronym for We Hope in God. They, in turn, branded their opponents as Tories, an Irish word meaning highwaymen or outlaws. It was largely the Whigs who presided over the replacement in 1688 of James II by his elder daughter, Mary II, and son-in-law, William III, though the Tory Earl of Danby also played a significant role and most Tories acquiesced in the change. Party divisions continued, however, mostly defined by attitudes to the monarchy, to religion and to foreign policy. To a twentieth-century observer like Namier these differences might seem slight, and they were certainly exaggerated by ambitious politicians in order to win (or retain) ministerial positions. Nevertheless, those who identified most closely with the 'Whig' tradition tended to be most in favour of limiting the monarchy, religious toleration (especially of Protestant Dissenters) and of prosecuting a warlike foreign policy aimed at curbing the ambitions of the 'absolute' French monarchy. The Tories retained a residual belief in the divine right of kings. Though they accepted the accession of William III and Mary II, and later of Queen Anne, they were divided about excluding the Stuart family from the succession after her death. Although many of them were not averse to the prospect of a Catholic king, they were fervent supporters of the Church of England, and opposed any initiative to remove the disqualification of Dissenters.

Opponents of high taxation, they also emerged as the peace party, luke-warm at best about the constant wars against France and its allies, which they believed to be ruinously expensive. There were social differences between the two parties – the Whigs were more aristocratic, while the Tories' strongest support came from the country gentry. Partly because of the suspected 'Jacobite' sympathies of some senior Tories, they were confined to the Opposition benches throughout the reigns of George I and II, a period of 46 years, and it was only the accession of George III which opened the possibility of office to them. They had gradually slumped in numbers during these years, as young men with serious political ambitions (and ill-defined political ideas) flocked to the Whigs.[8]

At general elections the great majority of seats were uncontested; only about one in five attracted rival candidates. This was because election campaigns were extremely expensive. In many two-member seats the Tories and Whigs refused to campaign against each other, each nomi-nating a single candidate. No-holds-barred elections, such as the noto-rious contests in Oxfordshire in 1754 and Westminster in 1784 (when Pitt the Younger made Herculean efforts to displace Charles Fox), were exceptional. Voting was very much a public event, with the polls being opened for up to 40 days or until the defeated candidates had conceded. Secret ballots were not introduced until 1872, which meant the landlords or employers of every voter could see how they voted. Very few of these dared to vote against their wishes. It is not surprising that a clear majority of MPs were aristocrats; in the 1784 election some 378 out of 558 came from titled families.[9] Namier lists the principal occupations of other MPs – lawyers, bankers, merchants (including those who had made their fortunes in India or the West Indies), civil servants, sailors and soldiers. Miscellaneous categories he mentioned included 'Robbers, Muddlers, Bastards, and Bankrupts.'[10]

Perhaps a majority of MPs were silent ones, rarely if ever attempting to speak, and many of them poor attenders. But they enjoyed listening to parliamentary 'stars', and no one could take it for granted that their votes would not be influenced by what they heard. Other leading MPs were renowned for their oratory, including Lord North, Edmund Burke and Richard Brinsley Sheridan, a brilliant Irish-born playwright who was elected as the Whig MP for the borough of Stafford in 1780. In the celebrity culture of the twenty-first century, Sheridan might have seen himself as a plausible candidate for prime minister. But political supremacy in the eighteenth century was determined by combat in the parliamentary cockpit; and here Charles Fox and the Younger Pitt were in a class of their own, revered as titans and hailed by their classically educated colleagues as the Demosthenes and Cicero of their time.

2

Fathers and Sons

IN February 1735 two young representatives of well-connected families were elected to the House of Commons, neither of them in a manner which would satisfy modern understandings of the democratic process. At a by-election on 17 February, the seven non-resident voters of Old Sarum, near Salisbury – the second-smallest constituency in the country and a notorious rotten borough – had all voted for the 25-year-old William Pitt. In doing so, they were following the instructions of the landowner, Pitt's elder brother, Thomas, who had earlier vacated the seat to represent the somewhat more populous, but still imperfectly democratic, constituency of Okehampton. Ten days later, Henry Fox, aged 29, was elected for Hindon, another infamous Wiltshire rotten borough, at his third attempt, and only after a great deal of skulduggery, including the bribery of the returning officer at the behest of the prime minister, Sir Robert Walpole.

The two men soon made their mark in the House of Commons, Pitt primarily through his oratory and Fox by his skill as a tactician. Within a few years, they were recognised as the two outstanding parliamentarians of their day. Sometimes they acted as allies, but eventually they emerged as irreconcilable rivals, foreshadowing the far more acrimonious and long-lasting divisions between their respective sons, Charles James Fox and Pitt the Younger. Henry Fox came from a strong Tory background, his father, Sir Stephen Fox, having been head of Charles II's household when he was in exile, before serving as Paymaster of the Forces, in which post he had made a large fortune, and having been for a long time Tory MP for Salisbury – the city whose expansion had made a ghost town of neighbouring Old Sarum. Sir Stephen was already 78 when Henry was born in September 1705, but lived for 11 more years. Together with his elder brother, Henry passed into the care of another Tory MP, Edward Nicholas. Despite these early influences, when he was elected Henry chose to attach himself to a leading Whig, John Hervey, the heir to the Earl of Bristol, who enjoyed the courtesy title of Lord Hervey. Hervey was a prominent figure at court, and was the author of a remarkably shrewd and candid memoir of the reign of George II, which was only published over a hundred years after Hervey's death because of the scandalous nature of many of his observations. The relationship between Hervey and Henry Fox was close enough for the latter to act as his 'second' in a 1731 duel with a leading Whig politician, William Pulteney. Hervey was bisexual, and his relationship with Henry Fox's elder brother, Stephen, was even more intimate.[1] He was a strong supporter of Robert Walpole, under whom he served as Lord Privy Seal, and consequently Henry Fox too became an ultra-loyal follower of Walpole, remaining loyal until Britain's first prime minister was finally driven from office in February 1742.

Fox promptly transferred his allegiance to Walpole's political heir, Henry Pelham, who served as prime minister for ten years from 1743. Pelham appointed Fox as a Lord of the Treasury, but the following year, at the age of 39, Fox caused a sensation by eloping with the 20-year-old Lady Caroline Lennox, daughter of the Second Duke of Richmond, a descendant of Charles II and his mistress Louise de Kérouaille, who had been created Duchess of Portsmouth by the 'Merry Monarch'. Richmond and his wife, who had previously been close friends of Fox, were horrified, suspecting him of being a fortune hunter, and cut off all relations with the couple for several years. Yet Fox was promoted in 1746 to Secretary at War, despite the opposition of Richmond (who was himself a Cabinet minister), and was soon marked out as a rising figure. In the words of the historian Eric Eyck, Lady Caroline's parents 'could no longer hide from themselves that here was a son-in-law of whom even a Duke need not be ashamed'.[2] And so in 1748, when their eldest grandchild, Stephen, was born, they overcame injured pride and 'took the first step towards a reconciliation.'[3] By the time the second child was born, on 24 January 1749, complete harmony had been restored. Perhaps in honour of the Duke's ancestry, this child was given the quintessential Stuart names of Charles James. It was by then evident that this supposed misalliance was a genuine love affair on both sides. Towards his children, Eyck continues,

> [Fox] showed a love which had only one great fault – that it was not tempered by some little strictness and firmness. This man, who pursued his aims in political life with ruthless energy, was at home as clay in the hands of his children, particularly his favourite, his second son Charles James, whose career was later to disclose all too clearly the effects of this paternal weakness.[4]

In his post at the War Office, which he retained for nine years, Fox became very close to the commander-in-chief of the armed forces, the Duke of Cumberland. The younger son of George II, he was widely known as 'the Butcher of Culloden' because of his ferocious repression of the supporters of the Young Pretender, Charles Edward Stuart, during the Jacobite rebellion of 1745. Despite his bloody martial reputation, Cumberland was respected as a decisive and level-headed political figure, and Fox effectively transferred his allegiance to him after the death of Pelham in 1754. Pelham was succeeded by his elder brother, Thomas Pelham-Holles, the Duke of Newcastle, and as the two most effective speakers among the small number of ministers in the Commons, both Henry Fox and William Pitt (Paymaster of the Forces) had strong claims to be appointed as Leader of the House, a key post when the prime minister was in the Lords. Newcastle offered the position to Fox, but would not relinquish control of secret service funds which were distributed to government supporters as a means of ensuring consistent majorities in the Commons. Fox could not accept these terms, and Newcastle chose instead to entrust the leadership of the Commons to Sir Thomas Robinson, 'who, though a seasoned diplomat, was completely without parliamentary experience or talents'.[5] It was a decision which explained why Newcastle had been so reluctant to relinquish the secret service money: he was adept at assembling theoretical parliamentary majorities through the careful allocation of 'sweeteners', but that was the limit of his political ability. Fox and Pitt were well aware that Newcastle had opted to appoint a mediocrity as Leader of the Commons because he feared that he would be unable to control better-qualified candidates. Rather than appreciating this backhanded compliment, the two men took it as a licence to join forces in opposition to Newcastle's government, without taking the usual preliminary step of resigning from it.

Circumstances had thrown together two fascinating, but sharply contrasting characters. William Pitt the Elder came from a West Country family whose notable representatives included government officials under both Elizabeth I and James I. In 1629 the senior branch of the family had acquired the substantial estate of Stratfield Saye, Hampshire.[6] Thus while the Pitts were not aristocrats, their elevated social position ensured that their daughters could expect advantageous marriages, and even younger sons had excellent prospects of securing comfortable positions within the 'respectable' professions, like the law, the Church or the army. For example, Pitt the Elder's great-grandfather, John, was the rector of Blandford St Mary in Dorset from 1645 to his death in 1672. However, the Reverend Pitt's son, Thomas (born 1653), was not content to eke out a nondescript existence thanks to the patronage of well-placed relatives. Rather than following his deceased father into the Church, in 1674 he travelled to India as an employee of the East India Company. However, he soon decided to take advantage of his 'insider' knowledge, and began trading on his own behalf. When he returned to England he had become sufficiently affluent to brush aside a £400 fine for breaching the East India Company's trading monopoly; he also made the dream investment for someone who enjoyed accumulating properties without actually occupying them, by purchasing Old Sarum and its two parliamentary seats (for £1,000). In 1698, the East India Company rehired Pitt in a more senior capacity, and he returned to India as its main representative, or governor, in Madras. In this new role of poacher-turned-gamekeeper he proved effective, extending the territories under the Company's control. His most celebrated exploit, however, was the purchase of an uncut 410-carat diamond for a sum estimated at around £20,000 (more than £3 million in 2018 values[7]). In hindsight this could be regarded as a one-way ticket to even greater riches, since the diamond seemed certain to fetch a much higher price on the European market. However, at the time it was a reckless gamble, given the chances that it would never reach that profitable destination. It is said that the diamond was transported to Europe in the shoe of Pitt's own son; but even that hiding place would not have protected the investment if his ship had sunk *en voyage*.

Thankfully for Governor Pitt, his diamond survived the journey and, after several unsuccessful sales pitches, it was bought by the Duc d'Orléans and used at subsequent French coronations, as well as being fashioned into a pommel for Napoleon Bonaparte's sword. Pitt obtained a profit from his hazardous investment, though nowhere near as much as he had hoped. The proceeds helped him to augment his property portfolio, incorporating Swallowfield Park in Berkshire as well as Boconnoc in Cornwall. 'Diamond' Pitt exhibited an enthusiasm for travelling, rather than settling at a specified destination; but some of his acquisitions suggest an awareness that control over parliamentary seats would prove shrewd investments for himself and his branch of the family. Indeed, he chose to elect himself for Old Sarum on four separate occasions during a parliamentary career which opened in 1689 and closed with his death in 1726. In 1728 there was a sensation at Old Sarum when a seat was contested. The Pitt family's candidate prevailed, although the usual script had been upset by a challenger who declared his candidature late in the day. The interloper was none other than the 22-year-old Henry Fox, who went down to a predictable but surprisingly narrow defeat (by two votes to one).

'Diamond' Pitt evinced an inability to suffer fools, even (or especially) when they cropped up within his own family. His son Robert – he of the accommodating footwear – was not immune from such parental strictures. However, surviving correspondence suggests that 'Diamond' Pitt softened in the presence of Robert's second son, William, who was born on 15 November 1708.[8] Perhaps he sensed that the family's energy and ambition would not die with him but had merely skipped a generation.

Governor Pitt was certainly glad to see 'Will' on his journeys to and from Eton College, which his grandson attended until 1726 (just after his grandfather's death), developing a marked aversion to the place in the process. In January 1727 he matriculated at Trinity College, Oxford, where he stayed for only one year. The death of his father Robert in May 1727 seems to have inspired a change of plan, and William switched to the University of Utrecht to continue (but not complete) his academic studies. This seems a somewhat eccentric choice, although Utrecht had a strong reputation at the time and attracted numerous scholars from England. Whatever the reasons for Pitt's attendance at Utrecht, they probably included a calculation that it would help to prepare him for a clerical career. By 1731, if not before, this plan had been abandoned and Pitt became a cornet – the lowest rank of commissioned officer – in the King's Own Regiment of Horse. The colonel of this regiment, Richard Temple, first Viscount Cobham, was a very distinguished soldier, whose nephew, George Lyttleton, had been a friend of Pitt's at Eton. Lyttleton persuaded his uncle to accept Pitt as one of his officers, but the asking price for the commission was £1,000 and William's personal resources fell far below this sum. The Walpole government stepped in and put up the money, regarding it as an ideal opportunity to reward a borough-owning family for its support, and to ensure its future loyalty.

William Pitt thus embarked on a career in the British army thanks to the self-interested calculations of corrupt ministers, and although 'Diamond' Pitt had not left William much money – a measly £100 per year – his determination to secure some political influence through the control of rotten boroughs had already paid off for his grandson. Much more was to follow. There would be no battlefield heroics from Cornet Pitt; indeed, his service under arms was so uneventful that he took some time off for a truncated version of the European grand tour. However, in 1735 one of the Old Sarum parliamentary seats fell vacant; and William Pitt, who through family marriages and personal relationships was already connected to some important political figures, seemed almost overqualified as a candidate for that borough. The only snag was that the family finances would have been improved if the spare Old Sarum seat could have been sold; but the idea of becoming an MP seems to have infected Pitt with the political bug, and once the prospect had been opened he was not prepared to give it up.

The election of William Pitt for Old Sarum was an object lesson for anyone who (like the Duke of Newcastle in 1754) was mulling over the possibility of entrusting secret service money to potentially unreliable hands. The lesson suggested that even the most careful calculations could give rise to unpleasant consequences. When the Walpole government had provided the means to establish William Pitt's military career, the controllers of the purse strings (i.e. Walpole himself and his closest advisors) had assumed that this would imbue the whole of the Pitt family with a proper sense of obligation. However, the immediate object of Walpole's generosity – William Pitt himself – promptly linked himself with a group of Cobham's younger relatives, known as 'Cobham's Cubs'. Cobham had fallen out with Walpole in 1734, when he had strongly opposed his Excise Bill, and the then prime minister retaliated by depriving him of the colonelcy of his regiment. Thenceforth Cobham became a bitter opponent of Walpole's, and instructed his 'Cubs' to oppose him at every turn. Cobham, a member of the powerful Grenville family, lived in the magnificent mansion at Stowe, in Buckinghamshire (since 1923 the site of the famous 'public' school). It was here that Pitt socialised freely with members of the Temple and Grenville families and met his future wife, Cobham's niece Hester Grenville (see Pitt family tree on p. xvii).

Like his new parliamentary friends, Pitt could claim that his opposition to Walpole was a question of principles more than personalities. 'Cobham's Cubs' were typical of Opposition or 'Country' Whigs, fiercely critical in particular of Walpole's foreign policy, which seemed unduly subservient to the interests of Hanover, George II's German birthplace and hereditary electorate. By contrast, Opposition Whigs presented themselves as 'Patriots', identifying British interests with territorial expansion outside Europe. These views were endorsed by George II's heir, Frederick, Prince of Wales, who in typical Hanoverian style was bitterly estranged from his father. Apparently oblivious to the possibility that Frederick was just using them as a means to embarrass the King, Pitt and his friends instead focused on the prospect of power once George II had been gathered to his ancestors. Unable to prove their usefulness in ministerial office, they were tempted to compensate through the violence of their parliamentary rhetoric – with the additional incentive that their 'patriotic' outbursts were likely to endear them to a significant element of extra-parliamentary opinion.

This intoxicating mix of 'populism' and deference – playing to the gallery with outrageous attacks on the King's government while also winning approval from the heir to the throne – would play a significant part in the rivalry between Charles James Fox and William Pitt the Younger. It turned out to be the making of the elder Pitt, although initially it looked like a serious misjudgement. Walpole enjoyed (or at least, *thought* he enjoyed) a way to deliver a decisive rejoinder to Pitt's incendiary rhetoric. An example could be made of the contumelious cornet, whose commission was abruptly cancelled in April 1736. If Walpole had made a mistake in offering patronage to the elder Pitt, he compounded the error by withdrawing support in this ruthless manner, which attracted considerable notice. Unlike his well-heeled friends, Pitt was sufficiently penurious to be portrayed as a martyr to the 'patriot' cause – someone who had been willing to sacrifice his chance of prosperity and martial glory if this was the price of exposing the corruption at the heart of government. In reality, Pitt had been stripped of a position which had brought him little tangible benefit, and (thanks to Walpole) had been relatively costless. Far from hurting him financially, Pitt's stance helped to secure him a position within the Prince of Wales's household, which more than doubled his annual income, and in 1744 he received the astonishing sum of £10,000 as a legacy from the late Sarah, Duchess of Marlborough, who was willing to reward anyone who had antagonised her enemy Walpole.

Between Walpole's misguided attempt to teach Pitt a lesson, and the Cabinet crisis of 1754 which brought his rivalry with Henry Fox to a head, Pitt established himself as a politician who would be highly dangerous either as an opponent or as a subordinate colleague. Having failed to silence Pitt by punishment, Walpole's successors tried to make him less relevant by isolating him. Just after receiving news of his legacy from the Duchess of Marlborough, Pitt found himself excluded from the government, headed by Newcastle's brother Henry Pelham, which found places for many of his key allies as befitted what was dubbed a 'Broad Bottom Ministry'. Although George II was prepared to overlook the verbal attacks of other Opposition Whigs if such forgiveness was a necessary step to the creation of a coalition government, he drew the line when it came to

Pitt, who had openly belittled his beloved Hanover. Pitt realised that he had gone too far; and since George II had been vigorous enough to take part in the Battle of Dettingen (1743) in his sixtieth year, it would seem foolish to expect a change of monarch any time soon. Pitt's speeches suddenly became more conciliatory; and when the Pelham government was reconstructed in 1746 the King gave way to ministerial entreaties that the pestilential Pitt should be included. At first, Pitt was fobbed off with the position of joint vice-treasurer of Ireland. However, in May 1746 he became Paymaster General of the armed forces, a position which Sir Stephen Fox had held for a total of 16 years and which Henry Pelham himself had filled between 1730 and 1743. Pelham's subsequent career suggested that this was a post well worth having in terms of its political opportunities, but it also offered the chance of material gain, since the paymaster was allowed to derive personal benefit from the considerable sums that passed through his hands. Like Pelham before him, Pitt refused to enrich himself in this dubious fashion, and his gesture, following on from his 'martyrdom' at Walpole's hands, cemented his reputation as an incorruptible politician. Nevertheless, the position offered limited scope for decision-making influence even for so forceful a politician as Pitt, and by 1754 the attraction of office-holding without power (or profit) had long since worn away.

Pitt and Henry Fox were now colleagues within a Whig government; for almost a decade, both had held offices which were intimately connected with Britain's armed forces. While it would be absurd to say that they had earned their positions entirely through their personal attributes, they had certainly made the most of their inherited advantages, and only jaundiced critics could deny that they were unusually gifted MPs. It is clear from their own testimony that they had considerable respect for each other. Indeed, their abilities were complementary. Pitt was a formidable orator who specialised in personal attacks without troubling himself too much on the score of consistency; therefore, anyone reading the parliamentary record of Pitt's speeches over his career would find numerous examples of self-contradiction. At the time, though, no one could have conducted such an inquiry, for the good reason that verbatim parliamentary reports were proscribed, leaving the public with brief excerpts or paraphrases. In any case, Pitt's reputation was built on his *performance*, rather than his logic – it seems that even when he delivered his weakest speeches in terms of content he could still command the Commons thanks to the supreme confidence of his delivery and his flashing, accusatory eyes.

By contrast, contemporary testimony suggests that Henry Fox was a hesitant parliamentary performer. Fox excelled in man-management, whereas Pitt, by comparison, had a more patchy record in this area. The obvious solution in the Cabinet crisis of 1754 was to combine these talents in a ministry which was nominally led by a member of the House of Lords – like the endlessly flexible Duke of Newcastle. Unfortunately, this would still leave the question of leadership of the House of Commons. Of the two most likely candidates, the power brokers of the time regarded Fox as far more acceptable than Pitt for this crucial position; but Pitt would not acquiesce in an arrangement which would land him with considerable political responsibilities without ensuring equivalent influence over decision making. As a result, what could have been a constructive partnership in government between a charismatic, crowd-pleasing orator and a supremely efficient man of business ended up being a temporary alliance of mutual convenience for the purpose of destabilising the administration to which both Fox and Pitt belonged. Rather than continuing to work in tandem, the two men increasingly became identified with entirely different approaches to government. Their contrasting qualities created rival legacies which made it very difficult (if not impossible) for their sons to cooperate, even though in the next generation the roles were reversed; this time it was William Pitt the Younger who exemplified efficient government, while Charles James Fox almost exactly reprised the populist persona cultivated by the elder Pitt.

In November 1754 Pitt, at the age of 46, married the 33-year-old Lady Hester Grenville. The couple had been acquainted for many years, and his new wife's brothers Richard (Earl Temple), James and George were Pitt's close political allies. For Pitt this alliance proved much more durable (and convenient) than his political flirtation with Henry Fox. Not only did it cement his relationship with Hester's family, but his new wife proved an indispensable source of support for him, bringing a degree of common sense into a household which would have been unsustainably chaotic under Pitt's sole stewardship. This belated plunge into matrimony, despite having many strategic advantages, was the product of emotion rather than calculation; the correspondence between Pitt and his wife is eloquent testimony to a deep and enduring love. Three children – Hester (born October 1755); John (1756); and Harriot (1758) – had already arrived before William was born on 28 May 1759. He was followed by a fifth and final child, James, in 1761.

Although his domestic circumstances provided Pitt with much-needed contentment, politically he was not mellowed by marriage. By 1754 Britain was being drawn into conflict with France in North America, and the government was anxious to secure its position in Europe. It signed treaties both with Hanover's neighbour, Hesse-Cassel, and more significantly, Russia, to provide troops in exchange for the payment of generous subsidies. To get these treaties through a largely hostile House of Commons was far beyond the powers of the mediocre Sir Thomas Robinson, and Newcastle reluctantly started conversations with Pitt to see if he could be persuaded to take his place. But the King was reluctant, and Pitt demanded not only the leadership of the House but also the right to exercise considerable influence over foreign policy as one of the two Secretaries of State, the most senior posts in the government apart from the First Lord of the Treasury. This was too much for Newcastle, but he was persuaded by Cumberland, who had the ear of the King, to make a fresh approach to Fox. Realising the strength of his bargaining position, Fox successfully held out for the terms refused to Pitt, and proceeded to demonstrate his parliamentary skills by successfully steering the subsidy bills through the Commons.

This state of affairs was deeply galling for Pitt, who faced the prospect of indefinite exclusion from high government office, unable to influence the course of a conflict in North America which had started badly for Britain. He vented his frustration by launching a comprehensive attack on the government's policies, finishing up with a jibe at Newcastle's expense. In an oft-quoted passage, after pretending to be fumbling around for an explanation as to why things had been going very much better for the government of late, he suddenly claimed to have found the solution:

I remember at Lyons to have been carried to see the conflux of the Rhône and the Saône; this a gentle, feeble, languid stream and, though languid, of no depth – the other a boisterous and impetuous torrent – but they meet at last; and long,' he added, with biting irony, 'may they continue united to the comfort of each other, and to the glory, honour and security of this nation!'[9]

If Fox was flattered to be likened to the torrentuous Rhône, Newcastle was mortified to be characterised as a feeble and languid stream, and it was no surprise when Pitt was dismissed from the government within a few days, together with his brother-in-law, George Grenville, and several other followers. War was formally declared on France on 17 May 1756, beginning a prolonged struggle on an unprecedented global scale. As a result of dramatic diplomatic readjustments, the Seven Years' War pitched Britain and Prussia against an alliance of France, Austria, Russia, Sweden and Saxony. For Britain the conflict began with a humiliating setback – the loss of Minorca to France, which a British fleet under Admiral Byng failed to prevent. Byng was selected as a scapegoat, and he was arrested on his return to Britain. Fox steadfastly defended the government position day by day in the Commons, but by October thought the position no longer tenable, and, fearing that he would be saddled with the blame for Minorca, submitted his resignation. The Duke of Newcastle had no alternative but to solicit help from Pitt, who spurned his advances. Newcastle had to admit defeat, and followed Fox out of office.

George II was enraged by Fox's resignation, which he attributed to political and personal cowardice. Although he remained deeply suspicious of Pitt, he needed at least one effective minister in the House of Commons, and it briefly seemed as if he would have to accept both of the objectionable aspirants in senior positions. He invited Fox to form a government, and the latter sounded Pitt out at a levee given by the Prince of Wales:

The rivals met at the head of the stairs, and were soon engaged in earnest conversation, which lasted full twenty minutes. 'Mr Pitt exceeding grave, Mr Fox very warm. They did not part amicably.' Neither of the two [contemporary] accounts of the discussion credits Pitt with having shown an ordinary modicum of civility.[10]

Pitt's refusal to serve under him induced Fox to abandon his attempt to form a government, and George II then approached a leading Whig peer, the Fourth Duke of Devonshire, a congenial but uninspiring politician devoid of personal ambition. 'I am sure that I can save this country, and that nobody else can,' Pitt told Devonshire,[11] agreeing to join his government as Secretary of State for the Southern Department, a post which gave him responsibility for conducting the war effort. Neither Newcastle nor Fox was included in the government, whose career was dominated by the fate of the luckless Admiral Byng, found guilty of neglecting his duties in a court martial in January 1757. Even Byng's judges recommended that the mandatory death sentence should be commuted, and Pitt made a genuine attempt to mobilise the Commons to save the admiral. He was bold enough to inform the King that Parliament was inclined towards mercy, to which George reportedly replied that 'you have taught me to look for the sense of my subjects in another place than in the House of Commons.'[12] It was a cutting rejoinder from an intransigent monarch who had sensed that his populist opponent had put himself out of step with a public which was thirsting for Byng's blood.

Byng was shot on the deck of his own ship on 14 March 1757 in an exemplary punishment, as Voltaire wryly noted in *Candide*, '*pour encourager les autres*'. Less than a month later Pitt was dismissed by the King, along with the First Lord of the Admiralty, his brother-in-law Earl Temple. James and George Grenville also left the government in solidarity. It was, however, easier for the King to dismiss ministers than to find viable alternatives whose surname was not either Pitt or Fox. The latter tried once again to form an administration, but by this time it was evident to most observers that Pitt had secured a decisive advantage in their personal duel, thanks to a network of supporters who now showed their feelings by orchestrating what Horace Walpole described as a 'golden rain' of civic accolades.[13] These tributes were led by the City of London, which made him an honorary freeman. Fox enjoyed nothing like this extensive extra-parliamentary following, but his ability to manage the Commons was still regarded as indispensable. If he could not take the leading role, he was still well placed to pursue two of his ambitions – to make a lot of money, and to acquire peerages for his wife as well as himself. After some complex negotiations, the King was finally persuaded that both Pitt and Newcastle (who still commanded a majority in the House of Commons) must be included, and Fox successfully held out for the Paymastership of the Forces, which he retained for eight years until 1765, duly amassing a huge personal fortune. Newcastle again became prime minister, but Pitt at last was the dominant force in the government, with unfettered control of war strategy. Devonshire happily slid into the largely ceremonial role of Lord Chamberlain.

Initially, the new government met with military setbacks. By September 1757 the Electorate of Hanover had been overrun by the French, after ineffectual resistance by forces under the Duke of Cumberland. George II was livid, though not sufficiently vengeful to order the execution of his son *pour encourager les autres*. However, Cumberland was compelled to resign from all his public offices. This was a further blow to Fox, who thus lost his best-placed patron. Pitt had hoped to relieve pressure on Britain's German allies through a diversionary raid on Rochefort on the south-west coast of France, but this ended in failure. By the end of the year, however, positive news had arrived: Britain had been victorious on 23 June at the Battle of Plassey in India, where the forces of the East India company, led by Robert Clive, had crushed the Nawab of Bengal and his French allies. Frederick the Great of Prussia had also ended a series of setbacks by defeating the French in November at Rossbach and the Austrians in December at Leuthen. Frederick's success gave Pitt a pretext to abandon his antipathy to Hanover, and in April 1758 the government agreed to generous subsidies for the Prussian king and 9,000 extra troops to supplement the Electorate's forces. In June a Prussian–Hanoverian army defeated the French at Krefeld.

It was the following year – the 'Year of Victories', also known as the '*Annus Mirabilis*' – which silenced Pitt's numerous critics. British forces annexed the island of Guadeloupe, repulsed French attacks in India, captured Quebec and Montreal after General Wolfe's dramatic victory in the Battle of the Plains of Abraham, and inflicted a serious defeat on the French at the Battle of Minden in Germany. Positive news from every front seemed to arrive with such regularity that Horace Walpole, not one of Pitt's greatest admirers, exulted that 'Our bells are worn threadbare with ringing of victories';[14] and the most spectacular successes followed hard on the heels of Pitt the Younger's birth in the May of that celebrated year. French plans to strike back at the enemy's heart by invading Britain were derailed in June 1759 when Admiral Rodney launched an assault on the port of Le Havre, resulting in the destruction of many vessels. In August a French fleet was routed at the Battle of Lagos, and in November a final attempt to challenge British naval power was seen off at Quiberon Bay.

Of course, Pitt's direct role in this military glory was grossly exaggerated at the time. To attribute everything to a single minister would scarcely be less absurd than claiming that the birth of the younger Pitt was a signal of divine approval for the British war effort. Given the speed of communications in those days, it would be ludicrous to suppose that many of the soldiers and sailors despatched by the British – let alone the ones whose rulers (like Prussia's Frederick the Great) received generous subsidies – fought with augmented courage because they were inspired by Pitt. Nevertheless, even in his short-lived spell as Secretary of State under the Duke of Devonshire Pitt had demonstrated administrative energies which matched his oratorical effusions: he could, in modern parlance, 'walk the walk' as well as 'talk the talk'. His insistence on the value of military operations outside Europe had paid off and secured a permanent reward in 1759 when Anglo-American forces struggling to drive the French out of Ohio County started to construct Fort Pitt, leading to the foundation of Pittsburgh. After forcing himself back into office in 1757, Pitt showed himself to be flexible enough to modify the anti-Hanoverian strategy which had won him so many admirers, even at the risk of alienating these devoted followers. Like Winston Churchill – whose character and career were not dissimilar – Pitt evidently regarded himself as a 'man of destiny', and seems not to have been unduly surprised by the way things turned out for him and his country.

However, Pitt was seriously affected by one hazard which was of limited concern for Churchill – the danger arising from bad relations with the monarchy. George II finally died in October 1760, to be succeeded by his grandson, the young George III. As we have seen, Pitt had been associated with George's father Frederick. He had not been insensitive to the new heir to the throne, and indeed had established good relations with the Prince's most trusted advisor, the Earl of Bute. However, George III ascended the throne with a determination to reassert royal authority. By 1760 Pitt had finally been accepted by George II; but he had proved his value in the face of what the King held to be well-founded reservations. Having succeeded in this uphill battle, Pitt believed that he had established the right to take his own decisions. But not even he could defy the rules of Hanoverian politics, which stipulated that amity with the monarch incurred the enmity of the heir. George III had duly reached the conclusion that Pitt was both 'ungrateful' and 'dishonourable'.[15] Since the immediate threat from France had receded, the public euphoria of the *Annus Mirabilis* seemed to be lapsing into a desire for the return of a peace which would allow Britons to gloat over most if not all of their existing gains.

If the advent of George III was an ominous development for Pitt, in Henry Fox it briefly raised hopes of a spectacular personal and political triumph. The new king became enamoured of Fox's teenage sister-in-law, Lady Sarah Lennox, a noted society beauty, and indicated to her closest friend and cousin, Lady Susan Fox-Strangways, that he wished to make her his queen. Fox, who was effectively Lady Sarah's guardian, did everything he could to encourage the match, pushing her to disport herself in front of the King as he rode daily past their Holland Park house on his way to Kensington Palace. But George was sharply rebuked by his mother, Princess Augusta, and by Lord Bute, who insisted that he should marry a German princess. On 8 September 1761 he was duly consigned to Princess Charlotte of Mecklenburg-Strelitz. Sarah, who was one of the bridesmaids at the wedding, did not appear notably distressed. She was, it was reported, soon consoled by a new pet – a hedgehog – for the loss of a crown, writing to Susan Fox-Strangways, 'Luckily for me, I did not love him, and only liked him, nor did the title weigh anything with me; so little, at least, that my disappointment did not *affect* my spirits above one hour or two I believe.'[16]

She was, however, promptly married off to the first remotely eligible suitor who presented himself, an undistinguished Whig MP, Sir Charles

Bunbury, whose lack of talent was matched by the smallness of his estate. Thoroughly bored, she embarked on a series of flirtations, one of which – with Lord William Gordon – led to the birth of a daughter, Louisa. Bunbury obtained a divorce, and Sarah was ostracised by 'polite society' for several years. She eventually found happiness in a second marriage to Colonel George Napier, a widowed and impecunious army officer. They had eight children, three of whom became generals in the British army. As for George III, he never forgot her, describing her during his illness in 1788 as his first love and awarding her an annual pension of £800 following George Napier's death in 1805.[17] Nor did he forget Henry Fox, who, he was told by Bute and his mother, had unscrupulously engineered his wooing of Sarah in order to increase his own influence at court and within the government. Thereafter, he was deeply prejudiced against Fox, and the episode probably coloured his feelings towards Fox's son, Charles James.

If Bute was influential enough to dissuade the infatuated King from marrying into the family of a political rival, he was unlikely to shy away from a showdown even with a minister as popular as Pitt. He merely awaited a plausible opportunity, which arrived in October 1761 when Pitt found himself isolated within the Cabinet (along with his brother-in-law, the Lord Privy Seal, Earl Temple), in an argument concerning the best way to address the threat of war against a new alliance between France and Spain. Pitt determined to make a pre-emptive attack on the Spanish fleet returning from South America laden with gold and other treasures. He was opposed within the Cabinet by Bute, who succeeded in rallying a majority of ministers against him. Pitt flounced out of the government, declaring: 'I will be responsible for nothing that I do not direct.'[18] This resignation was accompanied by a curious transaction, in which the King persuaded him to accept a pension of £3,000 per year and made Hester Pitt Baroness Chatham in her own right. To the ex-minister's backers, this was a distressing sign that he was human after all. Newcastle, who felt totally neglected by Bute, resigned the following year, apparently for good, after a marathon period in government service which had begun back in 1717. (He actually returned in 1765–6 as Lord Privy Seal in the first Rockingham government, but by then was no more than a 'passenger'.)

George III was thus able to instal Bute as prime minister – the first individual to hold that position who could plausibly be called a 'Tory'. Within a few months Bute had changed his tune and declared war on Spain, which was soon humiliated by the capture by British troops both of Havana in the Caribbean and Manila in the Philippines. Lord Bute admired Fox and wanted him to become a Secretary of State, but Fox preferred to retain his lucrative post as Paymaster General. Bute, however, feared difficulties in getting the House of Commons to ratify peace treaties with France and Spain, not least because Pitt was a likely opponent, and persuaded Fox to combine his moneymaking post with the leadership of the Commons. The King reluctantly complied with this arrangement, acknowledging that, at least on a temporary basis, 'We must call in bad men to govern bad men.'[19]

Fox showed that he had not lost his magical managerial touch, and the treaties were approved by a vote of 319–65. His methods were memorably recorded by Horace Walpole:

> [Fox] directly attacked the separate members of the House of Commons; and with so little decorum on the part of either buyer or seller, that a shop was publicly opened at the pay-office, whither the members flocked, and received the wages of their venality in bank-bills, even to so low a sum of two hundred pounds for their votes on the treaty. Twenty-five thousand pounds, as Martin, Secretary of the Treasury, afterwards owned, were issued in one morning; and in a single fortnight a vast majority was purchased to approve the peace![20]

Pitt spoke for more than three hours against the terms of the Treaty of Paris, but on this occasion his speech was widely judged to be more prolix than profound. From his perspective, his argument was unanswerable; although Britain was confirmed in many of its conquests in North America, the West Indies and Africa, and had regained Minorca, it had relinquished Guadeloupe and Martinique as well as islands off the Newfoundland coast which allowed the French to claim fishing rights in the area. The government's crushing margin of victory in the Commons suggested that the result had little to do with the quality of the speeches and instead reflected war-weariness as well as Fox's backstage manoeuvres. Egged on by Bute and the King, Fox – now clearly seen as a Tory – proceeded to exact revenge on those who resisted ratification of the treaty, starting with a clutch of Whig peers, including Newcastle, Rockingham and Grafton, who were stripped of the lord-lieutenancies of their counties. The Duke of Devonshire promptly resigned from his own position in sympathy with his colleagues. But Fox did not stop there. Hundreds of senior and even very minor officials who originally owed their appointments to either of the Pelham brothers were peremptorily dismissed. This operation (later dubbed 'the slaughter of the Pelhamite innocents') was designed to destroy the Whig oligarchy which had ruled the country for half a century, and to realise George III's long-cherished ambition of restoring monarchical authority after the long hegemony of 'bad men'. Fox, who was already unpopular, was now irredeemably damned among the extra-parliamentary elite; and when Bute went on to offer him the premiership for the third time, he refused without hesitation. Instead, his reward consisted of the peerage for which he had long been angling. He hoped for an earldom, or at least a viscountcy, but was offered a mere barony, becoming the first Lord Holland, a title he took from his London home, Holland House. Although this effectively marked the end of Fox's political career, it also seemed to have brought his duel with Pitt to a successful conclusion.

Pitt, however, was far from finished. Although he had never been a slave to consistency, he (unlike Fox) was acutely conscious of the rhetorical utility of appeals to principle. In February 1764, during the controversy aroused by the expulsion from the House of Commons of his supporter John Wilkes, he spoke passionately about the rights of Parliament and of the British people. In January 1766 he attacked the Stamp Act, which had helped to trigger disturbances in North America, and instead asserted the right of Parliament to legislate for the colonies but not to tax their inhabitants. This position was complex, but the main thrust of his argument – that the Act should be repealed – was conveyed with his characteristic clarity. While denying that American colonists could be represented 'virtually' by Westminster MPs, Pitt also questioned the way in which Britons themselves were represented.

It was safer for Pitt to throw stones at the system now that he had escaped from rotten boroughs and since 1757 had sat for the city of Bath (although that constituency was dominated by the oligarchical Corporation and boasted only 30 voters). Nevertheless, the speeches of 1764–6 completed Pitt's political legend: he would be remembered as a fearless champion of the people at home as well as a great war leader. The Stamp Act had been passed under the premiership (1763–5) of Pitt's brother-in-law George Grenville, from whom he had grown increasingly estranged. George III detested Grenville but was running short of options now that his favourite Lord Bute had withdrawn from the political fray in the face of savage press criticism, particularly from Wilkes and his supporters. Pitt suddenly looked more attractive, especially since at times he seemed to favour the King's own preference for a government which transcended party divisions and focused on the national interest. Maybe George III's decision to offer him a pension had been an inspired long-term insurance policy. After several approaches, Pitt finally agreed to form a ministry in July 1766.

At last it seemed that Pitt had reached the summit even of his vaulting ambition, and he emphasised his supremacy over all his old rivals by insisting that no previous prime minister should serve in his ministry. There would certainly be no place for the recently ennobled Lord Holland, who had finally lost the Paymastership in 1765 and lived on for another nine years in a retirement which was occasionally disturbed by the possibility that he would be forced to disgorge some of the wealth he had accumulated as Paymaster General. In this respect he had been a considerable beneficiary of Pitt's grandiose foreign policy, since there was much more cash to rake in from Britain's expanded armed forces. In 1769 the Lord Mayor of London, William Beckford, delivered a petition to Parliament which characterised Fox as 'the public defaulter of unaccounted millions' (according to rumour, Fox's profits had amounted to £400,000 – not 'unaccounted millions', but still a sum far beyond the avaricious dreams of 'Diamond' Pitt). Lord Holland died a deeply disappointed man just five years later, in July 1774, all his remaining hopes resting on his darling son, Charles James Fox.

But if Pitt was undoubtedly the ultimate winner of his contest with Fox, he was not destined to enjoy his triumph. In part, his difficulties arose from a symbol of his relative success. While Lord Holland had been given a mere barony, in 1766 Pitt insisted on an earldom for himself. However, the Earl of Chatham could never hope to command the fervent following which he had attracted in his former guise as plain William Pitt. In accepting his title he had jettisoned his image as 'the Great Commoner'; those of his supporters who had cherished the idea that an 'outsider' could overcome Royal resistance and achieve great things had to accept that their old hero had become part of the Establishment. More materially, he was now a member of the House of Lords rather than the Commons, and even in those days this entailed a diminishment of Chatham's 'box-office' appeal. Finally, Chatham refused any office with specific responsibilities – not even First Lord of the Treasury, the official position which had come to be regarded as the designation of the 'prime minister' – and instead opted for the more ceremonial role of Lord Privy Seal. The Treasury was instead left in the hands of the third Duke of Grafton, a well-meaning young man but essentially a dilettante. Like Henry Fox, Grafton was descended from the bastard son of one of Charles II's many mistresses, in his case Barbara Villiers, Duchess of Cleveland.

Even at the time, it was possible to anticipate that these decisions would hamper Pitt's evident desire to keep overall control of policy. However, he was acting from necessity rather than making voluntary choices, at least in part. Aged 57 when he became prime minister, he had entered the veteran stage for eighteenth-century politicians. More seriously, his health had been erratic even before he seized his chance of parliamentary prominence; indeed, more than once illness had forced him to abandon his favourite stage for months at a time, and the fact that he was able to force himself back, without apparent effort, into the front rank of the Commons after such prolonged absences is in itself eloquent testimony to his unusual prowess. At the time, his ailment was usually diagnosed as gout, from which it seems that Pitt did indeed suffer; but his state of mind was also involved. Pitt's psychological history – episodes of considerable energy interspersed with periods of despondency – points to a diagnosis of manic depression, and this is supported by evidence relating to other close family members, especially his favourite sister, Ann, who was declared insane before her death in 1780.[21] His grandfather, Governor Pitt, was also decidedly eccentric, and the senior branch of the family spawned Thomas Pitt, second Baron Camelford, whose sobriquet 'the half-mad lord' was probably a generous estimate of his psychological equilibrium.[22] Camelford's career ended in 1804 when he was killed in a duel with his best friend; by a curious coincidence, he was mortally wounded in a meadow next to Holland House, headquarters of the Fox family.

Superficial support for some hereditary psychological malady is supplied by Pitt's theatrical approach to parliamentary performances. In later years, when he was no longer so sure of intimidating his listeners through his unassisted physical presence, he employed props such as bandages to emphasise that he was not at his best, and even in an era which was understandably prone to hypochondria – there was no aspirin or paracetamol to assuage minor aches and pains – this was going a bit far. In his personal affairs, Chatham emulated his grandfather in the acquisition of property, but apparently without the same eye to political advantage. Seemingly he just wanted to accumulate estates, whether or not they came gift-wrapped with a safe parliamentary seat; and once he had bought the properties, he was impatient to 'improve' them, whatever the state of his finances. If Pitt had not been a stranger to frugality, despite his gestures of self-denial, he would have died a very rich man. Following the bequest from the Duchess of Marlborough and the £3,000 pension he was awarded on leaving office in 1761, three years later he received a legacy of £1,000 from the famous Bath-based philanthropist Ralph Allen, and in 1765 Sir William Pynsent, a Somerset landowner who had never met his political idol, left him an estate worth around £3,000 per annum. To the Victorian observer, Chatham's ability to work his way through these windfalls and to die in considerable debt would in itself suggest a degree of mental instability, but in the eighteenth-century context such financial imprudence was less remarkable – after all, Chatham was a younger son of an untitled family, and could be forgiven for feeling that he had to spend a lot in order to keep up with the St Johns. Even so, Chatham's disregard for the spectacular imbalance between his outlays and incomings does seem to signify something more deep-rooted than eccentricity; and his favourite son turned out to be equally improvident.

Whatever the nature of Chatham's malady, his ministry proved to be a fiasco, with its main figure effectively an absentee prime minister, leaving a distracted Grafton to pick up the pieces. Charitable observers concluded that Chatham had had a severe nervous breakdown; others thought he had actually gone mad. George III showed remarkable patience with Pitt, and his ministry limped on for over two years until October 1768, when he was finally persuaded to stand down, with George vowing never to employ him again.

The circumstances of Chatham's departure from office might have reassured his political opponents that the volcano was finally extinct, but he was still capable of violent eruptions. He returned to public life a year or so later, apparently cured of his ailments, and made cogent criticisms of Lord North's government and its conduct of the war against the American colonists. Chatham appeared to be offering himself once again as a war leader, and one who could either achieve victory or, preferably, reach a peaceful agreement with the colonists – for whom he had a great deal of sympathy, though he was opposed to ceding independence. His proposed formula could be paraphrased as 'You should acknowledge Britain's sovereignty on the understanding that it will never exercise it in a way which will upset you.' But George III had burnt his fingers with Pitt once before, and was not going to risk a repeat performance by bowing to the popular clamour for a recall. Also, the King retained the illusion that a British victory was still possible until long after his prime minister, Lord North, and most of his colleagues had concluded that the game was up.

On 7 April 1778 Chatham made a spectacular appearance in the House of Lords, where, swathed in flannel and clearly in a depleted physical condition, he delivered a dramatic but largely incoherent speech opposing a resolution by the third Duke of Richmond (Charles Fox's uncle) to let the colonists go their own way. The man who had once declared 'If I were an American, as I am an Englishman, while a foreign troop was landed in my country, I never would lay down my arms – never! never! never!', now asserted: 'If the Americans defend their independence they will find me in their way.'[23] When Richmond replied to his arguments, he intervened a second time but collapsed in a sudden fit. He was carried out of a shocked House by his two grief-stricken sons and a son-in-law, and died a month later on 11 May 1778 at Hayes in Kent, a property which he had bought in 1754 and which was the birthplace of his son William. On the same day, the House of Commons voted that he should have an official funeral in Westminster Abbey, that a memorial to him should be erected, and that all his debts should be paid off at public expense.

Despite their earlier achievements, both Chatham and Holland died without a sense of fulfilment. Both were determined that one of their sons could, and should, achieve the unalloyed political success which had eluded them. Their eldest progeny seemed to lack promise, and both concentrated instead on their second sons, Chatham coaching the younger Pitt in oratory from the age of seven, and Holland giving the precocious young Charles every encouragement and opportunity to achieve great things. There was good reason to expect that the Pitt–Fox rivalry would be resumed in the next generation at some level, although it defied the laws of probability to think that the renewal could emulate the prolonged high-wire act performed by Lords Chatham and Holland.

3

Charles James Fox:
Early Life, 1749–74

H E nearly didn't make it. He was thought to be stillborn, and his apparently lifeless body was casually placed on a ledge; several minutes later, he suddenly uttered his first cry. Charles James Fox was born on 24 January 1749 at his father's rented London home in Conduit Street. He was the second surviving son of Henry Fox and his wife, the former Lady Caroline Lennox. His elder brother, Stephen, was born in 1748, and his younger brother, Henry Edward, in 1755. It was not long before Charles became the favourite of both parents, who found him exceptionally precocious and quick-witted, and with a very sweet nature. Neither Stephen nor the young Henry gave any sign of resenting this favouritism, and the relationship between the three brothers remained very close and loving throughout their lives. Their childhood was largely spent in Holland House, an impressive Jacobean mansion on the western edge of Kensington, which Henry Fox first rented and later purchased, and from which he took his title in 1763. It later became famous as the venue of the most notable of the Whig salons, presided over by the third Lord Holland, Charles's nephew. It was destroyed by enemy bombing in September 1940, but the 52 acres of its grounds were later sold to the former London County Council and opened to the public as Holland Park.[1]

History has chosen to credit Fox with both his given names, but in his lifetime he was almost universally known as Charles, or very often

'Charley'. Much more is known about his childhood than about any other eighteenth-century politician because of the plethora of letters about him written by his parents and family friends. Very many of these have survived in the Holland House archives (now in the British Library) and extracts have been published in numerous books, notably in the two-volume biography of Henry Fox by his kinsman, the sixth Earl of Ilchester.[2] The earliest such letter was written by Henry Fox to his elder brother, the first Earl of Ilchester, the day after Charles's birth. It was hardly flattering. 'He is,' he wrote, 'weakly, but likely to live. His skin hangs all shrivell'd about him, his eyes stare, he has a black head of hair, and 'tis incredible how like a monkey he look'd before he was dressed.'[3]

Before very long, however, his father was boasting of how 'pretty' Charles was and how exceptional he was in every way. Henry became the earliest and most passionate admirer of the young Charles, and was an exceptionally indulgent father. Stories circulated far and wide of his utter failure to curb him in any way. When he proceeded to smash up his father's very valuable watch, Henry just looked on, saying, 'if it must be it must be.'[4] When the elder Fox forgot a promise to Charles that he could watch a wall being knocked down, he ordered it to be reconstructed so that he could watch its second destruction. He did not complain when Charles threw an important dispatch onto a fire, and calmly proceeded to rewrite it. As a busy minister, in 1756 he wrote to his wife complaining that his duties prevented him from dining 'tête à tête with Charles', then aged just seven, who was 'infinitely engaging & clever & pretty'.[5] Instructions were given to servants, family and friends that Charles should never be constricted in any way: 'Let nothing be done to break his spirit. The world will do that business fast enough,' he was reported as saying.[6] Lady Caroline was uneasy that her second son was given so much latitude, but was not able to restrain her husband, and made no strenuous attempt to do so. She fretted, however, when she heard of the accomplishments of the much more strictly brought up younger Pitt, still an infant and nearly ten years younger than her second son. He 'will be a thorn in Charles's side as long as he lives', she presciently declared.[7] Charles grew up adoring both his parents, but made no effort to conceal his preference for his father.

Initially Charles was educated at home, but at the age of seven it became clear that his knowledge, of history in particular, was beginning to exceed that of his mother, who was attempting to teach him. At his own request, he was sent to a school in Wandsworth, run by a Frenchman, M. Pampellone, and attended by two of his older cousins. He took great pleasure in outshining them, particularly in Latin, and it was probably due to the headmaster's influence that he grew up speaking an excellent if at times idiosyncratic French, with virtually no accent. A year later, in June 1758, he proceeded to Eton, where he joined his brother, Stephen (known in the family as 'Ste'), and a significant number of his aristocratic relatives and family friends. Unlike the elder Pitt, who had hated Eton, describing it as a 'stultifying and brutal place' and resolving that his own sons should never go anywhere near it,[8] Charles found it delightful and was immensely popular both with his teachers and his fellow pupils. It was at Eton that he acquired a lifelong love of the classics, and of French and, later, Italian literature. His tutors were amazed at his quickness and the breadth of his knowledge, but concerned about his short attention span. It was at Eton that his genius for friendship was first developed, and it was there that he surrounded himself with a group of young noblemen, many of whom were to be his companions for life – in success and adversity, in London gambling clubs and brothels, at the racecourses, in the House of Commons, briefly in government and in the long dispiriting years in opposition. What they found was a young man of extraordinary vitality, immensely gifted, warm, witty, open-minded, completely devoid of hypocrisy and incapable of bearing a grudge. In the later words of Edmund Burke, with whom he was closely associated for many years until the French Revolution finally drove them apart, he was a man 'made to be loved.'[9]

When he was 14, in May 1763, his father took him to Paris at the conclusion of the Seven Years' War. Here Henry Fox determined to ensure that Charles became a 'man of the world', introducing him to the pastimes of both sex and gambling and not objecting to his dressing as a dandy. Charles needed no encouragement, and plunged enthusiastically into a regime of debauchery. This had a lasting effect; he became an addictive gambler, which had a markedly deleterious effect both on his own life and on his father's fortune. The latter had repeatedly – and uncomplainingly – to bail him out of his losses. As late as November 1773, seven months before his death, he wrote the following note to his financial advisor:

> I do hereby order, direct and require you to sell and dispose of my long annuitys [sic], and so much of my other stock, estates and effects, as will be sufficient to pay and discharge the debts of my son The Honble Charles James Fox, not exceeding the sum of one hundred thousand pounds.[10]

It was not only Charles who helped to dissipate his father's fortune. His elder brother, Stephen, who was even more addicted to gambling and had extravagant tastes, was equally dependent on his overindulgent father, who was estimated to have spent at least £200,000 (approximately £18.5 million in 2018 values) to settle the two brothers' debts.[11] Fortunately, his youngest son, Henry Edward, led a relatively blameless life as an army officer, rising to the rank of general, and eventually finishing up as the governor of Gibraltar.

The teenage Charles spent four months in Paris, and became thoroughly Gallicised, conducting much of his personal correspondence in French and constantly writing poetry – most but not all of it doggerel – in the language of Voltaire, whom both he and his brother Stephen met. Voltaire was impressed with the young Charles, who returned convinced that France was the most civilised and agreeable of countries; but he had the good sense not to let this go to his head. When it was suggested that he should pay a second visit some months later at Christmas and the New Year, he wrote to his father:

> I am so fully convinced of the use of being at Eton that I am afraid of running the risk of not returning. I am resolved to stay there until Christmas twelve month: by this you may see that the petit maitre de Paris is converted into an Oxford pedant.[12]

So Charles completed his Eton education, and, still five months short of his 16th birthday, enrolled at Hart Hall (now Hertford College) in the autumn of 1764. He did not enjoy Oxford as much as Eton, but found it agreeable enough. He left after two years, without taking a degree, writing to his friend Sir George Macartney:

> I employed almost my whole time at Oxford in the mathematical and classical knowledge, but more particularly in the latter, so that I understand Greek and Latin tolerably well. I am totally ignorant in every part of useful knowledge. I am more convinced every day how little advantage there is in being what at school and the university is called a good scholar: one receives a good deal of amusement from it, but that is all.[13]

In 1766, he embarked on the grand tour, initially spending much time in Paris in the company of his brother Stephen and for a time his mother. He then proceeded to the south of France, and on to Italy soaking up culture and indulging in a wide variety of casual sexual encounters, both paid and unpaid, complaining in September 1767 to his friend Richard Fitzpatrick, 'I have had one pox and one clap this summer. I believe I am the most unlucky rascal in the universe.'[14] In a further letter to Fitzpatrick, in November 1767, he wrote that he had 'nul inclination pour le marriage, que c'etait même mon aversion, & que rien ne m'y pourroit engager.'[15]

L. G. Mitchell, who cites this passage, notes: 'He would not enter into a stable relationship until he was 35 and would not marry until he was 46.'

Henry Fox had never doubted that the destiny both of Charles and his elder brother, Stephen, lay in the House of Commons. In preparation for the general election of 1768, he made the necessary preparations, purchasing together with his own elder brother, the first Earl of Ilchester, the pocket borough of Midhurst, a small Sussex town. Ilchester's great-great nephew, the sixth Earl, described the transaction in the following terms:

> The possession of certain plots of land, or hovels, unfit in many cases for habitation, constituted the right to a vote in this type of borough. When the title-deeds of the hereditaments were accumulated in one ownership, an election became a simple matter. A few days before the

appointed date the proprietor would apportion the property among his servants or representatives, with instructions to return the two members whom he indicated, and to re-execute the deeds in his favour, as soon as the business was concluded.[16]

The two candidates indicated were Ilchester's son, Lord Stavordale, and Charles James Fox. Nobody seemed to mind that Fox was away in France and had never set foot in Midhurst, or that he was only 19 and the minimum age for candidates was 21; he duly took his seat, and made his maiden speech in April 1769 when he was still only 20 years and four months. At the same election, and in similar circumstances, his elder brother Stephen was also voted in for the constituency of New Sarum (also known as Salisbury).

The new Member for Midhurst was an extremely attractive young man in every respect, other than perhaps his looks. He was no matinee idol, being swarthy and distinctly portly. Many people remarked that his features resembled those of his great-great grandfather, Charles II. He had no particular political views and seems – like very many of his contemporaries – to have regarded his election primarily as a means to advance his own social standing, to gain access to patronage for his relatives and friends and to open the way to ministerial office. His guiding light was always his adored father Henry, who had become Lord Holland in 1763 and finally (and reluctantly) relinquished his office as Paymaster General two years later. Because his father had become a Tory after serving under Lord Bute, Charles too declared himself a Tory and defended with great vigour every policy his father had ever espoused. From the outset, he became one of the most active of MPs, speaking no fewer than 254 times in his first five years. And what speeches they were! It was not very long before the whole House realised that here was an orator of the highest order, speaking with total self-confidence, often without notes and having been up all night cheerfully gambling away his father's fortune. Within a very few months the prime minister, Lord North (who sat in the Commons because his title was a courtesy one as the eldest son of an earl), determined to make him a junior minister so as to greatly reinforce the government's debating power in the chamber. George III, who detested his father and disapproved of Charles's dissolute ways, initially resisted, but eventually gave way to North's pleadings. So, in February 1770, a month after his 21st birthday, he was appointed to the Admiralty Board, where he diligently put aside his customary indolence and proved to be a hard-working and effective minister.

North's government was a hard-line Tory one, and Fox did not disdain from supporting some of its most reactionary measures. One such was the exclusion from the Commons of the campaigner for press freedom, John Wilkes, for alleged criminal libels. Wilkes was three times re-elected by his Middlesex constituents, but on the third occasion the House decreed that his defeated rival, a Colonel Luttrell, who got many fewer votes, should be seated instead. Fox firmly supported this, and led the demand for strong action to be taken against Wilkes and his main supporters. In a remarkable speech on 25 March 1771 he revealed utter contempt for the opinions of voters, which contrasted sharply with the views he was expressing two decades later when he proposed a toast 'to our sovereign lord, the people':

> What acquaintance have the people at large with the arcana of political rectitude, with the connections of kingdoms, the resources of national strength, the abilities of ministers, or even their own dispositions? [...] Sir, I pay no regard whatever to the voice of the people: it is our duty to do what is proper, without considering what may be agreeable: their business is to choose us: it is ours to act constitutionally, and to maintain the independency of Parliament.[17]

His attacks on Wilkes earned him the enmity of the London 'mob', and on 27 March both Charles and his brother Stephen were dragged out of their carriage and beaten up in the street in a riot against Lord North, who showed great courage in facing down his angry assailants. Nor was Fox without enemies in the House of Commons, where he dominated by his eloquence but upset many by his presumption. According to Horace Walpole, 'At 22 he acted and was hated as a leader of a party; his arrogance, loquacity and intemperance raising him the enemies of a Minister [i.e. a prime minister] before he had the power of one.'[18]

Among those irritated by Fox's insouciance was the prime minister, Lord North. An easy-going character, North was prepared to cut his young colleague a great deal of slack, but his patience was sorely tried. Perhaps this was the reason that he turned a deaf ear to Charles's frequent pleas for patronage for various relatives and dependants, which led to his entire family building up a sense of grievance for which there was little objective justification. Lady Caroline gave vent to this in a letter addressed to her youngest son, Henry Edward, in February 1772:

> Ld North has treated both your brothers with much slight. They have not obtained of him the smallest favor they have asked for Salisbury people or others they have apply'd for, and Ste[phen] says Ld. Radnor has got things he was refused.[19]

In the same letter, Charles's mother complained of North's 'most unpardonable neglect' in not advising him in advance of the Royal Marriages Bill, which he was expected to introduce in the House of Commons. This bill was George III's reaction to the 'unsuitable' matches made by two of his younger brothers, the Dukes of Gloucester and Cumberland. The former, the King's favourite brother, had not only married Maria, the glamorous but illegitimate granddaughter of Sir Robert Walpole and young widow of Earl Waldegrave, but had kept the marriage secret from his father for six years, only revealing it when his wife became pregnant and rumours spread like wildfire throughout London society. His brother then announced his marriage to Anne Horton, a 27-year-old widow two years Cumberland's senior and the daughter of a disreputable Irish peer, Lord Irnham, who had been described by Lord Bute's daughter, Lady Louisa Stuart, as 'the greatest reprobate in England'.[20] It also hardly added to Anne Horton's qualifications that she was the sister of Colonel Luttrell, who had been awarded John Wilkes's seat after he had been disqualified from the House of Commons.

Yet it was not only Charles's disgust that North had kept him in ignorance of the bill that led to his immediate resignation in February 1772 after less than two years in office. He genuinely believed that it breached what would nowadays be described as the human rights of younger members of the Royal Family. More importantly, he felt that he owed it to his father and mother, who might have fallen foul of such an act if it had existed at the time of their elopement. He was well aware of the strong opposition of his father to an earlier bill, introduced in 1753 by Lord Hardwicke, the Lord Chancellor at the time, which became the Clandestine Marriages Act and which Henry Fox suspected had been specifically directed at him. The new bill applied only to the descendants of George II, forbidding them to marry before the age of 25 without the prior permission of the Crown, and even above that age they were to give 12 months' notice in advance and either House of Parliament could veto the marriage. This Act is still in force today, and its most prominent 'victim' was the then 23-year-old Princess Margaret, who in 1953 was forced to wait two years before she could get married to Group Captain Peter Townsend, and then thought better of it. Charles now set himself to oppose the bill by every means, moving a series of amendments at the committee stage, and even attempted to repeal Hardwicke's bill.

Apart from his parents, Charles got very little credit for his resignation. The general view among Members of Parliament was that it was quite unnecessary and was a sign of his immaturity and self-indulgence; if he had remained in office he could have excused himself from introducing the bill in the Commons and even voted against it, as collective ministerial responsibility was not as strict in 1772 as it later became. Both George III and North were angry with him, but the latter badly needed his assistance in the House of Commons, and only ten months later invited him back to the superior post of a Lord of the Treasury. He remained in this post, working hard and loyally for 15 months, until February 1774, when his second 'resignation' (though it was, in fact, a dismissal) occurred. An article had appeared in the *Public Advertiser* criticising the Speaker of the House of Commons, Sir Fletcher Norton. It was written by the famous radical parson, the Reverend John Horne, popularly known as Horne Tooke, and the printer of the newspaper, William Woodfall, was summoned to explain himself at the bar of the Commons. He adopted a penitent tone, saying that due to pressures of work he had not actually read the article prior to agreeing its publication; he knew it was about the House of Commons, but was unaware of its provocative and scurrilous nature. Woodfall claimed that he had been a printer for 20 years without causing any offence, and asked for this to be taken into consideration in judging his case. Most MPs were satisfied with his explanation, and were willing to let him off with a warning, but Charles Fox, who regarded any criticism of the Commons as beyond the pale, moved that Woodfall should be committed to Newgate Prison. Lord North, who had agreed to support Fox's motion before hearing Woodfall's explanation, was acutely embarrassed. He now favoured leniency and asked Fox to release him from his promise, but Fox insisted that he keep to his word as a gentleman. A deeply unhappy North duly voted for Fox's motion, but recommended his followers to vote against, and it was defeated by 152 votes to 68. There was an immediate reaction against Fox, who was seen as arrogant and vindictive and was widely condemned for humiliating North, who – at that time – was highly popular in the House. At the very least, a large question mark now appeared against Fox's judgement.

North himself was appalled at Fox's conduct, but his anger was nothing compared to the rage of George III. Ten days after the debate, Fox received a curt note from the prime minister. It read: 'His majesty has thought proper to order a new commission of the treasury to be made out, in which I do not see your name.'[21] Fox, who had regarded the affair as a great jape, originally dismissed the note as a hoax, but it eventually dawned upon him that he might have done fatal damage to his political career. He was still only 25, and it was not easy to discern a route back for him to follow. This appalling setback was followed in quick succession by the deaths of his three closest relatives, each of whom he adored. On 1 July 1774, Lord Holland, whose health had been deteriorating for some time, died peacefully in his sleep in his sixty-ninth year. His wife, Lady Holland, who was already dying of cancer, followed him to the grave 23 days later, aged 51. Their eldest son, Stephen, who became the second Baron Holland, was able to enjoy his title for only a few months. Never in the best of health, he succumbed to dropsy in November 1774, at the age of 26. The title then went to his infant son, Richard Vassall Fox, who grew up to become the closest and most faithful follower of his Uncle Charles.

The deaths of his parents and brother led to a modest improvement in Charles's financial situation. His father's fortune was largely depleted,[22] but it was still sufficient for him to leave Charles an income of £900 a year, £20,000 in cash, small estates in Thanet and Sheppey and the family's holiday villa at Kingsgate, to which he was much attached. From his brother, he inherited a very valuable sinecure, the Clerkship of the Pells, bringing in £2,300 a year. Charles was beginning to have doubts about the justification of sinecures, and chose to sell the reversion to the government in exchange for annual payments of £1,700 for 31 years.[23] Even after the loss of his ministerial salary, this should have provided him with an adequate income to satisfy his own needs and those of any family he might create – if only he could conquer his gambling addiction. This was quite beyond him, and he was condemned to a life of dodging creditors, borrowing from moneylenders at excessive rates of interest and having to rely, when *in extremis*, on whip-rounds by his wealthy friends. So beloved was he that they frequently did this without complaining, feeling it was an honour to be able to help *le grand Charley*. Much of his gambling was done at all-night sessions at clubs like Almack's, Brooks's or White's, or at race meetings, especially at Newmarket, but he was always eager to place bets with personal friends or acquaintances about any passing event. So notorious did his gambling become, and so frequent his losses, that a ditty soon began to circulate around town:

> At Almack's of pigeons I am told there are flocks;
> But it's thought that the completest is one Mr Fox,
> If he touches a card, if he rattles a box,
> Away fly the guineas of this Mr Fox.
> He has met, I'm afraid, with so many bad knocks,
> The cash is not plenty with this Mr Fox;
> In gaming 'tis said he's the stoutest of cocks.
> No man can play deeper than this Mr Fox,
> And he always must lose, for the strongest of locks
> Cannot keep any money for this Mr Fox.
> No doubt such behaviour exceedingly shocks
> The friends and relations of this Mr Fox.[24]

4

The Early Career of Pitt the Younger:
A Chip off the Old Block?

REFLECTING in 1796 on his arduous path to political prominence, Edmund Burke wrote that he was not 'swaddled, and rocked, and dandled into a Legislator.'[1] He was comparing his relatively humble origins with the advantages inherited by grandees like the Foxite Duke of Bedford, who had attacked the award of a government pension to the debt-laden Burke. As so often in his later years, Burke had allowed his rhetorical powers to run away with him; if they were damaging to his enemy, Bedford, his remarks could also be applied to the prime minister, William Pitt the Younger, who had been very helpful in securing the pension.

It is not surprising that Pitt the Younger's biographers have tended to speculate about the biological and environmental factors which influenced their subject. In part, this reflects his extraordinary political precocity; if he had become prime minister for the first time at 42 rather than 24, it would seem less relevant to speculate about the respective effects of nature and nurture. But it also reflects the fact that he was the son of a remarkable politician. Although members of the same family have often played significant roles in British politics – not least in the eighteenth century, when family connections were such an important factor in political fortunes – it is very rare for a father and son to leave similar records of achievement, let alone the remarkable feat of holding the highest office under the Crown. Arguably, indeed, the story of this particular father and son is *so* remarkable that it has often been trivialised, an attitude captured brilliantly by the satirists Sellar and Yeatman, who wrote that George III's ministers 'were always called Pitt' and that they 'generally came in waves of two'.[2] The plight of Pitt-portrayers is made even worse by the fact that father and son also shared a Christian name, rather like the wave (or waltz?) of Johann Strausses which swept through Vienna from the 1820s.

In fact, if the two Pitts had not been so closely related, commentators from their time to ours would have mused over the sharply contrasting qualities of two of the greatest eighteenth-century leaders. More considered biographers have emphasised that, far from being a kind of Chathamite clone, the younger Pitt's character and appearance bore a much closer resemblance to members of his mother's family, the Grenvilles. The most arresting feature of the Earl of Chatham, for example, was his eyes; contemporaries were cowed by them, and even in his portraits one can detect 'the sneer of cold command'. If Chatham's eyes had been less remarkable, his large, fleshy nose would have attracted more comment. By contrast, one could detect more feeling in the eyes of his son; but this feature was not sufficiently noticeable to distract attention from the Younger Pitt's nose, which caricaturists invariably rendered as a Grenvillite beak.

Being the product of two political families did not necessarily give Pitt a genetic advantage; his elder sibling, John, was an amiable but indolent individual who would not have held office without his illustrious family connections.[3] In one important respect Pitt's pedigree might in fact have been a disadvantage; there is a strong possibility that the elder Pitt suffered from manic depression, and that this could have been passed on to his children. The younger Pitt's health was indeed a regular cause for parental concern, and in his later years he seemed vulnerable to mood swings, although he never exhibited his father's wild fluctuations between volcanic activity and physical and mental prostration. Notoriously, the belief that the younger Pitt had inherited his father's propensity to 'gout' – at the time a portmanteau description rather than a precise diagnosis – led to the prescription of port wine. Lord Rosebery thought that this prolonged his life, but modern opinion would suggest that it shortened it. In any event, it is a moot point whether Pitt actually inherited any maladies, or whether his father's erratic medical history induced a state of parental hypochondria in which his son's slightest cough or sniff was interpreted as an imminent threat to life. At least the doctors (who included Anthony Addington, Chatham's physician and the father of a politician who played an important role in the younger Pitt's life) added some outdoor exercise to their prescriptions.

In his private activities Pitt the Younger did follow his father's example to some extent. Both embraced the contemporary vogue for landscape gardening, in a departure from their usual lack of interest in aesthetic displays. The younger Pitt could never have acquired properties with the irrational fervour shown by 'Diamond' Pitt or his father, who bought Hayes Place in Kent after his marriage, commenced various 'improvements', then sold it after his surprise inheritance of Burton Pynsent, before buying it back again in 1757. Nevertheless, just like his father the younger Pitt seemed to combine a refusal to compete with the biggest-spending political families with a feeling that high office demanded a certain style of living, even if this exceeded his resources. His careful stewardship of national finances (even when circumstances forced him to borrow) contrasted to a ludicrous extent with an utter inattention to his personal affairs, meaning that the whole of his adult life was overshadowed by debt. Unlike Charles Fox, though, who spent on a scale which reflected his relish for life, it is doubtful whether Pitt received much satisfaction in return for his extravagance.

The obvious trait which connects the elder and the younger Pitt is their ambition to lead, rather than to follow. Both were completely satisfied that public affairs could only prosper under their overall direction. However, there was a crucial difference which surely would have been noticed more widely if the two men had not been related. For Pitt the Elder, political life was essentially about self-assertion; he was determined to prove his superiority over his rivals, and once he had done so he seems to have run out of impetus. His son was supremely confident of his abilities, apparently to the extent of taking his superiority for granted; but in his mind, his real work would only begin once his right to govern had been acknowledged. It would be unfair to say that the elder Pitt was an inspired actor whose main ambition was to give a good show, while his son was a decision maker who regarded the need for public performances as a necessary (and occasionally regrettable) distraction from business; but the descriptions are accurate enough to suggest that a sense of personal destiny divided the two Pitts as much as it united them.

Long before they could have any idea of John's limitations, Pitt the Younger's parents were ambitious on their second son's behalf. Even when the baby's orations consisted of screams and burbling, his mother wrote: 'I cannot help believing that little William is to become a personage.'[4] Before long the pardonable hyperbole of parentage turned into genuine pride, even something approaching awe. The child won a series of nicknames within the family, including 'William the Great', 'the Young Senator' and 'the Philosopher'.[5]

His father's antipathy towards Eton (which presumably encompassed other similar institutions), combined with concern for William's health, meant that his precocious talents were nurtured in seclusion from his peers. In 1765 the family engaged the Reverend Edward Wilson, a graduate of Pembroke Hall, Cambridge, as William's tutor and his father's chaplain. According to the usual account, Wilson provided the expected pedagogical fare – English history and literature, mathematics and the classics – while the trimmings were supplied by William's father, who enforced an intensive course in rhetoric, asking him to read aloud from authors like Shakespeare and Milton, making him translate the original language of classical authors into English as he read them and encouraging him to treat his audience as if it was Parliament itself. Probably the psychological impact of these lessons was out of proportion to their duration. According to Horace Walpole – admittedly an observer who was often unsympathetic towards the elder Pitt, but nevertheless, as the youngest son of another great politician, an apposite witness – Chatham 'could not bear' to be in close proximity to his children for long. Hayes Park, where the younger Pitt had been born, was redesigned to ensure that he could escape from his offspring.[6]

Pitt the Younger was being equipped for a political career, but his education did not preclude other ways of becoming a 'personage'. In hindsight it might seem that everyone concerned would have designated the boy for politics rather than the Anglican Church or the legal profession, but these provided good alternative prospects for an intelligent (male) child.

The final choice was likely to be made by William himself, who had been born when his father was in his fifty-first year. Fortunately for the elder Pitt, long before he died he could be confident that William shared his own preferences. Most of the younger Pitt's biographers record a family trip to Weymouth when William was seven, which was punctuated by tributes to his (absent) father, including the ringing of Yeovil's church bells. In the same year, according to the Reverend Wilson, William declared that 'he was glad he was not the eldest son, but that he could serve his country in the House of Commons, like his papa.'[7]

The latter anecdote is particularly thought-provoking because it must relate to 1766 – the year in which Pitt the Elder took voluntary leave of the House of Commons by accepting a peerage, thus lowering himself in the estimation of supporters (such as the inhabitants of Yeovil) who had hailed him as 'the Great Commoner'. It was also around this time that Charles James Fox's mother is supposed to have said that William was 'not eight years old and really the cleverest child I ever saw', before predicting, with an uncanny foresight that would have helped her son immeasurably during his regular gambling forays, that the child would 'be a thorn in Charles's side as long as he lives'. While the detail of such stories is open to question, it is surely significant that they cover a relatively brief period, when the younger Pitt was seven years old. Before reaching this age, the child had shown sufficient ability to make him the apple of his parents' eyes and possibly a worthy successor to his father as a prominent politician. However, although the younger Pitt had been born in the year of his father's greatest triumphs, it was not until 1766 that the Earl of Chatham was given the King's commission to form a government – that is, when the man who had shown so much relish for the journey to the political summit had finally arrived. From that point, Chatham had new reason to cherish the hope that he had emulated other great families by establishing a political dynasty. This was clearly on his mind as he undertook the burdens of office; in the preceding days he told his wife (presumably half in jest and half in earnest) that he anticipated 'many sage reflections from William, upon the public papers'.[8]

Although in his first years William Pitt the Younger had shown every sign of being a worthy successor to his father, the impression is that after

1766 these expectations increased. The effect on Pitt of this is shown by the tone of his letters to his parents; when reporting back to his father he used overblown language, but he adopted an easy, conversational tone when writing to his mother. William was obviously anxious to please his father, but it was an uphill and ultimately unavailing struggle. When writing those letters, he was least like himself.

In 1773, when William was 14, he matriculated at Pembroke Hall, the Cambridge college of his tutor Edward Wilson, who accompanied him and continued to supervise his studies for more than a year; after this, he was entrusted to another Pembroke fellow, George Pretyman. Pretyman, who later appended the surname Tomline, became a lifelong friend, although he differed from his former pupil on the crucial issue of Catholic Emancipation (see Chapter Fourteen). Despite initial hopes that William would be a star undergraduate, worries about his health caused lengthy interruptions to his attendance and his diligent reading seems to have deepened, rather than widened, his knowledge in favoured subjects like History, Philosophy and (especially) classical literature. His main debt to Cambridge was social; while Pembroke Hall had only a handful of students, these included Edward Eliot, whose father controlled several parliamentary seats in Cornwall (and who later married William's sister Harriot), and John Hamilton, later first Marquess of Abercorn. Trinity College housed many equally congenial companions. The friends Pitt made at Cambridge included the Earl of Euston, later fourth Duke of Grafton, and John Pratt, later second Lord Camden. Both of these were the sons of senior politicians who were well disposed towards Pitt the Elder. The Marquess of Granby (fourth Duke of Rutland after 1779), left Cambridge soon after William's arrival, but was elected as one of the university's two MPs in 1774 and became a follower of the elder Pitt. Also at Trinity was William Lowther, whose family enjoyed considerable influence over elections in the county of Westmorland.

Rather like Harry Potter at the fictional school of Hogwarts, William Pitt had moved out of relative isolation and stepped into a world where his name alone gave him considerable cachet even among aristocrats; the Earl of Chatham might have resigned in 1768, but he continued to be a force to be reckoned with. Pitt's new friends shared his fascination with the political world, which (thanks to their connections) they were all preparing to join. Indeed, rather than being dissipated representatives of decadent noble families – the kind of people who provided eighteenth-century England with its version of a 'celebrity culture' – the members of Pitt's circle tended to be serious-minded individuals who recognised political service as a duty.

The American War of Independence dominated public affairs during Pitt's Cambridge career, and it was natural for him to share his father's preference for concessions which might secure continued British rule. He attended numerous parliamentary debates, and although he suspended his critical faculties when his father was speaking, he subjected other orators to careful scrutiny, drawing on his knowledge of debates from the classical period but also showing a sensitivity to the nuances of contemporary political controversies.

As we have seen, William was present on 7 April 1778 when his father collapsed after delivering his final, impassioned speech on peace with America. Although he survived for just over a month, it seemed that a commitment to politics had killed Pitt the Elder, as surely as it had made him. His son could have interpreted the lurid events of April 1778 either as a warning, or as a signal to pick up the burden. William Pitt chose to heed the signal rather than the warning.

Chatham was initially buried at his beloved Hayes, but his remains were transferred to Westminster Abbey in June 1778. William was the chief mourner, and in a dignified report to his mother noted that although the public had shown considerable respect the court had snubbed the ceremony. Parliament voted to clear Chatham's debts of around £20,000, and granted an annuity of £4,000 to support the dignity of the earldom which passed to William's elder brother. But this meant that William was embarking on his career without adequate means, a situation which was aggravated by the fact that his mother's pension was often in arrears. He was forced to contract loans, especially in connection with chambers which he rented in Lincoln's Inn in preparation for qualifying to practice at the Bar.

In July 1780 Pitt travelled to the West Country to start his legal career. However, he had also been preparing to offer himself as a candidate at the next general election, which under the terms of the Septennial Act could not be held later than 1781. In fact, Parliament was dissolved in September 1780, and polling took place over the next few weeks.

There were already suggestions that a convenient berth would be found for William through his personal connections – Old Sarum was even mentioned as a possibility. However, William had remained in residence in Cambridge until the requirements of the Bar took him to London at the end of 1779, and he clearly felt an affinity for the university. Compared to Old Sarum this constituency was a democrat's dream; more than a thousand votes were cast in the 1780 contest, and there were five candidates for the two seats. Furthermore, since the electorate consisted of Cambridge graduates (rather than local property-holders), it was somewhat more discerning than the usual body of voters and not so susceptible to crude corruption. Pitt's chances were always slight; there had been a by-election in 1779 (when his friend the Marquess of Granby vacated his seat to take the family dukedom), and the first three home in that recent contest were all standing again in 1780. As it turned out, they occupied the same three places, with Pitt trailing the field. However, he applied himself seriously to the task of canvassing, and attracted 142 votes – more than his populist father had accumulated throughout his whole career on the hustings.

While doing nothing to mar Pitt's reputation, the Cambridge election was probably one of several instances when his natural optimism led him to act without considering the consequences of failure. By contesting Cambridge rather than taking an easier option, he had shown very clearly that he had no wish to seem dependent on any boroughmonger. In other words, he had actually made it harder for him to accept the well-intentioned offers of seats from friends and family. Meanwhile, the election had left Lord North in power, with a vulnerable majority and a policy towards America which Pitt warmly opposed. He was understandably impatient to enter the Commons long before the next general election, which could be as late as 1787.

Thankfully for Pitt, his Cambridge friend William Lowther had a father who found himself with a spare seat out of the nine that he controlled in the north-west of England. William Lowther had been returned for Appleby, but the grateful electors of Cumberland had also chosen him for a more prestigious seat in Carlisle. Sir James Lowther was not known to bestow his favours unconditionally; but on this occasion it was easy to strike an agreeable deal for both parties, on the understanding that their views on public matters were broadly similar, and that if they should disagree in future Lowther would be free to select another parliamentary champion to represent the good people of Appleby.

Thus when Parliament reassembled in January 1781 William Pitt capitalised on his good fortune in being the Earl of Chatham's second son, and took his seat in the Commons. He was committed to no 'party' (even in the imprecise meaning of that term in the early 1780s), but was obviously opposed to North's government. Anyone who knew him could be certain that he would cleave to his father's position on America, at least so long as that remained practical, but in other policy areas he would try to be true to Chatham's legacy. Fortunately for him, even in Chatham's favoured area of foreign policy that legacy was ambiguous; and anyone who wanted to follow his domestic agenda would be almost entirely free from principled commitments, except perhaps for a vaguely positive attitude towards electoral reform.

Despite its various upheavals Chatham's career could be used as an illustration and defence of the informal checks and balances in the British constitution. He had opposed government policy and had become a senior minister, despite serious royal reservations, because he clearly enjoyed significant public support, which had to be accommodated. People like Chatham could thus be seen as essential intermediaries between the Crown and the 'People'. Before his first attempt to gain a parliamentary seat, the younger Pitt had witnessed the kind of thing that could easily happen if the shock absorbers between the palace and 'the mob' failed to operate. The Gordon Riots of June 1780 have attracted insufficient attention from historians because the rioters were acting on the wrong sort of grievances; instead of rising up on behalf of 'radical' causes and thus anticipating the French Revolution, these were reactionary anti-Catholics who were lashing out against moderately progressive reforms. In his Lincoln's Inn Fields lodgings Pitt remained phlegmatic; but it is very likely that his close proximity to the rioting helped to inform his attitude towards future threats to public order, whatever their source.

As for the individual human being who prepared to make his maiden speech early in 1781, it will always be difficult to form an assessment since so much of the testimony, even from Pitt's contemporaries, is so heavily coloured by hindsight. In this respect it is particularly valuable that the budding philosopher Jeremy Bentham recorded his encounters with the younger Pitt in letters which have been preserved and published. In August 1781 he told his father about a social gathering which included several senior politicians and 'William Pitt the orator'. On a subsequent meeting Bentham was surprised to find that Pitt was 'very good natured', if 'a little raw. I was monstrously frighten'd at him: but when I came to talk with him he seemed frighten'd at me'. Subsequently Pitt challenged Bentham to a game of chess, and after losing complained of a headache; he refused a rematch on the grounds that 'his head would not bear more than a game at a sitting'. His reluctance to renew hostilities might have been reinforced by the fact that in the interim Bentham had played against his elder brother John, who had proved that he was not a complete dunderhead by trouncing the future founder of utilitarianism.[9] Bentham's account is consistent with the general view that Pitt could be funny as well as obviously clever, but also quite bashful and anything but a show-off, although he obviously didn't like losing.

Another anecdote of these years paints a less attractive picture. During the Gordon Riots of 1780 the MP and historian Edward Gibbon (1737–94), who was helping to organise the militia, attended a dinner at Lincoln's Inn. According to one of the diners, Gibbon took a prominent role in the conversation, but was cut down to size by Pitt when he offered his reflections on 'the fashionable levities of political doctrine' and was forced to make an undignified retreat.[10]

The story was told (and has been repeated) as an example of Pitt's youthful prowess; and it is indeed something to get the better of an MP more than twenty years one's senior, especially when that MP happens to be one of the greatest historians who ever lived. Even so, it is easy to sympathise with Gibbon's reported comment that Pitt's 'style of conversation is not exactly what I am accustomed to'.[11] After all, Gibbon had just been helping to keep London safe for privileged individuals like Pitt, and could be forgiven for thinking that he would not be harangued by people he had protected when he tried to relax from his duties. It seems likely that this breach of good manners was inspired in part by personal considerations: Gibbon was related to Pitt's Cambridge friend Edward Eliot; indeed, Pitt and Gibbon became distant relatives themselves when Eliot married his sister Harriot. Whatever the ultimate source of his animosity towards Gibbon, Pitt had felt strongly enough to try to turn Eliot against him in previous correspondence.[12]

William Pitt delivered his maiden speech in the House of Commons on 26 February 1781. On the following day he reported to his mother that 'I was able to execute in some measure what I intended.'[13] Pitt was being playful, rather than indulging in false modesty; he was well aware that others would already have told her about a triumphant parliamentary debut which exceeded all reasonable expectations.

The occasion, indeed, had gone so well for Pitt that a more cynical age could easily suspect the input of a star-struck stage manager. The House was debating a proposal for 'economical reform' – an attempt to curb the monarchy's powers of patronage, inspired by the Irish-born MP Edmund Burke. During the speech of Lord Nugent, an opponent of reform, George Byng, the MP for Middlesex, encouraged Pitt to reply. At first, the young MP seemed reluctant; but when Nugent sat down Byng and his friends called out Pitt's name, making it impossible for him to refuse.

If Pitt had auditioned the whole House of Commons, he could hardly have alighted on a more suitable supporting actor than George Byng. The nephew of Admiral Byng, the scapegoat/martyr of the Seven Years' War whose life the elder Pitt had tried to save, Byng had been returned in the 1780 election for Middlesex alongside the radical hero John Wilkes, and was thus one of the few members of the House to enjoy something akin to democratic legitimacy.

But Pitt was equally favoured by his antagonist. Robert Nugent, like Edmund Burke, had been born in Ireland; but unlike Burke, who prided himself on his principles, Nugent had earned his Irish peerage by offering his services to the faction which happened to be winning at any given time. Indeed, in the year after his clash with Pitt he became

'Father of the House', having continuously held a succession of seats since 1741. The highlight of his time-serving career had come in 1767, when he had held office at the Board of Trade under Pitt's father, the Earl of Chatham.

Thus, if Byng was the perfect prompter of Pitt's maiden speech, Nugent was the ideal stage villain. Now in his early seventies, he had never been more than a mediocre debater. As a beneficiary of royal patronage, he was bound to dislike the whole idea of 'economical reform'. But he thought he had seen a weakness in Burke's plan, and he had urged the House to reject it because it lacked detailed proposals. Once Pitt had overcome his reluctance to speak, he pointed out that Nugent had not read Burke's bill properly, and drew the attention of his audience to the specific proposals.[14]

If Pitt had not been presented with an open goal by the hapless Nugent, his speech might not have made such an impact. Nevertheless, it would have been regarded as an excellent start. The speech which he presumably prepared made a logical case for reform, and while the argument could hardly be welcome to George III at least it was garnished with expressions of loyalty. Pitt had learned a great deal from his observation of other parliamentary orators and was evidently anxious to avoid the mistake of his own father, who had done his best to burn his boats with the King's grandfather, George II, and had laboured long and hard to make up for his early offences.

Burke's motion was defeated, but even this foregone conclusion helped to reinforce the impression of Pitt's maiden speech, since Lord North's majority was just 43 votes (233 to 190), which in those times suggested that the Opposition probably had the better of the debate. Afterwards Burke was understandably exultant, to the extent that he lost his acute critical faculties and claimed that far from being 'a chip off the old block', Pitt was 'the old block itself'.[15] In reality, Pitt had given ample testimony that, as a parliamentary performer, he would be very different from his impulsive father. Fox's reported reaction to the speech was more telling. Some observers, writing with hindsight, hinted that he betrayed mixed feelings. It seems, though, that Fox was genuinely pleased that Pitt had spoken so effectively on his own side of this specific question, and invited Pitt to join his favourite club, Brooks's, in the hope that this might lead to a lasting alliance based on social ties as well as shared principles. Judged on his maiden speech, there seemed no reason why Pitt should not join Fox and Burke in the ranks of the Whig faction led by the Earl of Rockingham, so it was certainly worth trying to recruit him.

Although Pitt did join Brooks's, he preferred the company at another Pall Mall club, Goostree's, where he spent many evenings with a group dominated by his Cambridge friends. One of his regular companions at Goostree's was William Wilberforce, the wealthy and witty MP for Kingston upon Hull who had been elected to the Commons in 1780 while still an undergraduate of St John's College. According to Wilberforce, there was plenty of gambling at Goostree's as at other nearby clubs, and Pitt took an intense interest in these activities before deciding that the excitement was not worth the risk to his meagre resources.[16]

In the months after Pitt's maiden speech Lord North's government was buoyed up by an apparent improvement in the fortunes of war across the Atlantic. Nevertheless, MPs who were opposed to the government still had ample grounds for expressing their grievances. Pitt continued to speak in favour of 'economical reform', and on 12 June 1781 he intervened in a debate on Fox's motion for peace with the American colonists. Provoked into speaking by a suggestion that his father would have approved of the war if the only alternative was American independence, Pitt described the conflict as 'unnatural, accursed, and unjust, its traces marked with persecution and devastation, depravity and turpitude constituting its essence, while its effects would be destructive in the extreme'.[17] This really did sound like 'the old block itself'; presumably Pitt felt under a filial obligation to emulate his father's fiery rhetoric on the subject of America. His passion certainly impressed Henry Dundas, who replied to the debate on the government side and praised Pitt for his 'first-rate abilities, high integrity, bold and honest independence of conduct, and the most persuasive eloquence'.[18]

If the government's American policy had continued to prosper Pitt's outburst would have seemed ill-advised. However, the war was about to take a decisive turn. Pitt had spent most of the summer replenishing his revenues through his legal work in the west of England, and in early October, when he wrote to his mother about a pleasant social occasion with some of his father's former followers, he was expecting a further period in which his energies would be divided between Parliament and the Courts. But Cornwallis capitulated at Yorktown just a few days later, and when the news reached London in late November Pitt did not hesitate in ending his vocational conflict and dedicating himself to politics.

In December 1781 he consolidated his reputation with two speeches. In the first, on 12 December, he exposed divisions within the government on its future policy towards America. Two days later, Pitt was strafing the stationary target presented by the government when he noticed that North was conferring with two of his most senior colleagues, including Lord George Germain who, as Secretary of State for the Colonies, was the prime target of Opposition rancour. Instead of chastising the ministers for their discourtesy, Pitt compared them to leading figures in the Trojan War. According to the MP Nathaniel Wraxall, the effect of this spontaneous use of bathos was 'electric, not only on the individuals to whom it was personally directed, but on the whole audience'.[19] Germain, whom Pitt had compared to Achilles, left the government a few weeks later, whereupon Pitt trained his fire on the First Lord of the Admiralty, the Earl of Sandwich. On 24 January 1782, Pitt explained that his criticism of Sandwich arose from political rather than personal considerations.[20] This was a reasonable precaution, since Sandwich was a member of the House of Lords and thus could not defend himself directly against personal attacks from MPs; but it was strangely inconsonant with notorious facts about Sandwich (i.e. that his record at the Admiralty was defensible, whereas his private conduct was reprehensible even by the standards of the day).

Political judgements are invariably coloured to some extent by personal considerations; and in Pitt's case the usual sources of friction were complicated by a determination to distrust those who could be accused of frittering away his father's gains. Lord North was the foremost among these unforgivable culprits. In early March 1782 a desperate government canvassed various ideas for ensuring its survival, including the promotion of Pitt and some of his friends to ministerial office. Significantly, Henry Dundas was associated with this proposal. Almost certainly this explains why Pitt, while supporting a motion of no confidence in the government on 8 March, made the remarkable declaration that 'I could not expect to form part of the new administration; but were my doing so more within my reach, I feel myself bound to declare that I would never accept a subordinate situation.'[21]

Since Pitt was several months short of his 23rd birthday, and had been an MP for little more than a year, this looks like an example of astonishing presumption; and it was regarded in that light by some contemporary observers. Subsequent historians have offered conflicting interpretations, even though Pitt's declaration obviously did him no lasting harm. Ultimately, those who regard his statement as a mistake base their verdict on the possibility that subsequent events might have been unhelpful to Pitt, making him look like an aspiring minister who had given a premature advertisement of talents which would never be needed. A more plausible explanation, however, is that Pitt was giving public testimony of his reasons for spurning the possible career path which, it seems, had already been offered to him (i.e. accepting voluntary restraints in return for a junior office, as his father had once done). Admittedly, Chatham had worn those restraints pretty lightly, but the younger Pitt was never going to emulate him by attacking a government of which he was a member. Leaving aside other considerations, Chatham had been an inspired politician who proved equal to senior government jobs without previous training. In contrast, Pitt the Younger had been coached for senior office from an early age. Overall, then, the best conclusion is that this was an occasion when overconfidence, rather than conceit, led Pitt into a public declaration of intent which was not absurd in itself but which was better suited to a private conversation.

Overall, even if William Pitt the Younger was 'swaddled, and rocked, and dandled into a Legislator', he had shown even before he entered Parliament that he was well suited to government. If anything, his deliberate courtship of a political career shows a deeper sense of vocation than that of his father, who had been forced to bulldoze his way to the top. In doing so, he had cleared many of the obstacles which might otherwise have held up his son. In his speech of 8 March 1782, the younger Pitt had made it clear that he proposed to vault in a single effortless leap over those which remained.

5

The Third Man:
A Stubborn and Determined Monarch

ONE person had a determining effect on the careers both of William Pitt the Younger and Charles James Fox: King George III. He raised one of them up so that he became the second-longest serving prime minister, a total of almost nineteen years. The other he cast down, to become by far the longest serving Leader of the Opposition (though there was no such official position at the time), for over twenty-two years. George was peremptorily dismissed in two lines by Walter Savage Landor, who wrote in his famous poem, 'The Georges':

> And what mortal ever heard
> Any good of George the Third?[1]

Yet he was a complex figure, and not all his actions in 60 years on the throne (during the last ten of which he was adjudged insane and his eldest son, later George IV, assumed the Regency) had a negative effect. George III was the third of the Hanoverian monarchs, following his great-grandfather, George I, and his grandfather, George II. His father, Frederick, Prince of Wales, never reigned, having died in March 1751 at the age of 44, when the young George was only 12. Frederick was a playboy and renowned libertine, who was estranged from his parents, both of whom positively hated him. He responded by intriguing incessantly against his father, with the aid of disgruntled Opposition politicians who hoped to be favoured when he became king. During Frederick's lifetime, Lord Guilford, a Gentleman of the Bedchamber, was responsible for George's education, but on the insistence of his mother, Princess Augusta, after the prince's death he was entrusted to the Earl of Bute, a little-known Scottish peer, who had been a friend of Prince Frederick. Bute was a close advisor to Augusta, and they were believed by Horace Walpole to be lovers. Walpole spread the rumour far and wide, though George's biographer, John Brooke, regarded it as highly unlikely, writing,

> Two persons less likely to engage in a love affair than Bute and the Princess could hardly be imagined. In 1755 Bute was forty-two, happily married to an attractive and devoted wife, and the father of a large family. He had never been suspected of gallantry. The Princess was thirty-six, the mother of nine children, and more famed for her discretion and good conduct than for her beauty or sexual charms. Everything we know of the character of either is evidence against a love affair.[2]

George was brought up in virtual seclusion by the Dowager Princess of Wales – as she was now known – at her residence, Leicester House (facing Leicester Square), along with his eight brothers and sisters, coming into contact with few adults apart from his tutor, Bute. Under Guilford, he had been a sullen and recalcitrant pupil, but Bute succeeded in bringing George out of himself. This was largely because George, who had adored his own father, responded to the earl as a father figure. Tall, handsome and highly esteemed (if not loved) by George's mother, Bute gradually succeeded in coaxing the young George into taking a lively interest in his studies. Though pedantic, the earl was a skilful teacher, and George learned his lessons all too well. What Bute taught him was that his two predecessors on the throne had grossly neglected their duties and had allowed a corrupt Whig oligarchy to encroach on the royal prerogatives and to rule the country in its own interests. The earl pointed the finger of blame in particular at Sir Robert Walpole and the two Pelham brothers, Henry Pelham and the Duke of Newcastle, who had followed Walpole in the premiership. Bute directed his pupil to the writings of Henry St

John, first Viscount Bolingbroke, who had been a leading Tory politician under Queen Anne. The viscount had disgraced himself by supporting the old Pretender and fleeing to France in 1715; he had only been partially amnestied upon his return to Britain ten years later. Unable to resume an active political career, he had devoted himself to writing a powerful series of books and articles condemning the Walpolian system of government.

Bute drew George's attention in particular to Bolingbroke's book, *The Idea of a Patriot King*, in which he argued that

> Britain's balanced constitution could be preserved only if the monarch acted on patriotic principles, ruling in the interests of the nation at large and choosing as his ministers men of property, probity and public virtue. If he did so all political parties would be remedied, all differences of principle resolved and the nation would unite in the pursuit of virtue and patriotic harmony.[3]

George may not actually have read Bolingbroke's book, but, through the mediation of Bute, he lapped up all the viscount's teachings and resolved to act accordingly. This included being himself a 'man of virtue', and it was notable that alone of the five Hanoverian monarchs he never took a mistress. George became very high-minded and – unfortunately, like Bute – self-righteous to a degree. He was determined to have his own way, and became exceptionally stubborn. His mother's constant urging of 'George, be a king!' he took literally.[4]

He grew up deploring all factions and parties, though his particular venom was directed at the dominant Whig faction, led at that time by the Duke of Newcastle. His grandfather was growing old and was not in robust health, and Princess Augusta and her entourage, including Bute, became increasingly anxious that he would die before George reached the age of 18, necessitating a regency. The Princess feared that George II's younger son, William Augustus, Duke of Cumberland, would be chosen for this role. A distinguished soldier, he was known as 'Butcher Cumberland' because of his brutality in pursuing Bonnie Prince Charlie's followers after the Battle of Culloden in 1745. But the Princess had no rational grounds for her belief that he would behave in the same way as Richard of Gloucester, who became Regent in 1483 on the death of his brother, Edward IV, and was then suspected of ordering the murder of Edward's two young sons and proclaiming himself king. Cumberland may have not been a very nice man, but he was very solicitous of his young nephew, and was a loyal friend and counsellor to him when he became king. Bute must have known that Augusta's fears were fantasies, but he made no effort to disabuse her of them.

In fact, George II survived until October 1760, when the young George was 22. He intended to make great changes, and, in the words of the historian Richard Pares, 'His policy, so far as he had one in 1760, was made up almost entirely of vindictive personal grudges against everything and everybody who had been connected with his despised grandfather.'[5]

Well before then the young George had made his plans for taking over the throne. He would immediately sack all his ministers and replace them with virtuous men committed to the national interest. As prime minister, he would instal his 'dearest friend', the Earl of Bute. This had been agreed between them long before. But when it came to the point, Bute began to get cold feet. The reason was that the Seven Years' War was going far too well, from George's point of view. As discussed in Chapter Two, 1759 was the most successful ever for the British army and navy. The French had been routed in Canada, India, West Africa, the Caribbean and even in Europe, where an Anglo-Hanoverian army gained a rare victory at Minden. Both the elder Pitt, the architect of all these victories, and the prime minister, the Duke of Newcastle, were consequently at the peak of their popularity, and Bute felt that it would be very badly received if they were turned out of office. George reluctantly agreed that the existing government should continue, but appointed Bute as a Secretary of State, equal in status – nominally, at least – to Pitt. Arguably this appointment was unconstitutional, as Bute belonged to neither House of Parliament. Although he was a Scottish peer, he was not one of the 16 Scottish representative peers who were elected by their fellows at the beginning of each Parliament to represent them in the House of Lords. In practice, as the only one who had the full confidence of the King, Bute became the most influential member of the Cabinet. Many of his colleagues believed it would only be a matter of time before he clashed with Newcastle and Pitt and forced them out of office.

The crisis came in October 1761. The Bourbon kings of France and Spain, who were first cousins, agreed a 'family compact' that they would coordinate their foreign policies. There was then a general expectation that Spain, which had remained neutral in the Seven Years' War, would soon enter the struggle on the French side. As discussed in Chapter Two, Bute's colleagues were right: this crisis came in October 1761 when Pitt and Bute found themselves at loggerheads over the best way to respond to France and Spain's 'family compact' to coordinate their foreign policies, an arrangement seen as a threat to Britain. When Pitt's proposal only received two votes, one from his brother-in-law, he stormed furiously out of the government. Newcastle hung on for another seven months, a virtual passenger in his own Cabinet, now completely dominated by Bute, grumbling that 'My advice or opinion are scarce ever ask'd, but never taken. I am kept in without confidence, and indeed without communication.'[6]

He submitted his resignation in May 1762. The King, who had taken a thorough dislike to him, and had been heard to remark, 'The more I know of this fellow the more I wish to see him out of employment,'[7] was delighted and offered him a pension, which the Duke proudly refused.

Bute, having displaced his rivals, now formally took over the premiership. Having been instrumental in preventing Pitt from waging war on Spain, he had now reversed his position, and within a few months British forces overran both Havana in the Caribbean and Manila in the Philippines. Peace was then made with both France and Spain, and a peace treaty was signed in Paris in February 1763. Under this, Britain gained Quebec, Breton Island, the mid-West as far as the Mississippi, Florida, Grenada, Dominica, St Vincent and Tobago, Senegal and Bengal, and recovered Minorca and the parts of Hanover which the French had occupied. It was a handsome reward for the war effort, but the elder Pitt fiercely denounced the peace treaty, saying that the war should have been continued until France had been driven down to its knees. Bute was concerned that the Commons might not ratify the treaty, and (as explained in Chapter Two) entrusted Henry Fox, as Leader of the Commons, to force it through by hook or by crook.[8] Fox duly delivered, but if Bute won the parliamentary battle, he lost the battle for public opinion, which rallied behind the elder Pitt. Bute (whose nickname was 'Jack Boot') became wildly unpopular, being the target of many demonstrations where jackboots and petticoats (an allusion to his rumoured affair with Princess Augusta) were burnt. Savage attacks appeared in the press, and he was lampooned in over 400 prints and broadsheets.

It was not just the peace treaty to which people objected, though; Bute was widely hated as a Scotsman who was believed to have crammed the administration with a host of fellow Scots. He became unnerved, fearing assassination. This belief was supported by an incident on 25 November 1762, where 'on his way to the opening of Parliament, he was hissed and pelted by the mob, and if the Guards had not been summoned his life would have been in danger.'[9] Unfamiliar with the capricious ways of the London mob, Bute concluded that it must have been bribed to attack him by his political opponents, and – fearing for his life – warned the King that he would soon stand down.

Bute resigned after only 317 days in office, recommending George III to appoint Henry Fox in his place while he remained the 'power behind the throne'. Fox, however, declined, persuaded by his wife that his precarious health would suffer if he took the post; in any event, he was now much more interested in becoming a peer (as Lord Holland). In the absence of any other Tory who was remotely qualified, George III was forced to choose yet another Whig prime minister. His choice fell on George Grenville, the elder Pitt's brother-in-law and a protégé of Bute, but this did not work out as George III and Bute intended. Grenville and his ministers, on threat of resignation, insisted that Bute should not advise the King behind the scenes, and indeed should no longer see him on a regular basis. George III grumpily agreed, but in fact was already largely disillusioned with Bute, who he thought had let him down badly by resigning, and he no longer regarded him as his 'dearest friend'. Few people believed that George had actually broken with Bute, who was widely suspected of being a secret – and malign – influence on the King for many years afterwards.

George III soon tired of Grenville, and sacked him after two years, in July 1765, and then tried out three further prime ministers, all at least nominal Whigs – the Marquess of Rockingham, Lord Chatham (the elder Pitt) and the Duke of Grafton – until 1770, when the last of these resigned. By then he had run through six premiers in the first ten years of his reign.[10] This was evidence of his impatience and immaturity and of his determination to choose someone who would unquestioningly carry out his wishes. In January 1770 he thought he had at last found his man. He appointed Frederick, Lord North, who had been Chancellor of the Exchequer since October 1767 and who was to remain prime minister for more than twelve years. North was five years older than George III, who had known him very well since childhood. They had been brought up in the same household, and had been playmates for several years. North was the eldest son of Lord Guilford, and was named after Prince Frederick, who was his godfather. In fact, they were quite possibly illegitimate half-brothers: Lady Guilford, who died in childbirth two years later, in 1734, appears to have been suspected by her husband of having an affair with the Prince. There is no direct evidence for this, but a strong case is made out by Professor Charles Daniel Smith in a book published in 1975,[11] where Smith reproduces a series of portraits in the National Portrait Gallery and the Courtauld Institute which show a striking resemblance between North and the Prince and no resemblance at all between him and Lord Guilford. Other pictures in the same galleries, of North and George III in their mature years, also show a marked resemblance. It is improbable that either the King or Lord North had any idea that they were related, but they had a great deal in common and got on extraordinarily well until North's belated resignation in 1782, after which George turned sharply against him.

North acquired the reputation of being the worst ever British prime minister (on account of the loss of all 13 North American colonies during his premiership), but he was a man of many qualities. A brilliant parliamentarian, he had the House of Commons eating out of his hand for almost the entire length of his premiership. He attended the chamber for long hours every day, and freely made himself available to every Member, always happy to listen to their concerns or even just to pass the time of day. When he spoke in the House, which he did very frequently, he had the gift of explaining even the most complicated issue in simple words, so that the most dim-witted of country squires could follow the argument (or at least thought he could). He was extremely jovial, and had the rare quality of being able to laugh at jokes made at his own expense. Many examples of this were in wide circulation, including the occasion when his neighbour at a banquet pointed to a woman seated opposite and asked: 'Who is that dreadful-looking woman over there?' 'That, Sir,' replied the prime minister, 'is my wife!' 'Oh no,' said his deeply embarrassed neighbour, 'I didn't mean *her*, I meant the monster sitting next to her.' 'That, Sir,' said North, 'is my daughter!'[12]

Frederick North's title was a courtesy one, as the eldest son of an earl. Throughout his time in office he sat in the Commons, and only entered the House of Lords, as the second Earl of Guilford, when he succeeded his father in 1778, at the age of 58. By then he was totally blind, and he died two years later. Lord North became prime minister in January 1770, and for the first five years his government, in which Charles Fox was to serve for more than half the time, was seen as being a great success – not only by George III, who was delighted to have found a minister keen to accommodate his every wish, but by a wider public which was impressed by the calm, orderly way in which it conducted its business. North himself, who retained the office of Chancellor of the Exchequer, won high praise for the way he handled the public finances and his success in reducing the national debt, which had been at a historically high level. In April 1775, however, war broke out with the American colonists, and the years of calm came to an end.

History has not dealt kindly with George III, whose reputation (particularly in the United States) could hardly be worse, though it has improved somewhat in recent years. He was highly conscientious, had many fine human qualities, and was an enlightened patron of science and the arts. Above all, he felt himself to be very British, unlike his Hanoverian predecessors, and shared the beliefs and prejudices of a wide range of his citizens, particularly in the countryside, where he was popularly known as 'Farmer George'. Nor did he see himself as in any way an opponent of the reforms ushered in by the Glorious Revolution. He proclaimed that the British constitution was the finest in the world, and claimed never to have exceeded the monarchical powers granted to William III and Mary II. What he did not comprehend was that a largely unwritten constitution was subject to continuous evolution, and that the conventions and precedents established during the reigns of Queen Anne and the first two Georges were equally binding on him. If he never broke the letter of the constitution, he certainly breached its spirit on numerous occasions.

6

From Tory to Whig

CHARLES Fox was dismayed by his loss of office under Lord North and devastated by the deaths of his parents and brother. Yet paradoxically these events liberated him politically, and thereafter he was his own man, constrained neither by any sense of obligation to North, nor by family expectations that he was obliged automatically to adhere to the views (and the feuds) of his father. He continued throughout his life loyally to defend Henry Fox's memory and all his actions, but he no longer regarded the leaders of the Whig Party as deadly enemies. The Duke of Newcastle was now dead, and his place as leader of the largest Whig faction had been taken by the second Marquess of Rockingham, with smaller groups clustered around the Bedford family and the elder Pitt, whose following was led by the second Earl of Shelburne after his death in 1778.

Socially, Fox mixed almost exclusively with Whigs, partly because of his membership of Brooks's. The club was founded in 1764 by a group of Whig noblemen, and Fox joined the following year, at the age of 16. Since 1778, it has been housed in a handsome Palladian building in St James's Street, just round the corner from Piccadilly. By then the club had become, together with Newmarket, 'as much home to Fox as the House of Commons'.[1] At Newmarket, he kept a string of racehorses periodically at risk of being sequestrated by enraged creditors. At Brooks's, he was a regular at the gaming tables most nights. In the Commons he was, by a wide margin, the outstanding speaker, with no rival in sight until after the younger Pitt was elected in 1781. The second most admired speaker among MPs was probably Edmund Burke, also a member of Brooks's, though no aristocrat and far from being a compulsive gambler.

Burke, an Irishman with a Protestant lawyer father and a Catholic mother, was 20 years Fox's senior, and had had to make his own way in the world. He had had the good fortune to be employed as private secretary to the Marquess of Rockingham, who had briefly been prime minister in 1765–6 and who was a Yorkshire territorial magnate with vast estates, including Wentworth Woodhouse, the largest privately owned house ever built in Britain. Rockingham had subsequently provided Burke with the pocket borough of Malton to represent, and Burke became the main spokesman for the Rockingham Whigs in the Commons. A skilful and elegant writer, he became their main theorist, putting together their often vague and skeletal aspirations into a convincing political programme. Two of his main themes were the necessity strictly to limit the powers of the monarch, and the importance of political parties that should agree on well-defined policies which they committed themselves to carry out if they secured office. This was a novel concept at the time, and deeply shocking to the King, but perhaps is the main reason why Burke is justifiably regarded as one of the progenitors of the modern political party.

Burke was completely bowled over by Fox, writing of him to an Irish friend, 'He is one of the pleasantest men in the world, as well as the greatest Genius that perhaps this country has ever produced.'[2] The two men became almost inseparable friends, and Burke became something of a mentor to Fox. Yet he was for a long time too diffident to attempt to recruit him to the Rockingham cause. It was not until 1777 that he sat down and wrote him an admonitory letter:

Though (as you are sensible) I have never given you the least hint of advice about joining yourself in a declared connexion with our party nor do I now – yet [...] I love that party very well, and am clear that you are better able to serve them than any man I know [...] For I much doubt, whether, with all your parts, you are the man formed for acquiring real interior favour in this Court or in any. I therefore wish you a firm ground in the Country; and I do not know so firm and sound a bottom to build on as our party.[3]

Even then, it took a year or two before Fox took the final step and formally aligned himself with the Rockinghamites. For a long time their views had been virtually identical about the American War of Independence and their common opposition to Lord North's premiership and George III's stubborn refusal to seek peace. Support for the American colonists had become the great cause in Fox's life and had given him the strength and conviction which he had previously lacked. He had shown evidence of this as early as the Boston Tea Party in 1773, when he had deplored the event but had fiercely opposed the punitive measures – known to the Americans as the 'Intolerable Acts' – imposed by the North government at the behest of George III. These included the closure of Boston's harbour and the stripping of the powers of the elected Massachusetts Assembly. The most powerful speech in the Commons opposing these measures was made by Burke, who memorably declared that 'Magnanimity in politics is not seldom the truest wisdom, and a great empire and little minds go ill together.'[4]

In the Lords, the now ageing Chatham put in a rare appearance, perhaps in the vain hope of advertising his availability to be recalled to office to avert the coming catastrophe, He made a persuasive speech, but George III, who had resolved never to employ him again after the fiasco of his government of 1766–8, was deaf to his entreaties. Fox himself followed Burke with a speech which was every bit as lively as his earlier efforts but conveyed a new seriousness and determination which was henceforth to characterise his many parliamentary interventions throughout the course of the War of Independence. Carefully prepared and extremely well informed, neither North nor any of his ministers were ever capable of offering an effective response. Fox completely dominated debates, but was unable to win a majority in the division lobbies. The war effectively broke out in April 1775 with the skirmishes at Lexington and Concord, followed by the Battle of Bunker Hill, outside Boston, three months later.

North, who had earlier declared airily that the dispatch of 'four or five frigates' would be sufficient to quell any trouble, now prepared for war à l'outrance, bolstered by a wave of patriotic fervour which embraced King, country and a clear majority in the House of Commons, confident of success. Parliament, however, agreed to the dispatch of peace commissioners, who were expected to negotiate with the rebels. When they duly arrived, however, they revealed that they were authorised only to accept the submission of the rebels and to offer pardons to those who repented their actions. In the meantime, the Declaration of Independence had been approved by the Second Continental Congress in July 1776, and George Washington had been placed in command of a newly raised Continental Army. There was now no turning back. Lord North recognised that he had no interest in (nor aptitude for) military strategy, and left the direction of the war to Lord George Germain while concentrating on his other prime ministerial duties, notably – in his other role as Chancellor of the Exchequer – to raise sufficient funds to pay for the war effort. Germain, previously known as Lord George Sackville, was a distinguished soldier who had been unjustly court-martialled and disgraced for alleged disobedience during the Battle of Minden in 1759. He had subsequently, however, been exonerated. North hoped to repeat the winning formula of the Seven Years' War, when the elder Pitt had presided over a series of stunning victories while the prime minister, the Duke of Newcastle, had raised the necessary cash.

It did not quite work out like that. Germain may have lacked the dynamic energy of the elder Pitt, but he proved himself to be a sound strategist and an efficient administrator. If the campaigns he planned did not yield the success he hoped for it was due more to the shortcomings of the generals in charge, in particular their failure to press home their advantage on several occasions after winning significant victories. For the first two years of the war the British forces (largely made up of German mercenaries from Hanover and other German states) generally held the upper hand, and American morale sank until it was revitalised by Washington's successful Trenton–Princeton campaign launched on Christmas night 1776. It then became clear that Britain was in it for the long haul, and hopes for a rapid conclusion of hostilities evaporated.

In Parliament, however, there was still a strong majority for continuing the war and a confidence that Britain would eventually prevail. Opposition MPs pressed for negotiations to achieve a compromise peace but were themselves badly divided in their objectives. The ageing Chatham, who still had hopes that he might be recalled to office, was in favour of maintaining British rule but making generous concessions to the rebel demands. Lord Shelburne went further, envisaging that the colonies should be granted a status similar to that of the electorate of Hanover, which under George III enjoyed effective 'home rule' while still recognising him as their sovereign. The Rockinghamites were ready to accept independence, which was also Fox's position, though he differed from them over their attitude to the North government. They insisted that the entire government should resign, and be replaced by a purely Whig administration, chosen by themselves. Fox agreed that North, Germain and Lord Sandwich, the First Lord of the Admiralty, would have to go, but otherwise sought a 'reshuffle', under which the Whigs, and hopefully himself, would share power with the remaining members of the existing Cabinet. Meanwhile, he and Rockingham's supporters paraded their sympathy with the American rebels, regarding them not as hostile foreigners but as free-born Englishmen fighting for their natural rights and demanding 'no taxation without representation'. The Rockinghamites compared the rebels with John Hampden and his followers who, more than a century earlier, had resisted Charles I's attempt to raise ship money without the consent of Parliament. They ostentatiously dressed in blue-and-buff-coloured garments matching the uniforms of Washington's army, and found it difficult not to appear to rejoice at every American success or British setback, which made them very unpopular with large numbers of people who regarded them as traitors. Fox was by a wide measure the most active and effective critic of the government, and did not spare his words in laying into North, Germain and Sandwich, and above all – sometimes by implication, but increasingly directly – the King himself. North, no mean parliamentary performer, was left to bear the full brunt of Fox's attacks, most of the other leading Cabinet members being in the Lords. He was no match for Fox's scintillating oratory, left speechless by such quips as: 'Not Lord Chatham, not the Duke of Marlborough, no, not Alexander nor Caesar had ever conquered so much territory as Lord North had lost in one campaign.'[5]

Then, in the summer of 1777, Germain launched his master stroke, sending General Burgoyne with a powerful army down the Hudson Valley from Canada to link up in New York with another army led by General

William Howe, brother of Lord Howe, who was commanding the British fleet. The objective was to cut off the rebellious New England colonies from the southern states where loyalist sentiment was stronger, enabling the British to re-establish themselves there before concentrating all their forces to subdue the north. Unfortunately for the British, this did not go according to plan. Burgoyne met with greater and more effective resistance than expected as he slowly made his way down the Hudson, and Howe, impatient of waiting for him, set off southwards himself and occupied the American capital of Philadelphia. After suffering several defeats, and despairing of being reinforced by Howe, Burgoyne surrendered his entire army when it became surrounded at Saratoga on 17 October 1777.

This proved to be the turning point of the war – though few people realised it at the time, apart from Lord North. He despaired of victory, certainly under his own leadership, and during the next four years on literally dozens of occasions begged George III to let him stand down. One of his most fervent appeals was in March 1778, when he suggested that the King should send for Lord Chatham, in the desperate hope that Chatham would be able to repeat his achievements during the Seven Years' War. But George III refused to countenance this, though he agreed that William Eden (later Lord Auckland), a close associate of North, should talk to a representative of Chatham to find out if he would be prepared to join North's government at a lower level. Eden met Shelburne, who told him that 'if Chatham became a minister he must become a dictator.'[6] A furious King George declared that he would rather abdicate than submit to 'such ignominy'. Unfortunately for North, this was just a few weeks before Chatham's collapse in the House of Lords and subsequent death (see Chapter Two). Eden also talked to Rockingham and then to Fox. Rockingham replied that he and his followers would only take over the government if they received a mandate to negotiate peace on the basis of immediate independence for the American colonists. Fox gave Eden a less adamant response. He would consider joining the government, he said, but not alone, and would insist on the resignation of Lord George Germain. Fox indicated that he would not hold out for one of the most senior posts, but would be willing to take on a relatively junior one, such as Treasurer of the Royal Navy. George III implied that this might be acceptable to him, telling Lord North that Fox should be offered a lucrative, but not influential post. Fox would be glad of the money, he wrote, and 'he never having had any principle can certainly act as his interest may guide him'.[7] But the King and North were unwilling to offer jobs to any of Fox's friends, such as his brother-in-law, Richard Fitzpatrick, and nothing came of the discussions. On several other occasions Fox received indirect approaches from North, but all proved abortive.

He subsequently sent a candid letter to Rockingham, discussing their respective responses to Eden's approach, which the Whig leader had effectively rejected in principle. Fox wrote:

> What you considered as a step of the most dangerous tendency to the Whig party, I looked upon as a most favourable opportunity for restoring it to that power and influence which I wish it to have as earnestly as you can do [...] It has always been [...] my opinion that power (whether over a people or a king) obtained by gentle means, by the goodwill of the person to be governed, and, above all, by degrees rather than by a sudden exercise of strength, is by its nature more durable and firm than any advantage that can be obtained by contrary means [...] You think that you can best serve the country by continuing in a fruitless opposition; I think it impossible to serve it at all but by coming into power, and go even so far as to think it irreconcilable with the duty of a public man to refuse it, if offered to him in a manner consistent with his private honour, and so as to enable him to form fair hopes of doing essential service.[8]

Yet he had some private doubts, which he revealed in a letter to a friend dated 3 February 1778:

> People flatter me that I continue to gain, rather than lose, my credit as an orator; and I am so convinced that this is all I shall ever gain (unless I chose to become the meanest of men), that I never think of any other object of ambition. I am certainly ambitious by nature, but I really have, or think I have, totally subdued that passion [...] Great reputation I think I may acquire and keep, great situation I never can acquire, nor, if acquired, keep without making sacrifices that I never will make.[9]

Meanwhile Fox continued to hammer the government in a series of parliamentary debates. During one of these, in November 1779, he gratuitously libelled one of North's supporters, William Adam, who promptly challenged him to a duel. They met at 8 a.m. on 29 November in Hyde Park, and a graphic description of what occurred was given in a letter written by James O'Brien to his wife, Lady Susan Fox-Strangways, Fox's cousin, with whom he had been infatuated at the age of 12:

> Mr Adam sent him a challenge on Sunday about 4 o'clock, in consequence of wch they went out on Monday morning early. Adam desir'd him to fire, wch he refused, saying 'You think yourself injured, fire'; which he did, and wounded Chas slightly slantwise in the right of his belly just above the waistband, pretty well aim'd you will say. Chas then fir'd and miss'd, on which Fitzpatrick step'd in and ask'd Adam if he was not satisfied, who sd 'No, unless Mr Fox wd sign the paper he had propos'd to him'. Chas said that was impossible [...] if he was not satisfied he must proceed, on which Mr A with the utmost care and deliberation level'd, fired, and thank God miss'd him. Chas then firing his shot into the air, the affair ended. It [...] ought to be consider'd as a determin'd plan d'assassination to get rid of an adversary they could not answer [...] I heard about it by accident abt one o'clock, and [...] ran away to him, and found him lying on the couch [...] He shook me very heartily by the hand and told me he was very well [...] thank heaven it was the slightest thing in the world.[10]

Fox added that he was in negligible danger as Adam had been 'using government powder'! Some years later Adam became a close family friend of Fox and helped him sort out his very rocky finances.[11]

Greatly influenced by Burke, Fox gradually extended his criticisms of both King and government to many other issues, and by the later 1770s had become a much more radicalised figure. He lined himself up behind Burke's proposals for economic reform, which provided for more parliamentary control over the King's Civil List and the abolition of a long list of sinecures, which were extensively used as *douceurs* to maintain a parliamentary majority for the 'King's Friends'.[12] At George's command,

Lord North skilfully fended off these demands by using every conceivable parliamentary device to amend, delay, evade or vote them down. Finally, the whole bill was defeated in March 1780, but the Opposition had a rare victory a few weeks later, on 7 April, when the Commons voted on two resolutions tabled by John Dunning, a supporter of Lord Shelburne. The first (and most famous) of the two read 'the influence of the Crown has increased, is increasing and ought to be diminished.' The second declared that 'it is competent for this House to reform the civil list or any part of public expenditure.' The first resolution was sensationally carried by 233 to 215, the second without a division. If there was any specific date on which Fox finally threw in his lot with the Rockinghamites, this was probably it.

At around this time, Fox – previously exclusively a 'House of Commons man' who disdained the views of voters – began to take serious notice of opinion 'outdoors', as it was rather quaintly known in the eighteenth century, or 'popular opinion' in more modern parlance. In particular, he responded to a growing call for parliamentary reform, which comprised a series of distinct demands, by no means all of which were simultaneously held by all would-be reformers. These included the abolition or restriction of rotten or pocket boroughs; an increase in the number of county seats, widely seen as less corrupt or more democratic than the boroughs; more frequent elections; and a widening of the franchise, though only a few 'advanced' reformers believed this should go as far as universal male suffrage and virtually nobody at that time envisaged votes for women. Agitation for such reforms was especially great in Yorkshire, perhaps unsurprisingly, as the county had one of the most democratic franchises in the whole country. With 20,000 electors, it was by far the most populous constituency, and there was widespread dismay that it had no greater representation than the two members chosen by the seven electors of Old Sarum. The Yorkshire Association, a powerful body led by the Reverend Christopher Wyvill, was established to press for parliamentary reform, and parallel associations were soon established in 25 other counties. One of these was Wiltshire, a county closely associated with the Fox family, and on 27 January 1780 Charles Fox was invited to address a meeting of 150 freeholders in Devizes, which was, apparently, the first public meeting which he had ever addressed. A few days afterwards, he spoke at a far larger gathering – estimated by his friends to be 'three to four thousand'[13] – at Westminster Hall, adjacent to the House of Commons. Here, flanked by a host of London Radicals (including his former enemy John Wilkes, now restored to fame and fortune as a popular Mayor of London and again MP for Middlesex), he enjoyed an oratorical triumph. He was nominated on the spot as Whig candidate for the Westminster constituency, the largest of all the borough seats with an electorate of 12,000.

The general election followed in September 1780, and the government made strenuous efforts to prevent his being returned for such a prestigious seat, spending £8,000 of secret service money in support of the two ministerial candidates. One of these, Admiral Rodney, was a war hero, and few doubted that he would top the poll. The other, Lord Lincoln, son of the second Duke of Newcastle, was Fox's rival for the second seat, and started off as the clear favourite. But Fox entered into the campaign with gusto and gradually overhauled Lincoln, the final result being:

Rodney 5,298
Fox   4,878
Lincoln 4,157

This victory transformed Fox's position in the House of Commons, and was an emphatic endorsement of his newly proclaimed radicalism. Previously he had represented a derisory number of voters – only 200 at Midhurst when he was first elected in 1768, and a mere 13 at Malmesbury, to which he had transferred in 1774. Now he had more electors than anybody, except the two Yorkshire MPs, and could denounce rotten boroughs and other electoral malpractices without apparent hypocrisy. The overall election result was mildly encouraging for the Whigs, who picked up 11 more seats in the counties and around ten in the boroughs,[14] but the government still maintained a comfortable majority in the House as a whole.

Apart from his oratorical superiority, Fox had the advantage over North of being formidably well informed, not only about the progress of the war on the ground but also of the course of international diplomacy. He received regular correspondence from a number of serving officers, including Burgoyne, a former close friend and gambling companion, and from his brother-in-law, Colonel Richard Fitzpatrick, who had served in America in 1777–8 and had fought in two major battles. In Paris he was also in touch with Benjamin Franklin, now the US ambassador to the French court, whom he had befriended several years earlier. A frequent visitor to Paris was the MP for King's Lynn, Thomas Walpole, a nephew of Sir Robert Walpole. In February 1778, four months after the Saratoga capitulation, he wrote to his cousin, Horace Walpole, asking him to pass on to Fox some news he had just heard: that France had signed a treaty of alliance with the American rebels. When Fox questioned North about this in the Commons, the prime minister and the entire House was reported as being 'thunderstruck', as they had no idea that it had happened.[15] North was utterly humiliated. Soon afterwards, both France and Spain, anxious to recoup their losses in the Seven Years' War, entered the war on the American side, and in an act of great folly Britain declared war on Holland. This meant that the three other great maritime powers were united against the British and control was lost of the English Channel, sparking real fears of invasion.

The war dragged on for several more years with fluctuating fortunes for both sides, but the Americans grew steadily stronger with the support of a French army commanded by General Rochambeau and the Marquis de Lafayette. Meanwhile, a French fleet under Admiral de Grasse temporarily gained control of the sea, wreaking havoc on British-held territories in the Caribbean and preventing reinforcements reaching British forces in the southern states. Here, commanded by Earl Cornwallis, the British were achieving notable successes, defeating the American General Gates at Camden on 16 August 1780, and subsequently overrunning Georgia and both Carolinas before entering Virginia from the south. There Cornwallis established himself at Yorktown, on the York River, to await reinforcements being sent from New York. But these were held off by de Grasse in the Battle of Chesapeake Bay, and never arrived. In the meantime, powerful American and French forces under Washington, Rochambeau and Lafayette mounted a siege, which began on 6 October. Bombarded from land and sea, the British forces, outnumbered nearly three to one, raised the white flag on 17 October, and Cornwallis surrendered his entire army of more than 7,000 men. This effectively ended land operations on the American continent, but in April 1782 Admiral Rodney succeeded in defeating de Grasse's fleet at the Battle of the Saintes, thwarting a Franco-Spanish invasion of Jamaica.

When Lord North learned of the Yorktown surrender, he exclaimed: 'Oh God, it is all over.'[16] Neither Lord George Germain nor (more importantly) the ever stubborn George III agreed, still deluding themselves that an ultimate victory was yet possible. The House of Commons disagreed – and in a series of divisions over the next few months the government's majority steadily declined. Finally, on 8 March 1782, following a motion brought by General Henry Conway, a leading Whig MP and former Cabinet minister, it fell to a mere nine votes. Immediately afterwards North received a delegation of independent MPs who informed him that they would withdraw their support in a subsequent motion of no confidence, being 'of opinion that vain and ineffectual struggles tend only to public mischief and confusion.'[17] North at last summoned up the resolution to insist on his resignation. He wrote what became a famous letter to the King, gently explaining to him his constitutional responsibilities, saying, inter alia:

> Your Majesty has graciously and steadily supported the servants you approve, as long as they could be supported. Your Majesty has firmly and resolutely maintained what appeared to you essential to the welfare and dignity of this country, as long as this country itself thought proper to maintain it. The Parliament have altered their sentiments, and as their sentiments whether just or erroneous must ultimately prevail, Your Majesty having persevered so long as possible, in what you thought right, can lose no honour if you yield at length, as some of the most renowned and most glorious of your predecessors have done, to the opinion and wishes of the House of Commons.[18]

The King was furious with North, saying that he had 'deserted' him, and henceforth was implacably opposed to him. Yet he had no alternative but to accept his resignation and to appoint a prime minister from among the ranks of the Opposition, to negotiate peace not only with the American colonists, but with their three allied powers.

7

Peace with America:
The Rockingham and Shelburne Governments

L ORD North's premiership came to an end on 27 March 1782. It had lasted for 12 years and 58 days, including almost all of the seven-odd years of the American War of Independence. Ending the war – and negotiating peace not only with the Americans, but also with France and Spain – took until September 1783, another 18 months, and involved no fewer than three governments, each of them short-lived, led respectively by the second Marquess of Rockingham, the second Lord Shelburne and the third Duke of Portland.[1] In the formation and conduct of each of these governments, either Fox or Pitt (or both) played a leading role, and it was during these years that their now bitter rivalry reached its zenith. When North resigned, it was apparent that his successor must be a Whig, and probably Lord Rockingham, leader of by far the largest Whig faction. Yet George III was desperately anxious to avoid this and deputed the retiring Lord Chancellor, Lord Thurlow, to sound out possible alternative candidates. He first approached Lord Gower, who had been Lord President of the Council for eight years under North and was previously an adherent of the Duke of Bedford. Gower declined the honour, and Thurlow then sounded out Lord Shelburne, the leading follower of Pitt the Elder, who was more than willing to become prime minister, but realised that Shelburne did not command enough support among MPs to assume the role. It then became apparent to the King that he had no choice but to appoint either

Rockingham or – even worse, from his point of view – Fox to head the new government. He could still not bring himself to deal directly with the Whig leader and insisted on using Shelburne, whose supporters would help make up Rockingham's majority, as a go-between. According to Shelburne's own account, the King expressed to him his 'bad opinion of Lord Rockingham's understandg. & His horror of C. Fox. His preference for me compared with the rest of the opposition.'[2]

In his biography of Fox, L. G. Mitchell comments: 'From almost the Ministry's inception, George flattered Shelburne with the notion that, if he could only break with his Rockingham allies, he, with royal backing, should be sole minister. Shelburne, in effect, became a royal agent in the Cabinet.'[3]

Rockingham accepted office only on his own conditions. These were that he, rather than the King, should name the other members of the Cabinet; that three measures of economic reform, including a new version of Burke's bill which had been defeated in the previous Parliament, should be introduced; and that there should be no royal veto on American independence.[4] If Rockingham had realised that George intended it to be effectively a joint premiership with Shelburne, who would share rights of patronage and would have exclusive access to the 'closet', it is extremely unlikely that he would have agreed to serve. The other ten members of the Cabinet were equally divided between followers of Rockingham and Shelburne. Rockingham refused the King's request that the Lord Chancellor, Lord Thurlow, should remain in office, and they were unable to agree on a successor, so the post remained unfilled and its duties put into commission. Additionally, General Conway, as Commander-in-Chief, normally attended the Cabinet and had full voting rights. Fox and Shelburne were both Secretaries of State, the first for Foreign and the second for Home Affairs, the first men to be so designated. Previously, they had had interlocking duties as heads of the Northern and Southern departments, the former of which was considered senior to the latter. Fox was, additionally, Leader of the House of Commons, and was generally seen (and certainly by himself) as the dominant member of the government. His uncle, the Duke of Richmond, was Master General of the Ordnance, and Lord John Cavendish, a keen Rockinghamite, was

Chancellor of the Exchequer. Burke was not included in the Cabinet but served as Paymaster General.

Lord Rockingham was a somewhat implausible figure to be prime minister. He was painfully shy, making him a poor speaker, and suffered from poor health. He had never been an MP, and had held no ministerial post before becoming PM for the first time in 1765, when he was seen as a mere figurehead (with the Duke of Cumberland being the real leader of the government, although his royal status prevented him from assuming the post). Cumberland's sudden death after four months left him with responsibilities for which, in his own words, 'howsoever unsuitable I might be for that office from my health and inexperience'.[5] His government lasted for a single year before being ejected by an impatient King to make way for Lord Chatham's disastrous premiership of 1766–8. By then he had repealed the Stamp Act and initiated policies which, if persisted in by succeeding administrations, might well have averted the American Declaration of Independence. For the next dozen or so years he was effectively the leader of the Opposition, declining numerous offers for him or his followers to take ministerial office. They would only do so, he insisted, if the King would agree to their policy demands. In this stance he was utterly consistent, always insisting that the role of the monarch should be tightly restricted. On 9 March 1778, he informed the House of Lords that 'The King can have no interests, no dignity, no views whatever, distinct from those of his people'.[6]

This was the pure essence of Whiggism, and is sufficient reason for George's extreme reluctance to instal him in the premiership. Some of Rockingham's followers had resented his preventing them from becoming ministers, but they remained loyal to him. He was greatly respected and highly popular, despite occasional grumbles at his indolence and excessive devotion to horse racing (his first government was composed almost exclusively of members of the Jockey Club[7]). Rockingham's popularity contrasted sharply with Shelburne, who was by a wide margin the least popular politician of his day. Born William Fitzmaurice, the son of an impoverished landowner from County Kerry, in the isolated south-west of Ireland, his fortunes had been transformed when his father unexpectedly inherited a vast income and estates in 1751, on the condition that he changed the family name to Petty. Shelburne's father subsequently received an Irish earldom and an English barony, and the young William embarked on a highly successful military career, distinguishing himself at the Battle of Minden (1759) and being promoted to colonel at a very young age and acting as an aide-de-camp to the young George III. Aged 24, he was elected to Parliament in 1761, but never took his seat, as his father's sudden death precipitated him into the House of Lords. He was then taken up by Henry Fox, the Paymaster General, who unsuccessfully proposed him as a Secretary of State in George Grenville's government: Shelburne was vetoed by the King, and later fell seriously out with Henry Fox when the latter became Lord Holland. A man of great intellectual distinction, with very independent views, Shelburne proved an awkward colleague in the posts he subsequently held, including as Secretary of State in Chatham's government of 1766–8. The historian Charles Stuart commented: 'He was touchy and interfering as a subordinate, uncooperative as an equal and secretive when in command.'[8]

Seen as a dissembler and intriguer, Shelburne became widely distrusted, and he in turn distrusted all his colleagues and was dubbed 'the Jesuit of Berkeley Square', a reference to the location of his house, which he had bought from Lord Bute. John Wilkes nicknamed him 'Malagrida' after a Portuguese Jesuit who had been executed on trumped-up charges of plotting to assassinate the Portuguese king.[9] Shelburne was, of course, not a Catholic, but his Irish background may have led to the suspicion that he was.

It was perhaps inevitable that he and Fox should clash sooner or later, but within days of taking office they were at daggers drawn. As Foreign Secretary, Fox assumed that he would be in charge of the peace negotiations, but the colonies were technically under control of the Home Office. Shelburne promptly claimed that he should be responsible for the peace talks with the Americans, while Fox should oversee those with France, Spain and Holland. Both sets of talks were taking place in Paris, where Benjamin Franklin was the American ambassador, given almost plenipotentiary powers. Both men appointed their personal representatives for the talks, Fox choosing Thomas Grenville, a younger son of former prime minister George Grenville, who was Lord Chatham's brother-in-law. Shelburne's choice was an elderly Scottish merchant, Richard Oswald, who proved to be a hopeless diplomat and was no match for the wily and unscrupulous Franklin. At their first meeting, Franklin presented him with a proposal that Britain should cede the Canadian provinces, which Oswald agreed was a reasonable proposal; Oswald duly submitted the proposal to Shelburne, who turned it down without bothering to inform the Cabinet.

A sharp difference soon emerged between Fox and Shelburne concerning recognition of American independence. Fox believed this should be granted unconditionally at the commencement of the negotiations, while Shelburne urged that it should be withheld as a bargaining chip which could be traded later for concessions to the claims of loyalists whose property had been destroyed or appropriated during the conflict. Fox's view was upheld at a Cabinet meeting on 23 May 1782, but a month later the decision was reversed at a meeting where Rockingham was absent, due to what was thought to be a trivial illness. Fox lost by a single vote, which was believed to be General Conway's,[10] and announced on the spot that he would resign, but he agreed to postpone his resignation until Rockingham's return. On the very next day – 1 July 1782 – the prime minister died from influenza.

The only previous occasion on which a prime minister had died in office was in 1754, when, on the death of Henry Pelham, George II had invited the surviving members of the Cabinet to name his successor. They proposed the Duke of Newcastle, Pelham's elder brother, who had been a Secretary of State for the previous 11 years. Based on this precedent, Fox sounded out his fellow ministers, and proposed to the King that the post should go to the third Duke of Portland, a leading Whig peer, who was currently Lord Lieutenant of Ireland. But the King had other ideas. Even before Rockingham's death, he had been planning to reduce Fox's influence, if not to get rid of him entirely. On the previous day Shelburne had written to the King, reporting the result of the Cabinet meeting and asking for consultations about the next steps to be taken. Shelburne apparently assumed that he would now take over the government, and his confidence was based at least in part on a 'satisfactory conversation'[11] which he had held with the younger Pitt.

The fact that Pitt was regarded as a central figure in a major government reconstruction, barely a year after his maiden speech, is remarkable in itself. In fact, Shelburne had already tried to entice him into the ranks of the Rockingham government, offering him in March 1782 the fairly lucrative but lowly position of vice-treasurer of Ireland. (Chatham himself had held that position for a few months in 1746.) The remuneration, around £5,000 per annum, would have been very helpful to Pitt, but acceptance would have made a mockery not just of his recent rejection of any 'subordinate situation' but also more generally of his self-adopted persona as a politician who wanted to influence major decisions, either as a backbench orator or a minister.

True to his sense of mission, having rejected the government's offer Pitt had volunteered for a leading role in the campaign for electoral reform. Like his impassioned denunciations of the American war, this risked making Pitt *persona non grata* to the decidedly anti-reformist George III, and of course both he and his father had entered the Commons in the first instance as representatives of boroughs which exemplified the defects of the existing system. However, Chatham had spoken out in favour of reform, while retaining his primary focus on foreign affairs.

The younger Pitt was given awkward reminders of his association with this cause after he became prime minister, but in fact his record was perfectly defensible even from a 'conservative' perspective. His main allies in 1782 were the impeccably moderate clergyman Christopher Wyvill and his Yorkshire Association. On 7 May 1782 Pitt introduced a motion to approve the establishment of 'a Select Committee to take into consideration the present state of the representation of the Commons of England'.[12] His speech was a shrewd attempt to unite all the members of the House who had any interest in reform – the handful of radicals who sympathised with the idea of universal franchise in all parliamentary constituencies, as well as those who much preferred the status quo but accepted that limited changes in the franchise might be an acceptable way to appease any Britons who had been influenced by the arguments in favour of American independence.

In short, Pitt had crafted an argument which no rational MP in the circumstances of 1782 could have found objectionable. However, the success of his motion would lead to the creation of a committee which might reach very different conclusions, opening the way to such horrors as shorter parliaments and even the extension of voting rights to all adult males. Even those MPs who liked Pitt's speech – which implied at most a desire to abolish the most rotten of boroughs and the reallocation of those seats to counties where the right to vote was wider, albeit still confined to property owners – recoiled at the mere mention of more radical ideas. Pitt's cousin Thomas Pitt claimed that the motion would promote 'a principle of equal representation', which was a travesty of the case being made but still sufficient to propel paranoid landowners into the 'nay' lobby.[13] The proposal was thus doomed to defeat, but it is difficult to see how anyone could have fared any better with such a self-interested audience; he only lost by 161 votes to 141. He was also warmly praised for a speech of 21 June, when he supported a bill introduced by his brother-in-law Lord Mahon which among other things was designed to outlaw certain corrupt electoral practices. In a reversed rehearsal for contests to come, Charles Fox took a key role in ensuring that the unsatisfactory status quo prevailed.[14]

Although neither could know it, Fox and Pitt were about to arrive at a crossroads, and events were about to send them down very different paths. Within a few days of their disagreement over electoral reform, Fox had offered to resign, and then Rockingham had died. In his letter to George III, Shelburne had asked about 'The weight which Your Majesty would think it proper to give Mr Fox in case of any new arrangement.'[15] George III replied:

> It may not be necessary to remove him at once, but if Lord Shelburne accepts the Head of the Treasury, and is succeeded by Mr Pitt as Secretary for the Home Department and British Settlements, [...] it will be seen how far he will submit to it.[16]

Thus, at this stage, Pitt was earmarked as a Secretary of State – a very senior government office, and not necessarily 'subordinate', since Shelburne himself had recently carried considerable weight in the same position. Armed with the King's commission, Shelburne invited Fox to remain in office, but he declined, confident that if he was supported by the other Whig notables, Shelburne would be unable to form a viable government.

But Fox was to be disappointed. At a meeting on 6 July of some 40 leading Whigs, he received overwhelming support, but it was not unanimous. The most significant dissenter was Fox's uncle, the Duke of Richmond, who declared that, though he had previously been a critic of Shelburne, he had now revised his opinion, and was not prepared to resign. His son-in-law, General Conway, also decided to remain in office; Admiral Keppel, the First Lord of the Admiralty, while sympathising with Fox, said that he felt he could not relinquish his post before a peace treaty was signed. Although Lord John Cavendish, the Chancellor of the Exchequer, and most of the non-Cabinet ministers, including Edmund Burke, sided with Fox, this was not sufficient to prevent Shelburne from going ahead. The meeting ended, with Fox very angry and Richmond in tears.[17]

Although Fox's precipitous resignation was widely criticised as showing poor judgement, his barely 100 days in office as Foreign Secretary added greatly to his reputation. Horace Walpole, previously only a lukewarm admirer, wrote in May 1782 to a friend:

> He already shines as greatly in place as he did in opposition, though infinitely more difficult a task. He is now as indefatigable as he was idle. He has a perfect temper, and not only good humour but good nature; and which is the first quality in a prime minister of a free country, has more common sense than any man, with amazing parts which are neither ostentatious nor affected.[18]

Eric Eyck added that 'Horace paid him the highest compliment he could bestow by comparing him with his own father, Sir Robert Walpole.' While a minister, Fox gave up gambling entirely, and started – belatedly, at the age of 33 – to put some order into his private life. He had never previously had a steady relationship, just a series of one-night-stands and assignations with prostitutes, and had fathered two illegitimate children, a boy and a girl, Harry Fox and Harriet Willoughby, for each of whom he took responsibility. Both were disabled, and Fox was extremely fond of them. When the French diplomat Talleyrand was exiled in London in 1793, he came to dinner with Fox and his family and friends, including Sheridan, at his London home. Throughout the meal, he later recounted, he was astonished to see:

> The first orator in Europe conversing with his son, but only with his fingers. This boy was deaf and dumb [...] Fox confined his attention almost entirely to his son, talking to him in sign language, 'while their eyes glistened as they looked at each other.'[19]

Harry Fox, said to be the 'very image of his father', lived only to the age of 15. Charles himself was no Prince Charming, being described by the contemporary parliamentary chronicler, Nathaniel Wraxall, in the following words:

> His figure, broad, heavy and inclined to corpulency, appeared destitute of elegance and grace [...] in his dress [...] he had then become negligent to a degree not altogether excusable [...] in 1781 he constantly, at least usually wore in [the Commons] a blue frockcoat and a buff waistcoat neither of which appeared in general new and sometimes appeared to be threadbare.[20]

Yet Fox was undeniably highly attractive to women in society, who flocked around him, drawn by his wit, intelligence and amiability. It is unlikely that he had sexual relations with any of them, with the probable exception of the glamorous Whig hostess, Georgiana, Duchess of Devonshire. It was with her protégée, Mary Robinson, an actress known as 'Perdita' because of her performance in that role in *A Winter's Tale*, that Fox began an affair in the summer of 1781, and he lived with her for several months. Robinson had been the mistress of the Prince of Wales, who at the age of 17 had fallen desperately in love with her and promised to settle £20,000 on her when he came of age. He had soon tired of her, however, and she had embarked on a career as a *grande cocotte*, flitting from one Whig noble to another while trying to blackmail the Prince by threatening to publish the compromising letters he had sent to her. 'Prinny', who in defiance of his father had fallen in with a group of rakish Whigs, including Fox, deputed him to negotiate with 'Perdita' for the return of the correspondence, and he struck a deal in exchange for £5,000 and an annuity of £500, which George III reluctantly paid from his privy purse. 'Perdita' took a fancy to Fox, who certainly was in no position to pay the market rate for her charms, and they both moved into her house in Berkeley Street. A highly intelligent woman, who later achieved renown as a poet and novelist, they got on well together, but after a while 'Perdita' ran out of money and returned to one of her earlier lovers. Fox then turned his attentions to Elizabeth Armitstead, an even grander courtesan, whose lovers included 'two dukes, an earl, a viscount and the Prince of Wales himself'.[21] Fox had known her for about ten years, but they had never been together before. She was now 33, only a year younger than Fox, and her long reign as 'the toast of the town' might have appeared to be approaching its end, but Fox was completely enamoured by her and commenced a relationship which was to endure to the end of his life.

Meanwhile, Shelburne was able to form his government, which was something of a patchwork affair. Fox was succeeded as Foreign Secretary by Lord Grantham, a former ambassador to Madrid and president of the Board of Trade, Lord Thurlow reclaimed his post as Lord Chancellor and Thomas Townshend, later Lord Sydney, became Home Secretary. But by far the most dramatic appointment was the 23-year-old William Pitt – not as Secretary of State, as originally intended, but as the successor to Lord John Cavendish as Chancellor of the Exchequer. Despite his youth, he was immediately seen as being Shelburne's deputy and the government's principal spokesman in the Commons, though Townsend was nominally the Leader of the House.

The first priority of the government was to complete the peace negotiations, and to secure parliamentary approval for the terms finally agreed in Paris in November 1782. These were very hard for the British to swallow, the Americans having got their way on virtually every issue. The Americans had secured unconditional acceptance of independence and a very favourable territorial settlement, giving them control of all the land between the Mississippi, the Ohio and the Great Lakes, with only Canada remaining in British hands, and without promising restitution to loyalists who had lost their property during the war. In addition, Britain restored

Senegal and Gorée to France and ceded Tobago, while the two countries restored to each other the various islands they had occupied during the war. To Spain, Britain ceded Florida and Minorca, though it kept control of Gibraltar, which had survived a determined Spanish siege.

Isolated in the House of Lords, and by his congenital inability to work on a basis of mutual confidence with his ministerial colleagues, Shelburne remained woefully ignorant of the flow of parliamentary opinion, which suggested that if he wished to remain in power he should seek to make an arrangement with either Fox or North. He did, however, ask the MP John Robinson – one of the 'King's Friends', who was largely responsible for advising which MPs should be offered bribes in order to win their votes and whose judgement was greatly respected – to make an assessment of his likely support. Robinson responded with a wildly over-optimistic report. This listed 439 MPs who were 'pros' or 'hopefuls' and only 106 who were 'doubtful' or 'con'. Robinson warned that the allocations were highly speculative, but Shelburne, saying he had been shown 'a very good list', blithely proceeded on his way.[22] It was only late in the day that he realised that he might fall short and asked the King to put pressure on North to bring his followers into line. George III obliged with a letter, which began:

> Lord North has so often whilst in office assured me that whenever I could consent to his retiring he would give the most cordial support to such an administration as I might approve of, that I should not think that I either acted properly to my own affairs or placed the confidence in his declarations if I did not express my strongest wishes that he will give the most active support [...] to the administration formed with my thorough approbation on the death of Lord Rockingham, and that during the recess he will call on the country gentlemen who certainly give great attention to him to come early and show their countenance by which I may be enabled to keep the constitution from being entirely annihilated, which must be the case if Mr Fox and his associates are not withstood.[23]

It was obtuse in the extreme for the monarch to write in such terms to his former prime minister so soon after he had mortified him by refusing to foot the bill, out of secret service funds, for government expenses during the 1780 election. These amounted to some £30,000, which North had personally guaranteed and which he could ill afford.[24] North replied evasively:

> It was true that he had, while in office, received the support of several independent country gentlemen, but he did not know whether he could venture to ask them to support the present ministry, and was afraid that he might give them some offence if he were to attempt it.[25]

Shelburne, nevertheless, resolved to approach North with a proposal to reconstruct his government to provide senior posts for the Tory leader and his main followers, and discussed the move with his Chancellor of the Exchequer. But Pitt flatly rejected a deal, saying that in no circumstances would he himself remain in the government if North was made a minister. Almost certainly this was an inherited antipathy, reflecting Pitt's belief that North was personally responsible for dissipating so many of his father's achievements. For his part, the generous-spirited North lost no opportunity to praise Pitt's best speeches, but this made no impression on the implacable Pitt. Remarkably, Shelburne decided that Pitt's services were more valuable than the votes of more than a hundred of North's followers, who were most unlikely to support the peace terms unless their leaders were offered government jobs.

At least Pitt was prepared to explore the government's sole remaining escape route by meeting Fox on 11 February 1783 – less than a week before the crucial Commons debate on the peace terms. Fox replied to Pitt's invitation by saying that he and his friends would be willing to consider the proposal, but they would only accept office if somebody other than Shelburne acted as prime minister. Pitt's reported claim that he had not come to see Fox in order 'to betray Lord Shelburne' is somewhat ironic, since in practice this is exactly what he had done himself by making his personal grudge against North a deal-breaker. In fact, this was probably the only time during their protracted duel that a combination between Pitt and Fox would have made sense. In relation to the American War, both had 'clean hands', at least compared to North and Shelburne. But parliamentary arithmetic made such a deal highly speculative at that stage, when Pitt still had a minuscule personal following in the Commons and his major asset – the apparent backing of the King – was outweighed by George's inveterate hostility to Fox. Thus the moment passed, and the two titans parted on bad terms.

Meanwhile, Shelburne's government was seething with discontent, aghast at his refusal to consult his colleagues either collectively or individually. William Grenville, Chief Secretary for Ireland, declared that 'Lord Shelburne's evident intention is to make ciphers of his colleagues', and sarcastically wrote to his brother, Earl Temple, that 'You will certainly think the mode of keeping a Cabinet unanimous by never meeting them at all an excellent one.'[26]

In January 1783 both Keppel and Richmond resigned from the government and joined Fox in opposition, and the former prime minister, the Duke of Grafton, also stood down as Lord Privy Seal. Fox, however, was already planning his return to office by setting out to woo Lord North, despite the fact that he had spent the better part of the previous seven years fiercely attacking him for his conduct of the American War. North for long remained uncommitted, largely because his own followers were divided on which side they should back. William Eden, later Lord Auckland, favoured a deal with Fox, while Henry Dundas, a cunning lawyer who was highly influential among his fellow Scottish MPs, was hot for supporting Shelburne and threatened North that his following would face annihilation in an early election if Fox and Pitt decided to gang up to form a new coalition. The normally shrewd Dundas miscalculated, and his advice proved counterproductive. Fox and North met at the house of George North, the former premier's son, on 1 February 1783, agreeing that they would join together to defeat the peace proposals when they were put to the House of Commons and subsequently would seek to form a coalition to replace Shelburne's government. They did not discuss the distribution of offices, but both agreed that the issue of electoral reform would remain an open question, the majority of Northites being strongly opposed, while the Rockinghamites were largely in favour, though several of their grandees were determined to hang on to their pocket boroughs.

The following day, Shelburne sent an emissary to North with an invitation to 'discuss matters' with him. North replied: 'I cannot meet Lord

Shelburne *now*. It is too late.'[27] North's motives were certainly mixed: he retained a great affection for Fox, despite all their differences, and an equal dislike for Shelburne. Above all, however, he was keen to obtain office for himself and his followers, still fearful that he might otherwise be impeached for his conduct of the war. The House of Lords met on 18 February 1783 to debate the peace proposals. No fewer than 145 peers were in attendance, the highest number so far during George III's reign. Lord Shelburne made heavy weather of defending the government's position, and when the vote was finally taken at 3.30 a.m., his government survived by the narrow margin of 72 over 59. 'Undoubtedly the smallest majority I ever remember in so full a House,'[28] remarked the King. Some hours later the Commons met, and North was one of the first speakers. He was sharply critical of the peace terms, and moved an amendment drawing attention to the plight of the loyalists. Fox followed suit, and strongly defended his new alliance with North, saying:

> If men of honour can meet on points of general national concern, I see no reason for calling such a meeting an unnatural junction. It is neither wise nor noble to keep up animosities for ever. It is not my nature to bear malice or to live in ill will. My friendships are perpetual, my enmities are not so. The American war and the American question is at an end [...] and it is therefore wise and candid to put an end also to the ill will, the animosity, the rancour and the feuds which it occasioned.[29]

When Pitt rose to reply he must have been torn by conflicting emotions. He was duty-bound to support the government, and indeed he felt that the peace terms were defensible in the circumstances; arguably Britain had conceded too much in the commercial clauses of the treaty, but this had been agreed in the overall interest of free trade, which he warmly supported. Nevertheless, the government was effectively carrying the can for North's ill-advised policy towards the colonies. It was no surprise that, when the Commons debate opened in earnest, Pitt was far from his best. His speech, delivered in the early hours of 17 February, included a barb against the brilliant dramatist turned Foxite MP Richard Sheridan, who responded by saying that Pitt reminded him of the character of the Angry

Boy in Ben Jonson's play *The Alchemist*. One historian has described this as 'one of the most crushing parliamentary retorts of all time'.[30] The government lost the ensuing vote, by 224 to 208. Although this showed that the Opposition ranks were not impenetrable, Pitt told his mother that he considered it a 'decisive' defeat, but not a dishonourable one.[31] Shelburne might well have resigned on the spot, but he held on for a further week in the hope of reversing the vote in a no-confidence debate led by Pitt's predecessor as Chancellor of the Exchequer, Lord John Cavendish.

The debate was dominated by Pitt. Thomas Pelham, a kinsman of two former prime ministers, wrote: 'Even his enemies or rather opponents unanimously acknowledged it to be the finest speech that ever was made in Parliament.'[32]

Pitt almost certainly knew in advance that his future prospects would hinge heavily on that performance, so it was probably nerves rather than illness or excessive drinking which caused him to vomit before he replied to Fox. His speech (see Appendix I), which lasted for almost three hours, opened with a comparison of the nascent Fox–North coalition to an 'ill-omened marriage'. That was predictable enough, but it ended with one of Pitt's self-aggrandising statements: 'in the name of public safety, *I here forbid the Banns*'. That set the tone for the rest of his speech. Pitt defended the peace terms, as he was bound to do as part of the government which had agreed to them. His argument, which attempted to rebut detailed criticisms of the peace, included the remarkable claim that the loss of Minorca was really a gain for Britain since the island had been 'Kept up at an immense and useless expense in peace, and never tenable in war'.[33] So much for the hue and cry which had consigned Admiral Byng to death and disgrace in 1757! The reasons for Pitt's bitter feelings towards Lord North were laid bare as he recalled being 'animated in my childhood by a recital of England's victories', but he now had to accept that 'the visions of her power and pre-eminence are passed away', thanks to North's incompetence.

Pitt felt able to heap praise on Lord Shelburne now that it was obvious that, however the present drama played out, he could not possibly continue as prime minister. Having done what he conceived to be his duty to falling comrades, Pitt proceeded to the true purpose of his speech, which was to pay tribute to an individual who was even more worthy than Lord Shelburne – himself. Although he had achieved next to nothing as Chancellor of the Exchequer, he presented his brief tenure of that office as a testament to his selfless sense of public duty. Plagiarising the refrain of all ambitious classical orators, he affirmed his willingness to retire from public life if necessary, 'not disappointed, but triumphant'. Again, this was stale material even for the undemanding eighteenth-century House of Commons, so Pitt had to spice things up with some personal abuse. Having belaboured Lord North, he turned to Fox, accusing him of 'avowing an indiscriminate opposition to whoever may be appointed to succeed. I will march out with no warlike, no hostile, no menacing protestations.'[34] This was a remarkable accusation from someone who had declared that he would not accept a subordinate role in any government, and who had already made it known that he would not serve under any possible successor to Lord Shelburne.

Pitt's speech may have gripped the House, but it shifted few, if any, votes, and the government was defeated by 207 to 190. Two days later, on 24 February, Shelburne offered his resignation. Ever distrustful, he was convinced – wrongly – that the King had connived in his downfall. George III however made no attempt to encourage Shelburne to remain in office, other than in a caretaker role until a new administration was formed. Instead he spent the next five weeks in a series of desperate attempts to prevent Fox and North from assuming office. These are described in great detail in John Cannon's book,[35] which is the definitive work on the subject. His first (and most hopeful) initiative was to invite William Pitt to form a government. This had originally been suggested by Henry Dundas, who effectively made himself Pitt's campaign manager. The King immediately summoned Pitt to ascertain whether he would be willing to serve, and gleefully informed Thurlow the same afternoon (24 February) that he had received the offer 'with a spirit and inclination that makes me think he will not decline'.[36] The following morning Pitt met with Dundas and another MP (Richard Rigby), and carefully went through a list of the entire membership of the Commons to estimate how much support he could rely on. Dundas then dashed a note off to his cousin, Robert Dundas, saying: 'I have little doubt that he will announce himself Minister tomorrow'.[37]

Pitt, however, was much more cautious, writing to his mother, 'I feel all the difficulties of the undertaking, and am by no means in love with the object [...] the great article to decide by seems that of numbers.'[38]

Over the next two days, he frequently changed his mind about whether to accept the King's offer, though he was confidently pressed to do so by Dundas and many others of his friends. Lord Thurlow in particular was exasperated by his hesitation, telling Dundas that 'to my notion the ball seems to be absolutely at his feet.'[39] But, perhaps remembering the 'very good list' which had misled Shelburne, Pitt informed the King on 27 February that only the 'moral certainty' of a majority in the House of Commons would allow him to go ahead.[40] The following morning Dundas made a final attempt to convince him that a majority could be obtained with Pitt at the Treasury and Lord Gower as Lord President of the Council, and left with Pitt 'perfectly resolved to accept', but within three hours he had changed his mind completely, and wrote apologetically to Dundas:

> What you stated to me this morning seemed to remove all doubts of my finding a majority in Parliament [...] I have since most deliberately reconsidered the ground, and after weighing it as fully as is possible for me to do, my final decision is directly contrary to the impression then made on me. I see that the main and almost only ground of reliance would be this – *that Lord North and his friends would not continue in a combination to oppose.* In point of prudence, after all that has passed, and considering all that is to come, such a reliance is too precarious to act on. But above all, in point of honour to my own feelings, I cannot form an administration trusting to the hope that it will be supported or even will not be opposed by Lord North, whatever the influence may be that determines his conduct. This resolution will, I am afraid, both surprise and disappoint you.[41]

For a young man of 23 to turn down the glittering prospect of becoming prime minister at more than ten years younger than any of his predecessors (or successors, for that matter!) showed a remarkable degree of judgement and self-control, in sharp contrast, many concluded, to his rival, Charles Fox. It was also an indication of his extreme caution – Pitt was not prepared to risk a 'fiasco' at the outset of his career and told the King 'it would be dishonourable not to succeed if attempted.'[42] George III had by no means yet exhausted his efforts to prevent Fox and North from taking office, and once more sent for Lord Gower, who indicated that he was only prepared to serve if he could find a formidable debater capable of standing up to both Fox and Pitt as Leader of the Commons. He was unsuccessful in his search, and the King's next resource was to send for Lord Guilford, North's father, with an offer to his son to resume his premiership, or alternatively to take a Cabinet post in an administration to be presided over by 'a peer not connected with any of the strong parties that distract this kingdom'.[43] North sent a somewhat convoluted reply to the effect that he would only accept such an arrangement with the consent of Fox, which he did not believe would be forthcoming. George then again sent for Gower, who told him that he thought that Thomas Pitt (William's cousin) might be prepared to lead the Commons. 'Mr Thomas Pitt or Mr Thomas anybody', replied the distracted King, but when Thomas Pitt was approached he replied that he was 'totally unequal to public business, but most certainly unequal to a task like this'.[44]

The despairing King now sat down and wrote a letter to his eldest son, the Prince of Wales, saying he intended to abdicate and retire to Hanover (which he had never visited), and see out his days as elector of the state, saying: 'The situation of the times are such that I must, if I attempt to carry on the business of the nation, give up every political principle on which I have acted.'[45]

He then drafted an abdication speech which he intended to make in the House of Lords. The letter was never sent, and the speech never delivered, though the drafts still remain in the royal archives. Instead, he made one last attempt to avoid completely giving way to Fox and North by accepting their coalition, providing that he could nominate a peer to the premiership. Fox replied that only his own choice – the Duke of Portland – could fill this role,[46] and on 2 April 1783, at the age of 44, the Duke kissed hands on his appointment. The triumphalism with which Fox and his friends greeted this event would perhaps have been tempered if they had been privy to the letter which George III had just sent to Lord

Temple, elder brother of William Grenville and another cousin of Pitt's. In this the King said he was 'the victim of the most unprincipled coalition the annals of this or any nation can equal', and continued:

> A ministry which I have avowedly attempted to avoid by calling on every other description of men, cannot be supposed to have either my favour or confidence and as such I shall most certainly refuse any honours that may be asked by them; I trust the eyes of the nation will soon be opened as my sorrow may prove fatal to my health if I remain long in this thraldom; I trust you will be steady in your attachment to me and ready to join other honest men in watching the conduct of this unnatural combination, and I hope many months will not elapse before the Grenvilles, the Pitts and other men of abilities will relieve me.[47]

8

The Fox–North Coalition and the King's 'Coup d'État'

G EORGE III's extreme reluctance to accept the 'Fox–North coalition', as the new government was inevitably called, had more than one source. Predominant was his belief that it encroached on what he regarded as his own prerogatives, above all his right to choose his own ministers, which he believed had never been challenged before, except by Rockingham one year earlier. In actual fact, his grandfather, George II, had had to give way, in 1746, when – by threat of collective resignation – the government of Henry Pelham insisted, against the wishes of the King, that the elder Pitt should be appointed to a ministerial post.[1] Almost as strong a motivation was his deep personal animus against Charles Fox. This went back a long way, starting with Lord Holland's intrigues to make his sister-in-law, Sarah Lennox, the King's wife or mistress, followed by what George III regarded as Charles's unsatisfactory conduct as a junior minister under Lord North. More recently, he had been appalled by Fox's friendship with the Prince of Wales, blaming him for his dissolute ways. Actually, the younger George needed no encouragement from Fox; he had already as a teenager embarked on a career of debauchery under the influence of two of his uncles, the King's younger brothers, William Henry and Henry Frederick.

It was not only the King who regarded Fox's irregular lifestyle as a disqualification for office. Dr Richard Price, a prominent Utilitarian with 'advanced' political views, who might have been expected to be a warm supporter of Fox, proved to be a strong critic, writing:

> Can you imagine that a spendthrift in his own concerns will make an economist in managing the concerns of others? That a wild gamester will take due care of the state of a kingdom. Treachery, venality, and corruption must be the effects of dissipation, voluptuousness, and impiety. These sap the foundations of virtue. They render men necessitous and supple, and ready at any time to sacrifice their consciences, or to fly to a court in order to repair a shattered fortune and procure supplies for prodigality.[2]

Yet it was not as if Fox was uniquely sinful among contemporary politicians; many others had kept mistresses and had recklessly gambled their fortunes away. The Earl of Sandwich was a byword for every kind of dissipation, but George III was happy for him to remain in office for 20 years as First Lord of the Admiralty and in other senior posts.

The new prime minister was William Cavendish-Bentinck, the third Duke of Portland, whose great-grandfather, Hans William Bentinck, had come from Holland with William III in 1689, marrying into the British aristocracy and inheriting vast estates. Portland himself greatly increased these by marrying Lady Dorothy Cavendish, daughter of the fourth Duke of Devonshire, and hyphenating his surname. (It is an intriguing fact that another future prime minister, Harold Macmillan, was to marry a Lady Dorothy Cavendish, daughter of the ninth Duke of Devonshire, over 150 years later, in 1920.[3]) Portland was a poor speaker, and not very bright, but had strong Whig principles, and due to his high social position and enormous wealth was readily accepted as Rockingham's successor as Whig leader in the Lords. A great admirer of Fox, he was happy to play a figurehead role as the head of the new government. The Cabinet resembled that of Rockingham, except that the supporters of Shelburne were replaced by the followers of Lord North, who became Home Secretary, nominally on a par with Fox as Foreign Secretary; but nobody doubted that Fox was the real leader of the government. Lord John Cavendish and Edmund Burke resumed their earlier posts as Chancellor of the Exchequer and Paymaster General respectively, and two of Fox's oldest and most intimate friends, the Earl of Carlisle and Richard Fitzpatrick, joined the government as Lord Privy Seal and Secretary at War.

Right from the start, George III made it clear that he would not ease the path of the new government by offering the customary amount of patronage. It had been envisaged that North should go to the Lords to strengthen the government's debating strength in the Upper House, that the Earl of Hertford should be given a dukedom and that peerages or advancement should go to half a dozen other government supporters. All these moves were blocked by the King, which meant that the over-all shape of the government was rather different than Fox and North had planned. The government's first task was to try to improve on the peace terms which had been rejected by the Commons. It had very little success, only winning slightly better treatment for British citizens in Tobago, a small modification of French fishing rights in Newfoundland and a clearer definition of British rights to participate in the gum trade, while efforts to negotiate a commercial treaty with the United States were abandoned. The Commons sullenly accepted the inevitability of approving the revised treaties, but not before Pitt had thoroughly enjoyed himself by demonstrating, with biting irony, just how minimal these improvements had been.

The King began quietly to prepare plans to evict the government as soon as a favourable opportunity arose. This might have been as early as June 1783, when there was a heated dispute concerning the establishment to be set up for the Prince of Wales when he came of age on 12 August 1783. Fox proposed an income of £100,000 a year, including the revenues of the Duchy of Cornwall. Both Lord John Cavendish and Lord North thought this too much, but the Cabinet agreed, and Portland formally put this to the King. George III exploded with rage, describing it as 'a shameful squandering of public money' and as an attempt 'to gratify the passions of an ill-advised young man'.[4] The most he was prepared to give from the Civil List was £50,000, with Parliament to provide a grant of £50,000 to pay the Prince's debts (then estimated at £29,000) and to meet the costs of setting up his own establishment at Carlton House. The King later backed down and agreed to a compromise plan, under which the amount of the

Prince's grant would be raised to £60,000, evidently concluding that this would not be an acceptable issue on which to turn out the government, even though public opinion was predominantly on his side. He was not yet sure that he could find an alternative prime minister, as Pitt and his friends were still hesitant. 'Prinny' reluctantly accepted the settlement but then proceeded to make massive extensions to his new residence, stuffing it with every conceivable luxury, with the result that his debts eventually grew to the astonishing sum of £269,878.6s.7¼d.[5] (approximately £37 million in modern terms).

Fox was nervous that the King might move against the government during the summer parliamentary recess, but was reassured when the Commons reassembled in the autumn and he obtained very healthy majorities whenever the House divided. The biggest challenge to its authority was expected with the introduction of the India Bill, which Burke had been steadily working on throughout the summer. Its purpose was to ensure parliamentary control over the activities of the East India Company. Founded in Elizabethan times as a trading company, it had metamorphosed, especially in the years following the Battle of Plassey in 1757, into a vast imperial power, controlling a territory which greatly exceeded that of Britain, both in terms of area and population. It had its own private army of 67,000 men, and was steeped in corruption, many of its officials making large fortunes and riding roughshod over the rights of the Indian population. The company paid out huge dividends to its shareholders, but by 1783 its finances were in disorder and it was facing bankruptcy. Henry Dundas, who served under Shelburne as Lord Advocate, had tried to introduce a modest reforming bill, but the government fell before it could make any progress. Burke, who had closely followed Indian affairs over several years and who felt a strong moral obligation to act, was determined to carry through a much more radical measure, which he described as 'the great Magna Carta of Indostan.'[6] He was strongly backed by Fox, who could justly claim to be co-author of the bill. Before its introduction, Fox attempted to bolster the government's position by approaching Pitt with an offer of a senior ministerial post, which the latter abruptly declined. He informed his cousin, Earl Temple, of the offer, who promptly reported it to the King.

The central provision of the bill was to invest control of the company in a parliamentary commission of seven, with eight assistants who would oversee the commercial dealings of the company. They would be directly appointed by Parliament, would have security of tenure for at least three years, and the Crown would have no say in either their appointment or dismissal. Fox announced the names of the seven proposed commissioners; all were supporters of the government, including Lord North's eldest son, George North. This enraged Pitt and other Opposition MPs, who feared that this would deliver into Fox's hands the vast array of patronage which the company had at its disposal, notably including control of many pocket boroughs. Fox, they believed, would use this power to compensate for the King's withholding of his own patronage powers. The directors of the company, and the city interests who were its principal investors, took fright and began a vociferous campaign against the bill, aided by a barrage of critical articles in the press, many of them attacking Fox in the most venomous terms. A vast number of prints and cartoons were circulated around the country most of which also pictured Fox – and sometimes also Burke – in an unfavourable light. The most famous of these, by the caricaturist James Sayers, is on display at the National Portrait Gallery. Entitled 'Carlo Khan, the Great Potentate of Leadenhall Street' (Leadenhall Street was the headquarters of the East India Company), it portrays Fox making his triumphal entry into the company premises astride an elephant bearing the face of Lord North and preceded by Burke as herald with banner and trumpet.[7] Meanwhile, Pitt hastened to mobilise parliamentary opposition to what he described in a letter to the Duke of Rutland as 'The boldest and most unconstitutional measure ever attempted, transferring at one stroke, in spite of all charters and compacts, the immense patronage and influence of the East to *Charles Fox, in or out of office.'*[8]

Pitt predicted that Fox would have difficulty to get the bill through the House of Commons, and appealed to Rutland to use his influence to encourage as many MPs as possible to come up from the country to vote against it. The stage was set for a dramatic confrontation between the two outstanding parliamentary orators of their day. Fox prepared for the contest with some trepidation, writing to his mistress, Mrs Armitstead:

They are endeavouring to make a great cry against us, and will I am afraid succeed in making us very unpopular in the city. However, I know that I am right and must bear the consequences, though I dislike unpopularity as much as any man [...] I know I never did act more upon principle than this moment when they are abusing me so. If I had considered nothing but keeping my power, it was the safest way to leave things as they are, or to propose some trifling alteration, and I am not at all ignorant of the political danger which I run by this bold measure; but whether I succeed or no, I shall always be glad that I attempted, because I know that I have done no more than I was bound to do, in risking my power and that of my friends when the happiness of so many millions is at stake.[9]

The second reading of the bill was scheduled for 27 November 1783, and Fox was on his best form in recommending it to the House. 'It was well known,' he said,

that the Company's government of India was nothing more than a system of 'anarchy and confusion'. Its servants ignored its instructions and thought only of satisfying their own 'rapacity'. No confidence could be put in the Company's capacity to reform itself. Indeed, the government was called upon to save it from imminent bankruptcy. The Company's administration of India had been predicated on 'the miseries of mankind'. This is the kind of government exercised under the East India Company upon the natives of Indostan; and the subversion of that infamous government is the main object of the bill.[10]

He went on to give a magisterial speech which greatly impressed Members from all parts of the House. General Burgoyne, for example, now an MP for Preston, wrote to the Lord Lieutenant of Ireland, Lord Northington, reporting:

He went through a dissection article by article of this complicated and artful statement in a manner that did wonderful service to his cause, mingling the most convincing reasoning with a knowledge and accuracy of figures that would have made strangers believe he had been educated in the bank [...] Our friends are in the greatest spirits, the most sanguine not having expected so great a majority; the opposition are much depressed.[11]

Pitt responded with a highly aggressive speech, in which he described the bill as 'one of the boldest, most unprecedented, most desperate and alarming attempts at the exercise of tyranny that ever disgraced the annals of this or any other country.'[12]

Horace Walpole was not the only observer to conclude that Pitt had overreached himself and had been decisively worsted by his rival, writing to his friend, Sir Horace Mann:

Mr Pitt's reputation is much sunk; nor, though he is a much more correct logician than his father, has he the same firmness and perseverance. It is no wonder that he was dazzled by his own premature fame [...] Had he [en]listed under Mr Fox, who loved and courted him, he would not only have discovered modesty, but have been more likely to succeed him than by commencing his competitor. But what [have] I to do to look into futurity?[13]

The government's majority on second reading was a very healthy 109 – 229 votes to 120 – and it increased to 114 two weeks later on the motion to go into committee on the bill. This debate was dominated by Edmund Burke, 'in full spate, dwarfing all other contributions in an enormous three-hour survey of India and her problems and culminating in a sustained panegyric on Fox.'[14] The way ahead for the bill seemed clear, though Fox still expected that Pitt and his friends would fight tooth and nail to obstruct it during the committee stage. In the event this did not happen, as Horace Walpole explained in a further letter to Sir Horace Mann:

The opposition in the House of Commons were so humbled by their two defeats that though Mr Pitt had declared that he would contest every clause in the Committee [...] he slunk from the contest, and all the blanks were filled up without obstruction.[15]

What neither Walpole nor Fox knew was that Pitt had withdrawn from the contest at the behest of King George. The King had decided that the time had come for him to move against the government, and that he would use the House of Lords as his instrument to destroy both the bill and the Fox–North coalition. He entered into a conspiracy with Lord Thurlow, the former (and future) Lord Chancellor, and George Nugent-Temple-Grenville, the third Earl Temple, to bring this about. Temple, the eldest surviving son of former prime minister George Grenville, was now the head of the Grenville family, which had become notorious for its cupidity, manifested both in its ability to contract highly advantageous marriages and to secure a record number of sinecures. The earl, who had collected his first sinecure at the age of 11, as a Teller to the Exchequer, was by no means the least grasping of the Grenvilles. He had been Lord Lieutenant of Ireland in the Shelburne government and was not averse to seeking other high offices, though his main ambitions at this stage were for a dukedom and a Knighthood of the Garter, both within the gift of the monarch.

The King considered the option of refusing royal assent to the bill, but this power had not been used since the reign of Queen Anne, who had vetoed the 1707 Militia Bill and was generally regarded as having fallen into desuetude. It had also become rare for the Lords to defeat a bill which had been approved by the Commons, although this was not without precedent. Thurlow advised the King that it should be possible to secure a majority against the bill in the Lords, but only if it was made clear that this was the King's will. George felt that he could not risk dismissing the government unless he had an assurance that Pitt was now willing to assume power, and deputed Lord Clarendon, a former minister in Lord North's government, to find out. Clarendon reported back that Pitt had now overcome his earlier scruples, and the King took two decisive steps to secure his objective. Firstly, he summoned the Archbishop of Canterbury and asked him to help secure the votes of the 26 bishops who were members of the Lords. Secondly, he gave Temple, who was Pitt's first cousin, a piece of paper carrying the following words:

His Majesty allowed Earl Temple to say that whoever voted for the India Bill was not only not his friend but would be considered by him as an enemy; and if these words were not strong enough Earl Temple might use whatever words he might deem stronger and more to the purpose.[16]

Temple lost no time in showing this to large numbers of his fellow peers, but Fox, unaware of what was going on, was convinced that his bill would secure a healthy majority in the Lords. Wild rumours were circulating that the King was plotting his downfall, but Fox refused to believe them, and when the bill reached the Lords on 15 December he, together with Pitt and other interested parties, clustered behind the throne to listen to the debate. It did not proceed as Fox had expected, in part because Portland, who introduced the bill, made a hash of his speech. The Opposition, led by Temple, moved the adjournment of the House as an indication of their disapproval of the bill, and when the House divided carried the vote by 87 to 79. Fox dashed off a hurried note to Mrs Armitstead, saying:

> We are beat in the House of Lords by such treachery on part of the King and such meanness on the part of his *friends* in the House of Lords as one could not expect neither from him or them.[17]

Two days later the bill was defeated at the end of the second reading debate by a slightly larger margin, 95 to 76. According to John Cannon, this was probably the largest division in the House of Lords in the whole of the eighteenth century.[18] It was estimated that some 27 votes were switched on account of Temple's and the Archbishop's activities. The bishops, however, were badly split, with 12 voting against the bill, and eight in favour. Thomas Orde MP, a supporter of Lord Shelburne, wrote to him giving a graphic report of the occasion, saying, 'I understand that some of the bishops seemed to feel very awkward and that those who still voted with administration cast a sad look of contrition towards those who might tell tales of them to high-judging Jove [George III].'[19]

Both the King and Pitt assumed that the government would resign upon the defeat of their bill, but Fox, confident that the Commons would continue to support him, defiantly backed a series of motions in the House of Commons condemning the King's conspiracy. One of these was to the effect that to report any opinion of the King in order to influence debates was a 'high crime and misdemeanour'. The second was that the House would hold an enquiry into the state of the nation on the following Monday. The third, designed to forestall a dissolution of Parliament, proclaimed that 'in view of the urgent need for some provision for the government of India anyone advising the king to prevent it was "an enemy of the people".'[20] In the debate on the motions, both Pitt and William Grenville attempted to justify the Lords' actions, Pitt brazenly denying that there had been any conspiracy involving his own cousin, Temple, and the King. He declared that the 'rumour' to that effect was but 'the lie of the day' and called on the ministers to resign. Immediately, he was rebutted by Lord North in what was widely acclaimed as a 'great' speech, in which North ridiculed the 'disingenuous and puerile argument' of Pitt and stoutly declared that 'The responsibility of ministers was the only security which Englishmen had against the abuse of the executive power.'[21]

After Fox had wound up the debate with another coruscating oration, during which he actually read out the text of the note which George III had given to Temple, the House proceeded to vote on the three motions before it. All were carried by large majorities. Fox and North breathed sighs of relief, confident that their position was safe, and that same evening met with Portland at his house to review the situation. At midnight, however, messengers arrived from the King demanding that they immediately surrender their seals of office. In an accompanying note to North, he wrote, 'I choose this method as Audiences on such occasions must be unpleasant.'[22]

A few hours later, on 19 December 1783, the King had an audience with Pitt, who was now 24 years old, and Temple, whom he appointed respectively as prime minister and Home Secretary. Temple had assumed that the Commons would immediately be dissolved and a new Parliament would be elected, but this was not to be. John Robinson had, at the King's request, made an assessment of the likelihood of the new government winning a majority in a new election, given that the King would be willing to extend the powers of patronage which he had conspicuously withheld from the Portland ministry. The historian Erick Eyck has left a graphic description of how Robinson applied himself to this task:

He goes through the constituencies one after the other, noting who has each in his pocket or has a decisive influence in it, how such-and-such a patron can be won over, how much money will be needed to do it, who has to be 'seen' and so forth. It won't be a very cheap business: it can't be done under two hundred thousand pounds. But if this sum is forthcoming [...] at least 116 seats can be wrested from the coalition and brought over to the new administration to be formed by the King – and that is more than enough to give a good majority.[23]

Yet, perhaps recalling how Robinson had got his sums wrong when advising Lord Shelburne, the King concluded that it would be too risky to go for an immediate dissolution and that it would be better to allow more time to grease the palms of the proprietors of so many seats. On learning this, Temple lost his nerve, and fearing impeachment by the existing Parliament resigned his post after three days. Nor did he receive the dukedom he had expected as a reward for his role in turning out the coalition. Instead, 12 months later, he became the Marquess of Buckingham (the dukedom had to wait until 1822, when King George IV appointed Temple's eldest son, Richard Temple-Nugent-Brydges-Chandos-Grenville as first Duke of Buckingham and Chandos). Temple never held office again, except for a second term as Lord Lieutenant of Ireland, in 1787–9. He was not the only one, though, who feared that the Commons would seek to impeach the King's conspirators and thereby put their lives in danger. The ever witty Horace Walpole dashed off a little ditty which he circulated to his friends:

> Master Billy you are silly
> Master Temple you are simple
> Thus to risk your heads in vain
> But a greater fool than you
> Is he (to give the Devil his due)
> Whom God grant long to reign.[24]

The same fear gripped many others, which perhaps explains why Pitt (who had a sleepless night following Temple's withdrawal) had great difficulty in assembling a Cabinet. Many prominent former ministers turned Pitt down, and in the end he was able to assemble a Cabinet of only seven members, of whom only he was in the Commons; just two of the other members had previous experience of high office – Lord Thurlow, who returned as Lord Chancellor, and Lord Gower, who became Lord President of the Council.

Few observers foresaw a long lease of life for Pitt's ministry; the general view was that it was unlikely to survive much beyond the Christmas period. A much-quoted remark made by an MP's wife, Mrs Crewe, was that 'Pitt may do what he likes during the holidays, but it will only be a mince-pie administration.'[25]

This was certainly the view of Fox and his colleagues, who were utterly convinced that their large majority in the Commons would soon drive Pitt out of power and restore themselves to office. Little did he know that it would be more than twenty-two years before he would resume his ministerial career.

The majority view among academic historians is that George III exceeded his constitutional powers and effectively staged a *coup d'état* in removing a government which enjoyed a large majority in the House of Commons. Some, however, take the view that Fox had been the author of his own misfortunes, and that had he shown better judgement, and more understanding of the King's sensibilities, the coalition would have been able to remain in power and carry through many of the reforms which it wished to pursue. For Fox himself the event was an unmitigated tragedy, the bitter memory of which had a decisive influence on his actions for the remaining 23 years of his life. He now looked upon the King as the devil incarnate, intent upon imposing a personal tyranny and lacking any scruples. Against Pitt he felt less animus but could never bring himself to serve under Pitt on the numerous subsequent occasions when approaches were made to him. Each time Fox indicated that he might be willing to serve, but only on a basis of equality, meaning that Pitt would have to cede the premiership to somebody else. This Pitt was never able to accept.

If Fox was devastated by his political setback, it was compensated to a considerable extent by developments in his private life, notably by the consolidation of his relationship with Elizabeth Armitstead. Born in obscure circumstances as Elizabeth Bridget Cane, there is no record of a marriage to a Mr Armitstead. He may have been one of her early 'protectors', or may perhaps have never existed and had been invented as a *nom de guerre*. Not a classic beauty, she was seen as a very attractive woman, tall and full-bosomed. Four times painted by Joshua Reynolds, and highly intelligent, she was a good listener, and Fox would pour out to her every detail of his political strife and spend hours reading to her from the classics and Italian, French and Spanish literature. By the autumn of 1783, when they had been living together for several months in great harmony, she suddenly took fright. She was 33, which was old for a member of her profession; she had also run out of money and was afraid of ending up on the scrapheap like so many of her fellow courtesans. Elizabeth resolved to leave Fox, but could not bring herself to tell him. She waited until he had gone for a few days to Newmarket for the races and a shooting party, and then sent him a letter breaking off their affair. Fox was distraught and immediately wrote back a four-page letter pleading with her to stay. It began:

> It is impossible to conceive how miserable your letter has made me. No my dearest Liz you must not no indeed you must not, the very thought of being without you so sinks my spirits that I am sure the reality would be more than I can bear. To talk of favours received from me is ridiculous, are not our interests one? do I live but in you? No my dearest Angel you must not abandon me you must not.[26]

Elizabeth could not resist Charles's entreaties and their attachment became permanent. They began to live together effectively as man and wife, though they only married in 1795 and the marriage was not publicised until 1802. Much of their time was now spent at St Ann's Hill near Chertsey in Surrey, where Elizabeth had been renting an idyllic country house, which she was able later to purchase. Here Charles for the first time was able to enjoy the pleasures of domesticity, including gardening and country walks. Many of his friends looked forward eagerly to paying weekend visits (though without their wives) and coined the verb 'to charley' to describe such visits. One of his most frequent visitors, from the age of nine onwards, was his nephew Richard, Stephen's son, who had become the third Lord Holland after his father's early death. Charles treated him like the legitimate son he never had, and they became devoted to each other, Fox regarding the boy as his political heir.

9

The 'Mince-Pie' Government

O N 19 December 1783, when Richard Pepper Arden announced to the House of Commons that his friend Pitt had agreed to serve as First Lord of the Treasury and Chancellor of the Exchequer, the supporters of Fox and North responded with ribaldry rather than rage. Nathaniel Wraxall thought that this was a reflection on Pitt's youth: as he put it, such a promotion at the age of 24 was 'an instance without precedence in our Annals, and will probably never be again realized!'[1]

Yet, as we have seen, in less than three years as an MP Pitt had proved a match for the best orators in the House and had already served for several months as a senior minister. While George III had not exactly advertised his prolonged courtship of Pitt, most MPs must have known that the King had identified him as the most promising alternative to Fox and North – and that Pitt had decided not to take up the invitation. Far from acting like an impulsive youngster, Pitt had shown judgement worthy of a far more seasoned statesman. Perhaps the laughing Coalitionists of December 1783 were really expressing relief that Pitt had finally made a schoolboy error by accepting an impossible commission from the King.

From a twenty-first-century perspective, the idea that service as Chancellor of the Exchequer could be regarded merely as an apprenticeship to a career in government seems absurd. Although recent holders of the post, like James Callaghan, John Major and Gordon Brown, have used it as a stepping stone to the highest office in the UK government, appointment as Chancellor is beyond the wildest dreams of most MPs – in itself the pinnacle of a very successful career. But things were different in the eighteenth century, when the prime minister's official title of First Lord of the Treasury was taken seriously. As a general rule, the post of Chancellor of the Exchequer had only been significant when it had been held by the First Lord, as it had been (for example) by Walpole and Henry Pelham. The precedent set by Walpole was one which Pitt himself would follow when he had the chance to combine the offices. Other holders of the position included deservedly obscure figures like John Aislabie (1718–21) and Henry Legge-Bilton (who served in the role on three separate occasions between 1754 and 1761).

However, the fact that the Exchequer had been offered to at least three other people before Pitt, when the Shelburne government was formed, gives a misleading impression. Pitt was always intended to be a crucial piece in the ministerial jigsaw, and it was more a question of where he would fit in. The fact was that the new government was top-heavy with peers, even by eighteenth-century standards, and was desperate to recruit talented representatives in the Commons. In this respect, Pitt was not really a 'subordinate' at all. The titular Leader of the House, Thomas Townshend – one of those who had turned down the job Pitt accepted – was not noted for his speaking skills, so Pitt was sure to play a prominent role in the inevitable clashes with the Opposition's crack team of orators.

Pitt also had the satisfaction of seeing his brother-in-law Edward Eliot appointed to a junior Treasury position, while other Cambridge friends, Richard Pepper Arden and John Pratt,8 also joined the government. Another congenial colleague was Henry Dundas, whose admiration for Pitt had arisen from professional dealings rather than previous acquaintance. Pitt was also able to move out of his chambers in Lincoln's Inn and take up residence in an even more prestigious property, Number 10 Downing Street, since no other senior minister needed to live there. In this respect he had already got the better of his father, who had never occupied the house. However, Pitt's comments to his mother suggest that he found the property a little large to suit his bachelor lifestyle.[2]

Although Pitt is rightly regarded as a notable reformer in the financial field, his first stint at the Treasury was unproductive in this respect.

Although proposals were developed for radical changes in the system of customs duties and for measures to cut administrative costs, neither of these schemes won parliamentary approval. While Pitt was Chancellor, major reforms introduced under the Rockingham administration (including Edmund Burke's much-vaunted Civil List Act) came into force; MPs and peers could therefore feel that they had done enough on this subject for the time being.

Pitt's actions in the months after the collapse of Shelburne's government were not those of a complacent politician who was hanging all his hopes on the retention of royal approval. Indeed, he seemed anxious to show his continued determination to cleanse the government of abuses, whatever their origins. After further consultations with Wyvill and the Yorkshire Association, he returned to the subject of electoral reform, this time presenting more concrete proposals for a redistribution of seats from boroughs to the counties and arguing for tougher sanctions against corrupt practices. He was disappointed by his heavy defeat – 293 to 149 – but had good reason to feel heartened by the support of a third of those who voted. There was also some satisfaction to be gained from the fact that the coalition partners Fox and North spoke on different sides of the question. Pitt also introduced a Public Offices Regulation Bill, to curb the misuse of things like official stationary. This bill was approved by the Commons but fell foul of the House of Lords.

Through these months, Pitt was sustained by his circle of friends, especially Wilberforce, who welcomed him for frequent visits to his home in Wimbledon. The fact that the same skin housed an austere ex-minister and a frolicsome practical joker has been difficult for observers to credit ever since the 1780s. It seems, though, that Pitt could only find a satisfactory psychological balance if he had full licence to indulge both sides of his character; thus, instead of brooding over the reception of his latest speech in these crucial months, he would meet up with his cronies for evenings which often incorporated embarrassing undergraduate pranks. The problem for Pitt was that if he did become prime minister he would have far fewer opportunities for his favourite mode of relaxation.

In September 1783 Pitt left England for a visit to France with Eliot and Wilberforce. He had the gratification of finding himself a minor celebrity in his own right, and not just as his father's son. The visitors met Louis XVI and Marie Antoinette and key figures in the government, along with the American ambassador to France, Benjamin Franklin. Apparently, the wife of Jacques Necker – the Swiss-born former French finance minister whose reforms helped to inspire Pitt's own thinking – hoped that the young Englishman might be persuaded to marry her daughter, Germaine. The match was never made, but in later years the pair formed a political alliance at a distance, when the girl who became Germaine de Staël generated a degree of personal irritation in Napoleon Bonaparte which not even Pitt could produce. If Germaine had ever become Mrs Pitt, she would probably have proved equally vexing to her husband.

The prospect of a new parliamentary session put an end to the tour, and Pitt had been back in London for three weeks before the Fox–North coalition unveiled its plans in the King's speech of 11 November 1783. Notoriously, this included proposals for a radical reform of British administration in India. Five weeks later the coalition had been forced to resign, and on 19 December William Pitt the Younger took office as the tenth individual to serve George III as prime minister.

Although Pitt tried to minimise his involvement in the events leading up to the fall of the Fox–North coalition, he can scarcely be absolved since he was the key figure in George's plan and could have vetoed the enterprise at any time between March and December 1783. As we have seen, the coalition was an unpleasant obstacle to Pitt's ambitions. Although he had denounced it in memorable phrases, in constitutional substance his argument was little better than a parliamentary exhibition of sour grapes. He had ample reason to hope for its downfall by fair means or foul, and if possible to hasten this process.

In a parallel universe where the plot to instal Pitt as prime minister had come unstuck in spectacular fashion, or if it had worked and he had immediately plunged his country into a humiliating disaster, he would have been hard-pressed to defend himself even against a charge of treason against the state. Ultimately, though, he could have claimed that in the circumstances of 1783 no government could hope to implement constructive reforms without enjoying at least the grudging approval of the King, and that since the coalition was clearly deficient in this respect it was the duty of a patriotic politician to provide an alternative. If anyone had claimed that George III's plot to undermine the coalition exceeded constitutional bounds, Pitt could have accepted the argument in principle while pointing out that in practice, by making it known that members of the House of Lords who supported the coalition's Indian policy would not be the King's friends, George had exploited the kind of informal influence which was characteristic of Britain's uncodified constitution. The King had not resorted to armed force, as his government had done in America. And he had deployed his remaining powers of persuasion on behalf of an aspiring prime minister who had demonstrated a firm intention to attack constitutional abuses, whether or not this would tend to reduce royal influence in future.

Thus when Pitt emerged as King George's champion in the fight against Fox, he could boast of a solid if unspectacular record as a 'man of business' and was recognised as an orator whose initial success was not just a flash in the pan. Nevertheless, he had accepted the King's invitation to become prime minister in circumstances which he would never have chosen, and his task was intimidating. The announcement of an impressive ministerial team might have done something to subdue Opposition mockery, but even hardened place-seekers flinched from the prospect of holding office in the face of an enraged Commons majority. A former premier, the Duke of Grafton, turned down the post of Lord Privy Seal, saying he could see 'nothing to encourage me to come forward'.[3] Others who turned Pitt down included Lord Sackville (formerly Lord George Germain) and other former ministers including Earl Camden, and Lords Grantham, Cornwallis, Beaufort and Richmond, and even Pitt's brother-in-law, Lord Mahon.

The politicians who were happiest to bear the stigma – like Edward Thurlow, who had served as Lord Chancellor under North, Rockingham and Shelburne despite being on the wrong side of every important political controversy – tended to be those whom Pitt would have gladly done without. The obnoxious Thurlow had to be reappointed as Lord Chancellor because he was close to the King and was an effective debater in the House of Lords. Lord Gower (President of the Council) and the Duke of Rutland (Lord Privy Seal) were respected as individuals, but they were not noted for parliamentary prowess or administrative ability. Lord

Sydney, who had served in the Shelburne government as Home Secretary, resumed that position under Pitt; but he had never been an outstanding performer, and must be one of the most mediocre people to have a great city named after him, thanks to the identification in 1788 of Australia as an ideal home for deported convicts. The Foreign Secretary, the Marquess of Carmarthen, could boast of a splendid political pedigree and was not devoid of diplomatic talent, but he lacked charisma. The third Duke of Richmond, a former affiliate of the Rockingham Whigs who had shared Pitt the Elder's hopes for conciliation with America, agreed to resume his former role as Master-General of the Ordinance but stayed outside Pitt's Cabinet.

Overall, Pitt's colleagues seemed to have been assembled from a truncated list of titled people who, for one reason or another, had decided to quarrel with the Fox–North coalition. A record of loyalty to the elder Pitt was certainly not a guarantee of inclusion; if so, the Earl of Shelburne would have been the first to be approached. Instead, Shelburne was snubbed. This decision suggested that the younger Pitt, like almost everyone else, had found it difficult to work with Shelburne. In addition, the inclusion of his former superior within Pitt's government was likely to give rise to questions of precedence – and Pitt had said that he would never serve in a 'subordinate' position. Perhaps Pitt had in mind his father's eccentric stipulation, when forming his last government, that no former prime minister should be included. Finally, there was no chance that Fox would ever agree to serve in a ministry alongside Shelburne, but if the latter was excluded it was not impossible that Fox would accept an offer from Pitt at some point; Fox would at least be deprived of his most obvious reason for refusal if such an offer was made. In their last private conversation, Pitt had told Fox that he had not come to betray Lord Shelburne as the price of their cooperation; by omitting the latter from his government, Pitt had shown that he was ready to make that sacrifice so long as it was not seen as a quid pro quo. However, when feelers were put out to Fox the latter turned the tables by declaring that he would not take office without Pitt's bête noire, Lord North.

Whether or not Pitt was serious in his attempt to enlist Fox, he was certainly not fishing in an overstocked talent pool. Less than three days into his ministry his initial choice as Foreign Secretary, his cousin Earl Temple, resigned. Temple's decision has been explained by historians in various ways, ranging from pig-headed pique (his failure to receive a dukedom) through cowardice (fear that he would be punished for his prominent role in the King's whispering campaign against the Coalition's India Bill) to public-spirited self-immolation (on the grounds that his part in the Coalition's downfall would make him a liability to Pitt's government). Whatever Temple's reasons, his defection seems to have caused the new prime minister considerable disquiet. His first biographer, Tomline, even claimed that this was the only political development which ever deprived Pitt of sleep.[4] This seems rather odd, since Pitt (whose ability to sleep through critical events became legendary) would endure much greater strains in subsequent years; and while he had appointed Temple in the genuine hope of securing his services for more than a couple of days, the disappearance of such a tempting target for Opposition ire was not without its advantages. Unlike his biographers, Pitt might have been thinking of his family's recent history. The previous Earl Temple had refused to serve in the elder Pitt's government because of his self-importance, precipitating a bitter and prolonged personal feud. Although the current holder of the Temple title was the previous Earl's nephew, the circumstances of his resignation were unusual enough to suggest that history might be about to repeat itself (Temple also happened to be married to the daughter of Earl Nugent, the fall guy of Pitt's maiden speech, so a breach in their relations might have enjoyed marital support). Certainly Pitt made sure that he parted from Temple without acrimony. In December 1784, after a tactful interval, Temple was made Marquess of Buckingham.

As parliamentarians departed for their Christmas break, it was not certain that Pitt would still be in place when they reassembled. Superficially, indeed, it looked as if the leaders of the supplanted Coalition held all the winning cards, meaning that their opponents could be forgiven if they left the game even before it had begun in earnest. Pitt was rather like a US president confronted by a hostile Congress; lacking a majority in the Commons, he could not hope for the passage of any constructive legislation. As in the case of the US, he needed cooperation from the legislature just to keep the ship of state afloat; and if the majority in the Commons had chosen to obstruct the necessary bills (relating to the collection of the Land Tax and the maintenance of military discipline) Britain would have become ungovernable. However, Pitt had a card up his sleeve: he could advise the King to dissolve Parliament, even though it was less than halfway through its official seven-year term, and hold a new election. The result could not be certain, but it was unlikely to produce a House of Commons which was *more* antagonistic towards the new government. Nevertheless, Pitt was opposed to an immediate dissolution of Parliament, feeling that he needed time to consolidate his credentials as a prime minister who was much more than the King's nominee.

Thus over the Christmas of 1783 both Pitt and his opponents were aware that they possessed very potent weapons, which they were strongly disinclined to use except *in extremis*. Before the recess the Opposition had allowed the Land Tax bill to pass, and Pitt had announced that there would be no immediate election. Rather than simply marking time while he waited for the most favourable circumstances, Pitt decided to grasp the nettle which had fatally stung the Coalition. While Fox railed against the government, tabling a series of critical motions and winning the subsequent votes, Pitt had been preparing his own legislation on the governance of India. Although the parliamentary situation was highly unpromising, it was the ideal time to strike a deal with the East India Company, which had been seriously alarmed by the Coalition's abortive reforms. Mainly the work of the indispensable Dundas, the new proposal was based on consultations with the Company, and avoided the most controversial aspects of the Fox–North proposals, also proposing a six-strong 'Board of Control' appointed by the Crown. Instead of being irremovable during its specified term of office, this body would be responsible to Parliament, and its two governmental representatives were likely to be replaced with each change of ministry. In theory, at least, the Board of Control had no powers of patronage; all appointments in India would be made by the Company. These concessions did not persuade the House of Commons, which rejected Pitt's bill on 23 January 1784 by 222 to 214.

By the standards of what had been expected to be a 'mince pie' government, and in the context of the overwhelming majorities which the

Coalition's Indian policy had received from the same House of Commons just a few weeks earlier, this slender defeat was a victory of a kind for Pitt. But from the constitutional angle it was a serious setback. The Coalition had fallen because it had been unable to win parliamentary assent for its policy on the governance of India, but its supporters could argue very plausibly that they had only been defeated in the Lords because of illicit royal interference. Now Pitt's proposals on the very same issue had been rejected by the people's representatives in the Commons, even though the new government had enjoyed two key advantages – the unconcealed support of the King, and the ability to learn from the Coalition's mistakes and address the obvious flaws in the ill-starred Fox–North Bill. Pitt's dependence on the favour of George III was cruelly exposed. If the Coalition's proposals for India had been beaten in the Commons even by a single vote few would have questioned the King if he had seized on this pretext to dismiss his ministry. There could only be one explanation for the fact that defeat over India proved fatal to Fox and North but had no effect on the position of the 'mince-pie' ministry.

Nevertheless, if the issue of India had produced a constitutional stalemate in which neither of the alternative ministries could pass their preferred legislation in the current Parliament, the obvious tiebreaker would be a general election which would allow the voters to pass judgement on the contestants. This escape route from the current impasse was even more appealing because circumstances had changed so dramatically since 1780, when the last general election had been held. The supporters of Fox and North, in combination, enjoyed a considerable majority in the Commons thanks to that election; but back in 1780, very few of the voters would have expected them to combine. Thus, an 'appeal to the people' would have been a chance for voters to deliver their verdict on the formation and record of the fallen Coalition, as well as an opportunity for them to decide whether or not Pitt's government was more deserving of their confidence.

The big problem for Fox and his supporters was their concern that Pitt's position would be strengthened considerably by a general election. Immediately after the defeat of Pitt's India Bill, Fox challenged the new prime minister to rule out a dissolution of Parliament. No doubt digesting the various implications of his defeat, Pitt decided not to respond. His taciturnity infuriated Fox's supporters, who demanded a new guarantee that Pitt would not call a general election to help him out of his quandary. Given time for cool reflection, even a mediocre politician would have realised that Opposition barracking merely drew attention to the strength of his own position: the Coalition's supporters were obviously *afraid* of a general election. But Pitt had no time to reflect in the heat of battle, and he had obviously decided that his interests would be served best if he stayed in his seat and said nothing.

He certainly could not have anticipated that his opponents would deliver themselves into his hands at this point. But this is precisely what happened, thanks to an intervention by General Henry Conway. A former soldier who had served as Secretary of State for the Northern Department in the government of Pitt the Elder, Conway had first held senior office in 1757 and was thus hardly an excitable parliamentary parvenu who would lose his head in the heat of battle. However, Conway had not always been helpful to Fox, especially in May 1782, when his vote in favour of Shelburne's terms for peace with America had convinced the latter that he should resign from the Rockingham government. Now, provoked beyond endurance by Pitt's refusal to respond to Fox's challenge, Conway jumped to his feet to denounce the minister's 'sulky silence', before alleging that the government 'existed by corruption' and had already started bribing the voters in advance of a general election. He challenged Pitt 'for the sake of his own honour' to clarify his position.[5]

Having assumed that he was taking aim at an open goal, Conway had in fact sliced the ball into his own net. In terms of eighteenth-century debate, by involving Pitt's 'honour' he was inviting an extension of the quarrel from Parliament to the duelling field. More seriously, by alleging bribery he had put the onus on himself to prove his charges. Pitt would have been forced to answer anyway, given the personal nature of Conway's attack, but while he framed his reply, he realised that Conway had inadvertently handed him the best way of defending himself both personally and politically. He followed Conway's volley of vitriol by asking him to provide concrete evidence of governmental misconduct.[6] When, as Pitt expected, no such charges were made, he could feel that he had been given a new weapon to fight off his adversaries for as long as the old Parliament lasted. Although the real constitutional question was whether a government could stay in office if it lacked the confidence of the House of Commons, Pitt now felt entitled to restate it in terms more helpful to himself, and to claim that a government could not be dismissed unless it had been accused of a *specific* misdemeanour.

It was a flimsy reason for refusing to resign, but evidently it satisfied Pitt, who repeated it in a debate of 29 January. By that time, a significant number of independent MPs had become sufficiently concerned about the parliamentary position to hold a meeting at St Albans Tavern. More than fifty MPs attended, resolving to 'support the party which should in the present distracted moment manifest a disposition to union'.[7] Even the King felt obliged to play along with the subsequent negotiations for a ministry which might encompass the warring factions. He and Pitt were probably equally relieved to find an insuperable obstacle in Fox's insistence that the present government must resign before it could be reconstructed on a 'broader bottom'.

Ultimately a majority of the disappointed 'St Albans Tavern independents' decided to support Pitt rather than Fox, an outcome which was implied by the decision to hold the meeting in the first place. As such, the abortive call for a 'government of national unity' was another positive development for the prime minister in a month which contained plenty of good news to set against the awkward fact that he was being beaten time after time in the division lobbies of the House of Commons. On 16 January – a day which saw the approval by 21 votes of a motion describing the continuation of Pitt's ministry as an infringement of constitutional principles – the Corporation of the City of London flatly contradicted the Commons by sending a message to the King congratulating him on the apposite use of his prerogative. This was just the first in a remarkable series of 'loyal' addresses emanating from cities and small towns (mainly but not exclusively English), reinforcing the prospect that MPs who supported Pitt were likely to fare well in a general election. The evidence of public endorsement for Pitt was probably helped by his decision, after the death of Sir Edward Walpole on 12 January 1784, to award the latter's sinecure position of Clerk of the Pells to Colonel Isaac Barré, MP, on the assumption that he would, in turn, relinquish a handsome pension which he had been awarded by the Rockingham government.

This seemed to be a selfless decision by Pitt, guaranteed to win public applause. As a younger son he was relatively impoverished compared to the average member of the Hanoverian political class, and he had already accumulated significant debts in support of a lifestyle which was modest compared to his titled contemporaries. He could easily have awarded the Clerkship of the Pells to himself, as a perquisite of office which had fortunately fallen vacant. His refusal to do so was a practical illustration of his public spirit which could hardly pass unnoticed within the walls of Westminster and among those outside who followed political developments.

On closer inspection, indeed, Pitt's decision looks even more remarkable. Barré was not much better off financially because of the exchange of his pension for a sinecure (by the same token, Pitt's decision had saved the British taxpayer the cost of the pension). However, Barré's social position was certainly improved, since the etiquette of the eighteenth century elevated the grant of a sinecure above the award of a pension: at worst, a pension was a means of buying the services or silence of a real or potential government critic, whereas a sinecure was usually a reward for services already rendered. Barré's parliamentary 'services' had included an attack on the elder Pitt (back in December 1761) in terms which even Horace Walpole had deplored for their excessive brutality, but he had lost the sight in one eye in the most iconic of the battles associated with Pitt – the capture of Quebec – and by 1784 he was almost completely blind. Taking all these circumstances into account, even the most skilful spin doctor of the twenty-first century would have been hard pressed to find a more appropriate beneficiary than Barré for a prime minister seeking positive publicity. Even Pitt the Younger might not have been aware of the *bonne bouche* to this story. In 1774 another sinecure, the Clerkship of the Pells in Ireland, had been sold by its holder in order to pay off his son's gambling debts. The person who had sold that sinecure position (worth £2,000 per annum) was Henry Fox, who had been forced to sell off one of his ill-gotten gains in order to bail out his improvident son Charles.

However, there is a different (and, according to one's taste, possibly a darker) side to the story. Even in this early part of his career, William Pitt had shown that he was far more interested in power than in riches. He had no intention of serving as the King's puppet; but from Pitt's perspective George III had already done him the greatest possible favour by engineering his early rise to the premiership. The younger Pitt had no intention of falling further into the King's debt by accepting offices which would make him seem more dependent without adding anything to his political reputation; he had already repulsed many offers from the King without suffering as a result of his decisions. Turning down this sinecure must have been comparatively easy.

The St Albans Tavern initiative reflected a growing alarm at the depth of political divisions, and even before the negotiations broke down there had been a vivid illustration that the polarisation extended beyond Parliament. In addition to expressing its approval of the King's recent actions, the Corporation of the City of London had agreed to make Pitt an honorary freeman – thus enabling him to emulate his father, who had been the first person to receive that accolade. On 28 February 1784 a delegation from the City made the presentation to Pitt, accompanied by a large crowd. After the appropriate ceremonies (which included a flattering speech by the former radical firebrand, John Wilkes), Pitt's coach was dragged by his supporters on a tour of central London, taking in such landmarks as Carlton House, the residence of the Foxite Prince of Wales, and St James's Street, the location of Brooks's, Fox's political headquarters.

This kind of journey, offering partisans (or drunken loiterers) the chance to jeer and smash a few windows, was not unusual. But at a time of acute constitutional controversy it was a gratuitous provocation which Pitt was probably powerless to prevent. Predictably enough, once the coach and its uncouth attendants arrived opposite Brooks's, outraged employees of the club, and some of its members, launched an attack. As Pitt's brother, Lord Chatham, recalled almost forty years later, the coach was badly damaged and there were several injuries. Pitt himself could have been a casualty if Chatham had not intercepted several 'desperate blows'.[8] One of the assailants identified by Pitt was John Crewe, MP, whose wife's 'mince-pie' prediction was already looking a bit mouldy. Just a few days earlier Crewe had been included by Fox on a list of those whose personal and financial support justified the award of a peerage if the coalition should return to office. Thankfully for the prime minister, a relief party from rival club White's arrived to extricate him. Whether or not Pitt's life was ever in serious danger, contemporary sketches of this incident bear an uncanny resemblance to Parisian scenes from the French Revolution.

By this time, Pitt's replies to critical parliamentary motions had begun to seem formulaic, as if he were going through the motions before an imminent dissolution of Parliament. On 1 March, having recited his usual rebuttals to Opposition charges, he alluded to the apparent symptoms of public support for his government.[9] He lost the ensuing vote, but the margin was now merely 12. After a similar debate on 12 March the Opposition's majority was whittled down to just one. Once Parliament had passed the legislative measures which ensured the state's financial and military security, Pitt could begin to feel that he had weathered his first political storm. On 24 March the King dissolved Parliament.

According to the great historian William Lecky, 'No party ever went to the constituencies more hopelessly foredoomed to ruin than the Opposition which followed the banner of Fox and of North.'[10] In Lecky's view, the supporters of the former Coalition were 'foredoomed' because their alliance had offended public opinion even before the controversy over the India Bill. It was obvious that the 1784 general election was going to be decided at least as much by patronage as by opinion: since he enjoyed the confidence of the King, Pitt could draw on various sources of support, including the direct intervention of royal agents as well as backing from wealthy individuals who knew only too well the way the wind was blowing. It was no accident, for example, that George III, having declined to bestow titles upon supporters of the Fox–North coalition, suddenly proved more flexible after Pitt had taken office, and that people who controlled certain constituencies were suddenly recognised as worthy of ennoblement. However, it would be mistaken to suppose that such 'undemocratic' influences were decisive in the 1784 general election. In fact, since hardly any constituency in 1784 was remotely 'democratic' by twenty-first-century standards, it is tempting to reverse the charge against

George III and Pitt and to claim that most of the coalition supporters returned in that year would have gone down to defeat had it not been for corrupt practices of various kinds.

Nevertheless, government expectations that the new House of Commons would provide it with a majority of up to 180 MPs were based on an over-optimistic assessment of the power of patronage. The final reckoning was a 'working majority' for Pitt of about 120, although thanks to the fluid nature of partisan allegiances that number could hardly be guaranteed in every division.[11] Among those who had lost seats previously regarded as 'safe' were Lord John Cavendish at York and General Conway at Bury St Edmunds. In the first division of the new House, Pitt was victorious by 233 votes to 136. Numerically Pitt's majority was smaller than expected, but its *quality* was greater than his advisors had anticipated.[12] On balance, the most corrupt constitutions proved more loyal than expected to Fox and North, while Pitt's opponents lost ground in places with a broader franchise, like the counties. In a result which combined personal and political triumph, Pitt learned that his friend William Wilberforce had won one of the two seats allotted to Yorkshire without a contest, ensuring his 'promotion' from his previous parliamentary berth at the borough of Kingston upon Hull.

Pitt himself was enlisted as a candidate for three seats – the City of London, Bath and Cambridge University. Turning his back without regret on the Appleby constituency which he had never visited, Pitt's attention was riveted on his alma mater. This preference has not received adequate notice from any of his biographers, despite the paucity of alternative clues to Pitt's emotional life. Bath should have been attractive to him, for its social cachet as well as the fact that his father had represented it. In itself, being MP for the City of London automatically made a politician into a figure of national consequence. By contrast, as a constituency Cambridge University had not propelled many politicians to fame, although it had briefly been represented by no less a personage than Sir Isaac Newton.

The younger Pitt had no interest in representing Bath or the City of London, and did not campaign there. He did, however, make time to canvass the voters of Cambridge University. As a result, despite having come bottom of the poll in 1780 he swept to the top in 1784, beating his running mate, the Earl of Euston, who was the son of the university's chancellor, the Duke of Grafton. The previous Foxite incumbents had been beaten by two Pittites, one of whom was 'the old block himself'.

Just possibly, Pitt plumped for Cambridge University as his preferred seat, despite a host of easier options, simply because he wanted to efface the memory of a previous defeat. But this explanation of his behaviour in the euphoric mood of 1784, when he knew in advance that he could transform his unsustainable parliamentary position into a secure majority whenever he chose to throw the electoral switch, does not ring true. More plausibly, Pitt just wanted to represent this particular constituency because of a profound emotional investment in the place. Many Cambridge University voters were intellectually distinguished, but that was only part of the seat's attractions; more importantly, it was the place where William Pitt had struck up valued friendships as he emerged from the social seclusion of his early years.

But the William Pitt who had found emotional validation during his years at Pembroke Hall could not afford to wallow in his victory at Cambridge. Given the circumstances, he could be forgiven for thinking that his political career was at stake in the 1784 general election. He regarded the Opposition with personal animosity, and tried to animate friends like Wilberforce with the same spirit. Not even his comfortable victory could quench his partisan feelings: indeed, he was tempted to use his parliamentary majority to turn a rout into something approaching annihilation.

The Westminster election of 1784 was a more momentous event for Fox than for Pitt, but nevertheless it sheds a fascinating and somewhat lurid light on the latter's political persona. Historians have offered contrasting interpretations of Pitt's determination to overturn his rival's victory at Westminster by challenging the validity of his vote. In the course of a typically insightful and elegant discussion of the episode, William Hague has observed that 'the first instinct of a politician who has knocked his opponent to the ground [is] to find some means of preventing him from getting up again.'[13] The obvious rejoinder is that shrewd politicians should keep those instincts in check, and should consider whether it might be better to let the wounded opponent struggle back to his feet in order to prolong the punishment.

Fox's struggle to retain his Westminster seat had reached epic proportions. It was a two-member seat, and the government put up the very popular Admiral Hood, who had been second in command to Admiral Samuel Rodney in the Battle of the Saintes (1782), and Sir Cecil Wray, a former Foxite MP who had defected to the Tories. Fox was pessimistic about his chances but installed himself in Westminster, sending daily reports to Mrs Armitstead back in St Ann's Hill. He started off in early April clearly in third place. Five days later, on 7 April, the gap between him and Wray had widened considerably, and he duly reported the figures:

Hood 4797
Wray 4420
Fox 4126

> I must not give up tho' I wish it. I have serious thoughts, if I am beat, of not coming into Parliament at all, but of all this we will talk with you more as soon as this Business will let me go to you.[14]

It was not until 27 April that Fox succeeded in creeping past Wray, and on 17 May, when the polling closed, the final figures were:

Hood 6694
Fox 6234
Wray 5998

Hood and Fox were declared elected, but Wray refused to accept the result and demanded a scrutiny, confident that it would be overturned by a parliamentary vote as it was already evident that the Pittites would enjoy a substantial majority in the Commons. There would be no shortage of dirty tricks to expose to the scrutiny, though it was far from clear that most of them were the work of Fox's supporters. A rough idea of the malpractices employed may be given by the famous series of four paintings and engravings by William Hogarth, entitled *Humours of an Election*. The paintings, now on show at Tate Britain, dated from 1755, and referred to a notoriously corrupt campaign in Oxfordshire during the 1754 general election. There is little doubt that all the shady practices (and more) shown in the pictures were also present during the Westminster election, though it is far from clear that Fox was the main culprit. One notable feature of Fox's campaign was the large number of elegant women who campaigned on his behalf. These included two duchesses, Portland's wife and the beautiful Georgiana, Duchess of Devonshire, who was alleged to have sold kisses for votes. Georgiana vigorously denied this to her mother, Lady Spencer, but admitted that it was true that both her sister and another lady friend had been kissed 'so it's very hard I who was not sh'd have the reputation for it.'[15] Fox's victory was celebrated by a triumphal procession ending at Carlton House, where the Prince of Wales gave a breakfast in his honour.

Even if Pitt had failed to secure an overwhelming majority in 1784, the gamble of holding an early election would have been judged a success if he could have prevented Fox from retaining his Westminster seat. This explains why both the Opposition and the government (spurred on by the King) committed disproportionate resources to the Westminster contest, as indeed they had done in the 1780 election. Yet even if he had lost Westminster on the original, disputed poll, Fox would not have been finished as a political force. After all, his indictment of Pitt's government was founded on an argument about the corruption of the constitution thanks to undue monarchical interference. Fox could have continued to make that argument in the Commons, since his supporters in the north of Scotland had ensured his return for Tain Burghs as a precaution once things began to look sticky in Westminster. Tain Burghs, whose electoral process was idiosyncratic even by eighteenth-century standards (and which was controlled by Sir Thomas Dundas, a cousin of Henry Dundas, but, unlike him, a fervent Whig), was not the most promising bridgehead from which to make a comeback. But even as MP for Westminster – the most 'democratic' constituency in Britain – Fox would still have been forced to wait for national politics to turn dramatically in his direction if he was ever to pose a serious threat to Pitt's position. He would hardly be worse off as MP for Tain Burghs in a Parliament which lacked so many of his 'martyred' followers.

In other words, Pitt's determined support for the attempt to overturn Fox's victory at Westminster looks like a bid for supremacy in a war of propaganda rather than a realistic campaign to 'decapitate' the Opposition. Pitt's conduct during the prolonged controversy about the Westminster election should be put down to his inexperience, which persuaded him that the best way to remedy one mistake was to make another. Before he became prime minister, he had shown a degree of antipathy towards Lord North which the latter scarcely deserved. As soon as he gave way to the King's entreaties even Pitt had to accept that he had targeted the wrong foe, and that Fox was the chief obstacle to the realisation of his ambitions. Indeed, if he had adopted a more conciliatory attitude towards Lord North he would have made life much easier for himself in his first months as prime minister. Fox, however, was a very different kind of antagonist, who had contemplated the use of every conceivable weapon to make sure that Pitt's government would truly turn out to be a short-lived, 'mince-pie' administration. If Fox was prepared to throw down his gloves for a bare-knuckle fight, Pitt was ready to follow suit once he was in a position to exploit his opponent's weaknesses.

Unfortunately for Pitt, his attempt to prosecute a personal vendetta against Fox from a position of considerable strength was far less impressive than his repeated attempts to defend himself when he and his government had been on the ropes. On 8 June 1784, for example, he delivered a lengthy and legalistic speech on the Westminster election. He seemed to overlook the fact that, even if he was right in thinking that Fox had cheated more than his Westminster opponents, the number of individuals who had voted for him was way beyond the level of support enjoyed by most of the MPs who witnessed Pitt's dubious and dreary attempts to argue that Fox was an unworthy Member of Parliament. Presumably Pitt also failed to appreciate the possibility that his initiative would undermine his hopes for electoral reform. MPs could be forgiven for thinking that a more inclusive franchise would lead to more contested elections and a greater likelihood that the results of such contests would be challenged. Certainly any MP who regarded the Westminster Scrutiny as a crashing bore could regard the process as an excellent advertisement for the preservation of rotten boroughs.

Whatever they felt about other issues, on this subject Pitt's supporters gradually drifted away, so that during February and March of 1785 he began to experience the sinking feeling which Fox had suffered in the previous year when his anti-Pittite majorities had begun to erode. On 3 March 1785 the government was defeated by 38 votes in a division on the Westminster election, and what seemed to be turning into an interminable process was terminated. Fox was duly acknowledged as the properly elected MP for Westminster.

The battle over Fox's election lasted so long that, by the time it ended, the government was deeply embroiled in more constructive parliamentary debates. Most MPs proved sufficiently open-minded to overlook Pitt's mistaken vendetta with Fox, and to judge his policy proposals on their own merits. In itself, the fact that the House of Commons elected in 1784 approved so much of Pitt's agenda made the conflict over the Westminster result seem inconsequential and gratuitously vindictive. It was far more important that, in the 1784 election, the 'mince-pie' government had proved appetising in places where the voters could affect the outcome, and had made mincemeat of its opponents.

10

The Young Reformer

F OR Pitt, the general election of 1784 was a personal triumph, giving him the chance to excel in the only role which he had seriously envisaged for himself. By the same token, the election result was a serious setback for historians hoping to present a balanced picture of Pitt as a human being. Usually even very successful politicians rise to the pinnacle of their profession after a lengthy apprenticeship, and often they retire with many years of relatively active life ahead of them. Alternatively, individuals whose adult lives are dominated by politics at a high level (like Gladstone and Churchill) endure periods out of office when they are forced to devote at least some of their energies to activities which shed light on their personalities. In Pitt's case, these 'off-duty' periods were almost completely lacking. His apprenticeship was unprecedentedly truncated, in the remaining 22 years of his life after the 1784 general election he was only out of office for 38 months (during which he behaved like a prime minister on sabbatical, rather than a private individual), and instead of emulating the classical figures he admired so much by spending his last years in mellow retirement, Pitt died in office.

If Pitt had been forced to wait longer, it would probably be much easier to write about the private man as well as the minister. Then again, such was his impatience to exercise real power that it seems unlikely Pitt would have stayed in politics if his apprenticeship had been more prolonged. This is not to say that – to borrow Nye Bevan's description of Hugh Gaitskell – Pitt was a kind of 'desiccated calculating machine' who only came to life when confronted with a row of official statistics (neither, for that matter, was Gaitskell himself); even before becoming prime minister, Pitt had shown considerable charisma in congenial company. Nevertheless, after taking the top job he betrayed a marked disinclination to relax, revealing at best a preference to mix business with pleasure (particularly in the company of Henry Dundas) and at worst to find his only real pleasure in the conduct of business. This tendency was reinforced by a narrowing of his emotional outlets in the years after 1784. His sister Harriot, to whom he was especially close, died after giving birth to a child in September 1786, and this tragedy effectively deprived him of a second cherished companion because her widower, Pitt's friend Edward Eliot, was a changed man after his bereavement. Meanwhile William Wilberforce, who was probably Pitt's closest friend at the time of the 1784 general election, then embarked on a tour of Europe during which he became a devout Christian. From Pitt's perspective, Wilberforce had been transformed overnight from a boisterous associate with numerous shared interests to an obsessive evangelical who was more serious-minded than the prime minister himself.

Pitt was clearly susceptible to strong and sincere friendship, but, it seems, only when he felt able to trust someone completely; and even before he became prime minister he had good reason to doubt the sincerity of people who courted his friendship. Thus his default reaction to new acquaintances was to keep them at something more than arm's length. In Nathaniel Wraxall's famous description,

in his manners, Pitt, if not repulsive, was cold, stiff, and without suavity or amenity. He seemed never to invite approach, or encourage acquaintance [...] From the instant that Pitt entered the doorway of the House of Commons, he advanced up the floor with a quick and firm step, his Head erect and thrown back, looking neither to the right nor the left, nor favouring with a nod or a glance, any of the individuals seated on either side, among whom many who possessed five thousand a year would have been gratified even by so slight a mark of attention. It was not thus that Lord North or Fox treated Parliament.[1]

Wraxall drew an unfavourable comparison between Pitt's glacial public persona and that of the easy-going Lord North. In marked contrast to North, Pitt was determined both to *seem* and to *be* intensely serious about his task. While parliamentarians like Wraxall could wish that Pitt would let the mask slip from time to time, or at least to behave courteously towards powerful people who were existing or potential supporters, the young prime minister decided that it was better to cause offence by being brusque than to run the risk of looking weak and frivolous by exchanging pleasantries with MPs. If this was a mistake, in the circumstances of 1784 Pitt was at least erring on the safer side. To observers who focused on the underlying condition of the British state, those who had generated the dramatic period of political instability ushered in by the loss of the American colonies could only seem dangerously self-indulgent. Britain's attempt to crush the rebellion had been expensive as well as unsuccessful; it had also left the country in diplomatic isolation. Now that he was in a position to exercise real influence over Britain's response to these serious challenges, Pitt prioritised financial and administrative reforms. In these areas, he showed a combination of pragmatism and principle which, by the time of the next general election in 1790, had helped to ensure Britain's recovery from its serious setback across the Atlantic.

Pitt's financial inheritance was highly unpromising. At the end of the war, Britain's national debt stood at £234 million (around £15 billion in the values of 2018). Taxes raised approximately £13 million per year; of this sum, £8 million was used to service the interest on the national debt. In order to carry out even the limited duties of the peacetime British state, Pitt had no alternative but to increase the yield from taxation. His task was complicated by the understanding that although he should avoid imposing new burdens on the poor, he would have to win consent for his proposals from a Parliament monopolised by representatives of the propertied classes.

In Pitt's first budget as prime minister, on 30 June 1784, he expressed the hope that the necessity of tax increases would be understood thanks to 'the good sense and patriotism of the people of England [*sic*]'.[2] He proceeded to unveil a range of revenue-raising ideas which would moisten the eyes of a modern Chancellor of the Exchequer. Almost everything which distinguished a life of 'privilege' from mundane existence was either taxed for the first time or subjected to heavier imposts. It would be an exaggeration to say that in his search for revenue Pitt taxed everything that moved, but he certainly taxed a lot of things that moved quickly for the convenience of the well-to-do. It was typical of Pitt's approach that he increased the duty on relatively expensive wax candles and lowered it on the cheaper tallow versions. In his 1785 budget he raised the duty paid by employers of male servants, introducing a higher rate for individuals who could afford more than ten retainers. Having taxed hats and gloves, in 1786 he placed stamp duty on perfume, cosmetics and powder used on wigs.

Thankfully, Pitt was free from the compulsion which leads modern Chancellors to proclaim that they are 'tax cutters by instinct', but he did realise that in certain instance high government levies could be counter-productive. Duties on tea, which had helped to stir up trouble between Britain and the American colonists, were now causing serious trouble closer to home: they were high enough to encourage widespread evasion, greatly reducing the government's potential share in the thriving trade in that essential commodity while undermining the state's authority by making smuggling seem to be a patriotic activity rather than a crime. In his first budget, Pitt reduced the duty on imported tea from more than 100 per cent of its value to just 25 per cent. As a result, the smuggling trade was drastically undermined and domestic consumption of tea increased.

Pitt's first budget speech dispelled many doubts concerning his ability to govern, by showing that he could master detail as well as construct an argument. But, in the absence of administrative reform, his measures would have been far less effective in realising his aim of maximising revenue and reducing unnecessary government expenditure. In these tasks Pitt undoubtedly benefited from proposals which had been advanced under Shelburne's premiership, and from a general climate of opinion which made it unlikely that he would face concerted opposition. Given their own previous record, Fox and supporters like Edmund Burke could hardly attack the principle of 'economy'. As usual, however, Pitt was careful not to alienate vested interests; rather than abolishing superfluous posts within the administrative machine, his preferred approach was to leave them unfilled when vacancies arose (a process of 'natural wastage', in modern parlance). He also tried to curb the costly abuse of the privilege allowed to MPs of posting their letters free of charge – a forerunner of the 2009 parliamentary expenses scandal.

In 1787 Pitt launched a more direct assault on inefficiency by introducing the Consolidated Fund, a single account to receive government revenues which replaced the previous arrangement under which funds assigned to different purposes had been kept in separate accounts. By inviting potential creditors to compete for the privilege with sealed bids, he had also reduced the scope for corrupt practices when the government sought to raise loans.

If Pitt had only served as Chancellor of the Exchequer he would be remembered as a very significant holder of the post. The fact that he performed that role while he was also prime minister, with responsibilities across the whole range of government activity, only makes his achievement all the greater. However, it can be objected that, at least in part, his reputation in the economic field was inflated by the relative absence of qualified competitors. The limited parliamentary records from the mid-1780s give the impression of an eloquent and well-informed minister who held the attention of his audience not least because so few of them understood what he was talking about. These were the ideal conditions which would tempt a minister into a feeling of hubris, leading to the perpetration of avoidable mistakes.

In 1786, Pitt created a 'sinking fund' which, he convinced himself, would lead over time to the liquidation of the national debt. He conjured this vision, so pleasing to someone of his naturally optimistic outlook, with the help of the nonconformist clergyman Dr Richard Price. Price, who had been part of Lord Shelburne's retinue of intellectuals, had argued back in 1771 that a government which enjoyed a surplus of revenue over expenditure could invest the additional funds in a way which, thanks to the workings of compound interest, would quite rapidly pay down its debts. The idea of such a fund was not new – Robert Walpole had started one in 1716 – but Price imbued it with almost magical qualities, holding out the promise that a painful financial burden could be lifted from the British public even if they could not muster much in the way of 'good sense and patriotism'. Pitt's version also entrusted the management of the fund to commissioners, who would prevent the government from raiding it to meet unexpected demands for expenditure.

Even in the abstract, Price's dreams were open to puncturing considerations, which were freely expressed by Pitt's own brother-in-law, Lord Mahon. On the practical level, the plan depended upon a prolonged period free from serious international conflict. If Britain should become embroiled in a major war, the government's revenue surplus would disappear and instead of being a financial saviour the sinking fund could become a very serious drain on resources. In 1786, Pitt established £1 million as the annual sum to be allocated to the fund. Initially, while peace prevailed and the government enjoyed a budget surplus, the national debt was indeed reduced. However, the beginning of war with revolutionary France destroyed the rationale for the fund, which could only be replenished on an annual basis if the government resorted to borrowing more than it required to meet the cost of war. Thanks to its initial prestige as a symbol of careful financial management, the sinking fund long outlived Pitt, surviving in all its absurdity until the 1820s.

While the sinking fund saga showed that over-optimistic (even utopian) thinking could overcome Pitt's common sense on occasion, this was perhaps forgivable because in other instances he was capable of making a success of initiatives which would have daunted a less sanguine spirit. In 1786 Britain agreed a commercial treaty with France which greatly reduced the previously punitive import duties on the produce of each country. The deal was largely the product of necessity on both sides – French intervention during the American War of Independence had helped to deprive Britain of a captive market for which a substitute was urgently required, but that effort had exposed and accentuated France's own financial problems. Nevertheless, Pitt's decision to seize the opportunity was prompted at least in part by principle, since (along with his cousin, William Grenville) he had read Adam Smith's *The Wealth of Nations* (1776) in his first year as prime minister and embraced its arguments. His advocacy of the Commercial Treaty showed that he rejected the 'mercantilist' argument that a nation could only prosper at the expense of others, while accepting what came to be a characteristically 'liberal' view of international relations which assumes that states who regard each other as trading partners rather than economic rivals will never resort to violence to settle their disputes.

In recommending easier economic relations with France in parliamentary debates, Pitt was well aware that he was flying in the face of centuries of hostility between the two countries. For his part, Pitt saw no reason to regard the relationship between Britain and France as one of 'eternal enmity'. This was an irresistible challenge to Charles Fox, who denounced the deal because, unlike Pitt, he saw France in traditional English terms (i.e. as a country ruled by an absolutist monarchy, which would never relent in its mission to dominate the continent of Europe) and felt that France was thus bound to be a dangerous rival rather than a friendly power. Insofar as the Commercial Treaty would benefit the French economy, it would weaken Britain's ability to resist the unquenchable French thirst for European hegemony. However, Pitt was able to argue that Britain had got the best of the bargain, thanks mainly to the tough tactics of the chief British negotiator, William Eden (later Lord Auckland). The fact that Eden had previously been a junior minister within the Fox–North coalition made the apparent success of his negotiations with France an even more bitter pill for Fox to swallow. Leaving aside such personal and partisan considerations, the clash between Pitt and Fox over the Commercial Treaty suggested that Fox regarded international relations from an institutional angle – France was ruled by a despot, and as long as this lasted Britain should treat it as a hostile power – while Pitt felt that even under a theoretically absolute monarch it was still possible to do profitable business with France. Within a decade, these perspectives would be reversed.

The recruitment of Eden was just one example of Pitt's ability to enlist able individuals to the government's service as well as making the most of talented people who were already in place. Although these colleagues often held quite junior offices, they allowed Pitt to devise and execute effective policies despite the limited calibre of more senior figures, who had to be included in the Cabinet to lend a veneer of prestige or to ensure the support of their backbench followers. George Rose, for example, had served as Secretary to the Treasury when Pitt was Chancellor of the Exchequer; reappointed by Pitt in December

1783, he became an indispensable advisor on financial matters and had risen to the rank of joint Paymaster General by the time of Pitt's death in 1806. Richard Frewin, of the Customs Board, was a key figure in the creation of the Consolidated Fund. Evan Nepean, an undersecretary at the Home Office, was entrusted with a variety of crucial tasks including naval espionage. By 1804 Nepean had become very familiar with Pitt's approach to office holders, and wrote that 'he will not be trifled with by those who hold employments under the crown or are expecting favours from government.'[3] Pitt's most trusted colleagues were certainly not selected because of their social graces; some of the most influential, like Sir Charles Middleton, Comptroller of the Navy from 1778 to 1790, were distinctly spiky individuals.[4] In this respect there was a marked contrast between Fox and Pitt: in choosing his closest associates Fox always took personal friendship into consideration, while Pitt was rarely swayed by emotion.

Thus while it was easy for Pitt's admirers to present him as a financial wizard whose record in that field was at least equal to that of his father in the arts of war, his achievements were collective rather than unaided. Recent biographers, following John Ehrman, have also stressed the flaws in his record. He could have done more, for example, to sweep away corrupt practices within government departments concerned with revenue-raising. As one historian has put it, 'The image of his dedication to probity and efficiency, rather than his actual accomplishments, was in fact Pitt's greatest contribution to the eventual modernisation of British government administration.'[5] Apart from the sinking fund, which enjoyed widespread support but proved a predictable failure, other measures were either abandoned due to public opposition (like a tax on retail shops, introduced in 1785 and withdrawn 4 years later after provoking riots) or thwarted by political opposition before they could be put into practice.

Between 1784 and 1789, the most important of these setbacks was Pitt's failed attempt to apply Adam Smith's principles to trading arrangements between Britain and Ireland. Hitherto, these had been a source of considerable friction between the two countries, and Britain could be sure of coming out best from their quarrels due to its disproportionate economic strength. Having inherited a deeply unsatisfactory situation

1 William Pitt the Elder, first Earl of Chatham, painted in 1754 when
he married Lady Hester Grenville (studio of William Hoare).

2 Henry Fox, first Lord Holland, painted in 1762 when he was
Leader of the House of Commons (after Joshua Reynolds).

3 Fox as an adolescent, with his cousin, Lady Susan Fox-Strangways, in the garden of Holland House, while his young aunt, Lady Sarah Lennox, looks down from an upstairs window (Reynolds).

4 William Pitt the Younger, aged 29, five years into his premiership (James Gillray).

5 The young George III, in the second year of his
reign, 1761–2 (studio of Allan Ramsay).

6 The third Earl of Bute, mentor and 'dearest friend' of
George III, as Prime Minister in 1762 (Reynolds).

7 Pitt addressing the House of Commons in 1793. Fox is seated opposite, sixth from the right in the front row, wearing a black hat (Karl Anton Hickel).

8 'Paradise Regain'd': the Prince of Wales (later George IV) looks on as Fox woos his former mistress, Mary 'Perdita' Robinson (Gillray).

9 Fox (left) chats with Edmund Burke when they were still bosom friends (after Reynolds).

10 The second Marquess of Rockingham, leader of the
Whigs and twice Prime Minister (after Reynolds).

11 William Henry Cavendish-Bentinck, third Duke of Portland, who was Prime Minister of the 'Fox–North coalition' in 1783 (after Reynolds).

12 The second Lord Shelburne, standing under the gallows, looks glumly at Fox and Lord North, who displaced him from the premiership in 1783 (Gillray).

13 William Grenville, Pitt's cousin and close collaborator, who became
Premier of the 'Ministry of all the Talents' in 1806–7 (John Hoppner).

14 Henry Dundas, Lord Melville, a senior minister in both of Pitt's
governments, who was sacked in 1805 because of corruption charges
of which he was later found innocent (Thomas Lawrence).

15 'The Nuptial Bower': Pitt and Lady Eleanor Eden, with
Fox, as the Devil, spying on them (Gillray).

16 Elizabeth Armitstead,
former courtesan
who became Fox's
lover and later wife;
mezzotint (Reynolds).

17 Henry Addington, later Lord Sidmouth, who succeeded
Pitt as prime minister in 1801 (James Parker).

18 The Belgian sculptor, Joseph Nollekens, with his
famous bust of Fox (Lemuel Francis Abbott).

19 Pitt refused to sit for Nollekens, but he produced 72 copies of
a marble bust based on Pitt's death mask and on a portrait by John
Hoppner. They sold for 120 guineas each (Nollekens).

20 Richard Henry Vassall Fox, third Lord Holland, painted in Florence
in 1795 while he was on the 'grand tour' (François-Xavier Fabre).

which (to differing extents) was damaging both to Britain and Ireland, the supposedly pragmatic Pitt suggested a remedy which seems close to an experimental application of pure ideology: Ireland would be offered a trade deal on a basis which promised to foster its prosperity. On the one hand, Britain would treat it with a new degree of respect, as befitted a country with autonomous institutions, while on the other, Pitt clearly hoped that his deal would remove significant reasons for Irish resentment towards the British, thus verifying Adam Smith's linkage between free trade and peaceful relations. Given the geographical proximity of Britain and Ireland, the removal of economic grievances could pave the way to a peaceful union between the two countries – an eventuality suggested by the quid pro quo in Pitt's proposal, namely that as Ireland became more prosperous it would make a rising financial contribution towards the cost of British forces committed to its defence.

The initial plan was announced to the Irish Parliament in February 1785, but it ran into trouble almost immediately. Confronted with a prime minister who wanted to implement a rational settlement instead of bullying them into submission, Irish legislators assumed that Pitt was in a weak position, and duly demanded concessions. Once these had been granted, it was the turn of the Westminster Parliament to feel affronted; Charles Fox took the lead in expressing the claims of manufacturers who allegedly feared that their products would be undercut by unfair Irish competition. Pitt tried patiently to explain that British manufacturers could only gain from freer trade, given their competitive advantages; but the House of Commons would not be satisfied without some amendments which would protect their constituents, and these proved unacceptable to the Irish Parliament. The trade deal was dropped in August 1785.

John Ehrman has argued that '[t]he defeat of the Irish Propositions marked Pitt's most serious failure in his first two years in office.'[6] In hindsight, this seems understated – it could be regarded as one of the most serious missed opportunities in modern British history, and was recognised as such by the later prime minister Lord Rosebery.[7] What turned out to be a shotgun union between Britain and Ireland in 1800–1, accompanied by considerable skulduggery and bitterness, could have been a more organic process, leading to a much better understanding between the countries (if not to an enduring liaison). Pitt's failure to implement such a significant measure is striking evidence of the limits on his power, even in fields where he enjoyed extra authority thanks to his facility with figures. Between 1784 and 1789 there were other serious reverses over crucial government policies, notably the failure of the Commons to endorse a plan to augment the sea defences of Portsmouth and Plymouth. Senior ministers disagreed on this issue, and a Commons vote of February 1786 resulted in a tie which was broken by the Speaker's negative vote.

It is somewhat ironic if critical assessments of Pitt's financial and administrative reforms tend to overstate his ability to effect change, because they represent a reaction against earlier accounts which often portrayed Pitt as a dominant figure in these fields who refused to lend his authority to other political and moral causes. In particular, 'Whiggish' historians in the nineteenth century and after deplored his failure to exploit his parliamentary position after the 1784 general election to push through reform of the antiquated voting system. From their perspective, Pitt had never advocated the truly *radical* franchise reforms which the country self-evidently required. It is argued that he simply lost interest once his reputation as a reformer helped him to secure the prize which he coveted.[8]

In reality, this line of argument only seems plausible in the light of subsequent events, when Pitt really *did* experience second thoughts about parliamentary reform after the outbreak of the French Revolution. Between 1784 and the downfall of the French monarchy, even if Pitt was secretly working in his own interest without any regard to principle he would have hoped to expand voting rights; after all, the 1784 general election had proved that this was likely to *increase* his parliamentary majority. In reality, Pitt's proposed reforms had always been modest because he thought that was the best way of maximising initial support for a process of change which would (or at least *could*) satisfy more radical demands in the long term. He maintained this attitude after he took office, but he was acutely aware that in one crucial respect his task had actually become more difficult: now that he had become prime minister, he had to be far more sensitive to the King's opinions – and these were decidedly opposed to any revision of the franchise. Pitt's approach to the issue after 1784 certainly proves that he regarded reform as a desirable objective, but not a crucial one. However, that could have been gathered from his attitude before he became First Lord of the Treasury. Now he was in a position to implement many (if not all) of the policies he saw as necessary to the restoration of British fortunes after the loss of America. If he pushed too hard on the subject of parliamentary reform, he could forfeit the King's support and, potentially, lose key elements of his wider agenda.

Pitt, in short, wanted to keep the King on board, or at least to avoid giving the impression that he and George were steering in different directions. Thus, when he learned that the doyen of the reform movement, Christopher Wyvill, was claiming that proposals would be introduced as if they had been accepted by the whole Cabinet, Pitt wrote that he wished 'Mr Wyvill had been a little more sparing of my name.'[9] Pitt persuaded the King to declare a state of formal neutrality, but George made it clear that this was dependent on reform being made an 'open question', rather than an official government proposal. This was the best that Pitt could do, and it was clearly not good enough, since the King's vehement opposition was already widely known.

On 18 April 1785 Pitt asked the Commons for permission to bring in a bill which envisaged a limited expansion of the franchise and the transfer of up to 72 parliamentary seats from rotten boroughs to the counties. Far from being compulsory, the transfer would depend upon the consent of the voters in the boroughs, and a fund would be established to compensate those who benefited from the existing system. Even this very modest measure was defeated, by 74 votes.

Those who regarded Pitt as an omnipotent minister at this time can lay a much heavier charge against him – that through unnecessary caution he delayed the abolition of the slave trade. In October 1787 William Wilberforce recorded a conversation in which Pitt had encouraged him to use this humanitarian cause as the central purpose of his membership of the Commons. Their discussion took place in the grounds of Holwood House, a property located near Pitt's childhood home of Hayes in Kent. Pitt had bought Holwood in 1786, and (following his father's example) had embarked on a programme of 'improvements' to the house and grounds which did little to improve his personal finances. Wilberforce remembered that the prime minister had discussed the slave trade with him 'in the open air at the root of an old tree', which survived not only Pitt's ventures into landscape gardening but also his designs for Holwood House itself, which was rebuilt in the 1820s.[10]

In May 1788 Pitt identified himself with Wilberforce's crusade, but only to the extent of recommending an inquiry into the conduct of the slave trade. This suggestion was accepted by the Commons with hardly any opposition.[11] However, the mood in the House of Lords was more antagonistic, and proposals for a minor modification of the conditions of transportation for slaves were almost defeated there after a violent speech by Chancellor Thurlow. In these circumstances, the fact that Pitt continued to side openly with the principle of abolition (rather than technical improvements in the loathsome trade) is sufficient testimony to his sincere commitment. Battle was resumed in May 1789, after the Regency Crisis (see Chapter Eleven), and Pitt delivered one of his greatest speeches in support of Wilberforce's attempt to prove that the ending of the trade would not damage Britain's economic interests. He was backed by Fox and by Edmund Burke – a rare occasion when the greatest debating team in British parliamentary history could unite, free from partisan constraint, in a cause which engaged their moral passion. They should have been unstoppable, but Pitt diluted the effect by dealing with practical objections – notably, what would happen if Britain gave up the trade but other European countries tried to fill the vacuum? – too honestly to assuage the doubts of the self-interested. No definitive parliamentary verdict was delivered on Wilberforce's motion until the following year, when the situation in Europe and further afield had hardened sentiment against almost any kind of reform.

It was not as if Pitt had been indifferent to European developments before the outbreak of the French Revolution. Indeed, despite his lack of foreign policy experience he had been a keen and anxious observer from the start of his ministry, as the success of his economic strategy depended on a prolonged period of peace and, given Britain's diplomatic isolation in 1784, there was every reason to be sensitive to potential threats. Although Pitt hoped that the 1786 Commercial Treaty would lay the foundation for warmer relations with France, it was impossible to overlook immediate sources of tension, in particular the case of a pro-French 'patriot' faction which had seized effective power in Holland in 1785 from the hereditary ruler, the stadtholder William V of the House of Orange. To signal its support for William, Britain had signed a treaty of friendship with Holland in the first months of Pitt's premiership. Once in power, the Dutch patriots negotiated an alliance with France.

The fate of Holland was acutely interesting to the British, for strategic, financial and commercial reasons. Pitt came under pressure to intervene on behalf of the stadtholder, but he had to work hard to persuade some Cabinet colleagues as well as George III. In May 1787 the patriot army defeated forces loyal to the stadtholder, and George accepted Pitt's argument that Britain should take steps to assist the anti-French 'Orangeists'. However, the initial assistance came in the form of subsidies rather than a threat of military intervention. This prudent approach seemed to be vindicated in June when the patriots arrested the Princess of Orange, who was the sister of King Frederick William II of Prussia. This transformed Britain's diplomatic position from one of wary weakness to one of considerable strength. Frederick William had previously shown some sympathy towards the French – another ominous development for the isolated British – but now felt that the insult to his family must be redressed and prepared his forces for an attack on the patriots. Pitt stepped up his support for the Orangeists and offered to help a Prussian invasion, while maintaining communications with the French in the hope of a negotiated settlement. As it happened, the Prussians had little need of assistance, since their advance into Holland was barely opposed. On 18 September 1787 the stadtholder was invited back to The Hague, and patriot resistance was effectively over by 10 October, when Amsterdam surrendered.

Pitt received much of the credit for an outcome which could not have been more satisfactory from the British perspective. The praise was well deserved, not least because the prime minister had taken a leading role in the Dutch crisis, leaving the Foreign Secretary, Carmarthen, on the sidelines. His anxiety to maintain control over the direction of policy was exemplified by the cancellation of a rare holiday excursion which would have included a visit to Wilberforce's property near Lake Windermere, thus extinguishing any hope that the former MP for Appleby would ever set foot in the north-west of England.

The stadtholder had been reinstated in circumstances which meant that Britain was no longer isolated – good relations with Prussia, which Chatham had valued so highly, were restored, along with something like a 'balance of power' in Europe. This had been achieved without armed British intervention, but when in September 1787 the Cabinet had agreed to mobilise naval forces in preparation for action the response had been impressive. This was largely due to Pitt's close interest in naval matters and his insistence on a high level of expenditure even in peacetime. At a deeper level, Pitt's emphasis on economic strength as a decisive factor in international relations was apparently vindicated; the French had felt unable to back their patriot allies because of their domestic problems, while the British, thanks to economic revival, had been regarded as a potent force to be reckoned with even before they showed that they could flex their muscles.

It could even be argued that, as early as 1787, the younger Pitt had already proved himself a more 'complete' prime minister than his father could ever have been. He had made significant progress in finance and administration, and now he had been instrumental in securing a signifi-cant foreign policy success for his country. His methods had moved him further from his father's shadow; in foreign as in domestic policy, as in his oratory, he preferred to use a rapier rather than the bludgeon which Lord Chatham had wielded. He could be forgiven if he overlooked elements of the Dutch crisis which could lead to less happy outcomes in the future. What if France itself – rather than Holland – provoked intervention from other European powers and resisted in a way which threatened to inspire revolutionary movements across the whole continent (including even Britain itself, as well as Ireland, which represented Pitt's most important 'unfinished business')? Could Britain hope realistically to quench this spirit by subsidising sympathetic powers and mobilising its ships? If not, what else could it do? If still in office, Pitt would have to meet the final challenge presented by his father's legacy and prove himself a great war leader.

By late 1787 Pitt the Younger had certainly shown that he could deal with the King more effectively than his father. George III's attitude towards Lord Chatham had oscillated between hatred and hero worship, closing at a point of acute antagonism. It is possible that this kind of relationship suited George III, since it reinforced his self-adopted role as the permanent guarantor of political stability, checking the wayward impulses of his temporary ministers. By exercising cool judgement in domestic and foreign affairs and trying to anticipate the King's reaction to every key policy decision, Pitt was threatening to make the monarchy's constitutional role redundant. Having tried so hard to recruit Pitt, George III soon showed signs of (at best) taking him for granted, or even of looking out for reasons to feel irritated. Something had to give. On 22 October 1788 Pitt was notified that the King's health, which had been poor for some months, had taken a dramatic turn for the worse and that he was now in a condition 'nearly bordering on delirium'. This might not have come as a complete surprise to Pitt, who on the previous day had been forced to remain standing while the King harangued him for more than three and a half hours.[12] The confirmation that George was really ill threatened to cause him more than mere physical discomfort; it seemed likely to bring his premiership to an abrupt halt, for reasons which would have nothing to do with his previous performance in the role.

11

The Regency Crisis

KING George's *coup d'état* and Pitt's subsequent election victory knocked the stuffing out of Charles Fox. After that 'it was never glad confident morning again', as Robert Browning put it in his much-quoted poem 'The Lost Leader'. Fox was convinced that the King, to whom he now frequently referred in his private correspondence as 'Satan', would go to any lengths to keep him out of power, and that there was no prospect of regaining office so long as the King lived. Some of his friends thought that this was far from being a distant prospect. After all, Frederick, Prince of Wales, who had been completely estranged from his father George II, had died at the age of just 44 in 1751. George III – Frederick's son – had already lived longer than his father when the younger Pitt took office in December 1783, and he had been carrying the burdens of kingship for more than half of his lifetime. Although he had eschewed the usual Hanoverian habits and took regular outdoor exercise, his health had sometimes given cause for concern, notably in 1765 when a bout of illness prompted the passage of a Regency Act.

However, those who based their hopes of an early operation of the 'reversionary principle' by estimating George's life expectancy on Frederick's example were ignoring some salient facts. Frederick's death seems to have been hastened by an accident on the sporting field – possibly while indulging in his obsession for cricket. Other notable members of his family had enjoyed much longer innings; George II had died just before his 77th birthday, and Sophia, Electress of Hanover was only despatched to the eternal pavilion at the age of 83 (while running for cover during a shower of rain). If she had decided to brave the elements and had lived just two months longer she would have become Queen of England under the terms of the 1701 Act of Settlement. As it was, her son became George I in 1714 and lived to the age of 67.

It would be unfair to suggest that Foxite politicians had cosied up to 'Prinny' out of cynical calculation; he was already a bosom friend with many of them, notably including Fox himself. Having the prince (with whom he had shared more than one mistress) on his side was by no means an unmitigated advantage for Fox; indeed, he and his friends would have been well advised to keep the heir to the throne at arm's length. Cultured and superficially good-natured, George was dissolute, vain, extravagantly self-indulgent, lacking in judgement and profoundly untrustworthy, and his conduct over the Mrs Fitzherbert affair did great damage to Fox's credibility. Maria Fitzherbert was a young Catholic woman who had been twice widowed by the age of 29. The prince, six years her junior, fell violently in love with her, but she refused to become his mistress and only agreed to a more orthodox liaison after he had stabbed himself to prove the depth of his attachment. The marriage, which was conducted secretly on 15 December 1785, was illegal, under at least two grounds: firstly, he was prohibited to marry a Catholic under the Act of Settlement of 1701, and secondly, under the Royal Marriages Act of 1772, he could not marry before the age of 25 without the King's consent (he was 23 at the time). Hearing rumours that a marriage was about to take place, Fox confronted the prince. The man who had professed to prefer death to the prospect of life without his true love now showed his true colours by betraying both Fox and Mrs Fitzherbert. Perhaps he utilised unsuspected powers of dissimulation during the interview, or maybe Fox was too eager to believe what he heard. Whatever the reason, during a House of Commons debate on the prince's finances Fox was confident that he was leaving no hostage to fortune when he stated that the rumour of an illegal marriage was 'a calumny destitute of all foundation [...] propagated with the sole view of depreciating the prince's character'.[1]

Pressed by another MP, Fox went on to say that he spoke with 'direct authority', but was informed the next day by a fellow member of Brooks's, who had actually been present at the wedding, that he had been misinformed.[2] Fox was furious with 'Prinny', and didn't speak to him for another year. Mrs Fitzherbert, for her part, was so upset by Fox's remarks that she was never reconciled with him – showing a level of resentment which she spared 'Prinny' himself even after the latter informed her by letter in 1794 that her surreptitious services were no longer required.

Perhaps Fox was less enquiring – and more reckless in defending the prince – than he might have been because he had been demotivated by the manner in which he had been ejected from power. He could not give up his engagement with politics, but thenceforward gave more priority to his other interests, spending more time at St Ann's Hill and showing increasing reluctance to attend the Commons. Having been forced to accept the defeat of his own plans for reform of the East India Company, he diverted his parliamentary energies to the attempt to impeach Warren Hastings, the governor general of Bengal, for gross corruption. Twenty-two charges (later reduced to 20) were laid against Hastings, one of which was that he had attempted to fine Chai Singh, the Rajah of Benares, half a million pounds merely for *delay* in paying a due sum of £50,000. This was the subject of a brilliant speech by Fox, which persuaded the House, by a majority of 40, to go ahead with the impeachment. It also, according to Stanley Ayling, 'served finally to clinch in Pitt's mind the conclusion which he had been moving towards "after long and laborious study" that Hastings had indeed acted in a manner "disproportionate, arbitrary, tyrannical, shamefully exorbitant, repugnant to principles".'[3]

Fox was appointed as one of the 18 Managers chosen to conduct the prosecution of Hastings before the House of Lords, along with many of his followers, notably including Burke, Sheridan and the young Charles Grey. Burke continued to play a leading part in the proceedings, but Fox soon lost interest. The trial dragged on from 1788 to 1794, when Hastings was acquitted on all charges. The minutes of the Managers' meetings reflect Fox's fluctuating commitment: 'In 1787, he attended 2 meetings out of 10, in 1788, 6 out of 46, in 1789, 2 out of 26, in 1790, 3 out of 17; and in 1791, 8 out of 14.'[4]

For his part, while Pitt had decided that the case against Hastings was sufficiently strong to justify an impeachment trial, there was never any chance that he would let 'long and laborious study' of the subject develop into a habit. He was happy to leave the prosecution in the hands of senior members of the Opposition. Indeed, it has been suggested that Pitt's vote in favour of impeachment was prompted, at least in part, by an expectation of a protracted process which would divert his most dangerous opponents into a profitless field. According to this reasoning, having failed to exclude Fox from the Commons by means of the Westminster scrutiny, he seized upon the Hastings impeachment as a more ingenious way of achieving the same objective.

There are two serious problems with this interpretation of events: it could only be convincing if Pitt was a Machiavellian operator out of the top drawer, and if Fox and his colleagues were hopelessly naive. In hindsight the Opposition probably was mistaken in lavishing so much energy on the Hastings case, which was marked by marathon speeches that invariably ended only when the exhausted orators collapsed into the arms of the nearest spectator. But at the outset they clearly felt that a conviction would serve their purposes, not least because it provided another chance to expose misgovernment in India and thus to revisit the subject which had served as George III's pretext for destroying the Fox–North coalition. Fox had attacked Hastings during debates on the ill-starred India Bill, and George had made no secret of his support for the governor general on his return to England. Indeed, given the crowd-pulling appeal of the trial in its early stages, one is tempted to depict the Opposition as opportunists rather than Pitt's puppets. After years of impotence, the impeachment process made them the talk of the town; and although their speeches are forgotten today, their eloquent utterances were brought to the attention of public schoolboys for many decades, ensuring the kind of lasting renown which Fox and his friends would have considered to be a reasonable return for their efforts.

In late October 1788, when George III fell dangerously ill, Charles Fox was travelling in Italy with his mistress, Mrs Armitstead. In keeping with his general practice of keeping a balance between his public and private activities, Fox had not revealed his travelling arrangements even to his closest allies – the eighteenth-century equivalent of an Opposition leader turning off his mobile phone. As a result, the Duke of Portland had to send a messenger on a cross-continental quest to track him down when the gravity of the King's situation became clear. Fox arrived back in London on 24 November, after a journey of nine days. It was not the ideal preparation for what turned out to be the greatest political opportunity of his life; and to make matters worse, he was seriously ill with dysentery, even giving rise to reports that he was dying or already dead.[5]

The King's condition seemed equally grave. On 5 November, George III had exhibited such dramatic symptoms of insanity that he had to be placed under physical restraint. The obvious diagnosis, at the time, was that he had contracted a fever which could quickly prove fatal. Even if George did not die, Parliament was due to meet on 20 November; and if he was unfit to take a full part in the legislative process the government would be faced with a constitutional dilemma, if not a full-scale crisis.

It is possible, as some have suggested, that Pitt felt special sympathy for the King's plight because his own father had experienced psychological problems in his later years. Others might think that the prime minister's conduct during the Regency Crisis of 1788–9 was dictated throughout by a desire to preserve his own position. As usual, the most likely explanation is that Pitt's motives were mixed. On the one hand, he was obviously reluctant to step down as prime minister, having seen himself as destined to fill that office and having done nothing to suggest that he was unfit for the role. Nevertheless, he was well aware (as were all well-informed observers) that a change of monarch was likely to result in his dismissal, with Fox as his substitute. Although he had been careful not to give any further cause for displeasure when dealing with the Prince of Wales, Pitt was astute enough to realise that no attempt to ingratiate himself with the prince was likely to alter the latter's preference for Fox. An undercurrent of animosity remained, even when Pitt exerted himself to arrange another settlement of 'Prinny's' gargantuan debts (as he did in 1787).

There were, though, other considerations beside Pitt's personal position. What if the full powers of the Crown were bestowed on the prince but his father subsequently recovered? Rightly renowned for his ability to resent injuries, whether real or imagined, a rehabilitated George III would have additional reasons for hating Fox and his colleagues if they took advantage of his illness. Pitt and any fellow ministers who were deemed to have shown loyalty would be reinstated without delay. But this would mean that the government had been subjected to two violent upheavals; and, given the Crown's extensive powers of patronage, the purges on both occasions would have extended far beyond the Cabinet and left hardly any area of public life unaffected.

Thus, as so often in Pitt's career, duty to self and to country could be made to point towards the same line of conduct. On this occasion his course seemed clear – to delay any transfer of royal authority for as long as possible, and, if a decision proved unavoidable, to place limitations on the powers of any regency. Accordingly, Pitt pushed back the opening of the parliamentary session – from 20 November, to 4 December and then to 8 December – before establishing a committee to take evidence from the King's doctors. In fact, on 3 December five doctors had given separate testimony to a meeting of the Privy Council, broadly agreeing that George's condition might improve but without indicating when this could happen.[6] Two new physicians had been brought in, including Dr Francis Willis, a retired clergyman who had presided over a sanatorium in Lincolnshire for almost three decades and who was recommended by the Queen. Although Willis was freely accused of partisanship (and quackery), he was less free from partisan taint than some of George's other attendants – including Pitt's own nominee Dr Anthony Addington, who had acted as both medical and political advisor to the Earl of Chatham, and whose son Henry was now a Pittite MP. Confined to his palace at Kew, the King was exposed to a mixture of benevolence and barbarity by Willis, including restraint in a straitjacket and the application of 'blisters' to the royal legs.

While George was accommodating himself to Willis's ministrations, on 10 December 1788 the House of Commons held its first debate on the crisis. Pitt accepted that the King would, at best, be unfit for business for some time, and that Parliament should act. However, he recommended the appointment of another committee to look at previous instances when a regency had proved necessary. Since Pitt could make no direct allusion to the real rationale for delay, any objective witness to his speech could only convict him of blatant time-wasting, enough to make a referee brandish a yellow card. The Opposition, however, was not 'impartial', and its senior figures saw red. Fox retorted that

> [t]he circumstances to be provided for did not depend upon their deliberations in a House of Parliament. It rested elsewhere. There was a person in the kingdom different from any other person that any existing precedents could refer to [...] In his firm opinion, his Royal Highness the Prince of Wales had as clear, as express a right to assume the reins of government and exercise the power of sovereignty during the continuance of the illness and incapacity with which it had pleased God to affect his Majesty, as in the case of his Majesty's having undergone a natural and perfect demise [...] His Royal Highness chose rather to wait the decision of Parliament with a patient and due deference to the Constitution, than to urge a claim which he was persuaded could not reasonably be disputed. But ought he to wait unnecessarily?[7]

The advice that one should bring digging operations to an abrupt end when finding oneself in a hole applies with special force in the parliamentary context, where there are usually plenty of ill-wishers who will notice the predicament. On this occasion, Fox seems to have realised that he had made a bad mistake and instinctively started trying to fill up the hole by saying that he would not oppose Pitt's motion and had merely wanted to warn MPs against unnecessary delay. The self-inflicted damage might have been limited if Fox had sat down at this point, but he was unable to lay down his spade. He added that 'His Royal Highness, he was convinced, must exercise the royal prerogative during, and only during, his Majesty's illness.'[8] At best, this qualification was superfluous; at worst, it gratuitously drew attention to a real nightmare scenario in which the prince might try to act as de facto ruler even after his father had made a full recovery.

It is easy to sympathise with Fox, whose own ill health must have contributed to a feeling of being goaded beyond endurance by a prime minister whose speech ostensibly combined outrageous cheating with a shabby attempt to flatter the institution which made the rules. However,

Fox could have begun with a promise not to oppose Pitt's motion, followed by a suggestion that although precedents might be useful, the country was faced with an entirely new situation and that the work of the committee could be allowed to proceed only on the understanding that Parliament retained the right to reach a decision either before it had reported, or in a way which contrasted with its findings. This at least would have furnished Fox with a decent reason to abstain on the motion; more importantly, it would have got him through a vexatious parliamentary occasion without offering any obvious openings for a counter-attack from Pitt.

As he prepared his response to Fox, Pitt might have remembered his prepubescent days, when he had pored over the record of political speeches and pointed out the ways in which the arguments of long-dead orators could have been improved. He had been offered a perfect opportunity to put that training into practice. According to an eyewitness, during Fox's speech,

> the countenance of Mr Pitt was seen to brighten with exultation, at the mistake into which he perceived his adversary was hurrying [...] slapping his thigh triumphantly, he turned to the person who sat next to him, and said, 'I'll *unwhig* the gentleman for the rest of his life!'[9]

Pitt had seen an opportunity to claim that Fox had committed the ultimate sin of eighteenth-century British politics by departing from the principles which had been used to validate the Glorious Revolution of 1688–9 and the deposition of James II. There was room for debate on the application of those principles to the present case. However, Fox's words implied that the Prince of Wales deserved to be congratulated for obeying the constitution but that it would be understandable if his patience was exhausted, since ultimately his right to rule was more important than parliamentary deliberations. The popular hero of the 1784 Westminster election had come dangerously close to sounding like an advocate of the divine right of kings. To make matters worse, most (if not all) of the MPs who listened to Fox on that day were well aware that the personal character of the Prince of Wales fell far short of divine standards; indeed, many must have known that the heir to the throne and prospective regent had fooled Fox into misleading the Commons by lying about the status of his relationship with Mrs Fitzherbert.

Fox might be 'unwhigged', but he was unruffled, assured as he was that the King would not recover and that his triumph was only a matter of time. On 12 December his ally Richard Brinsley Sheridan, who was being provided with regular bulletins on the King's condition, went so far as to warn Pitt that he was in danger of 'provoking' the Prince of Wales into action in defiance of Parliament.[10] Understandably, the crisis encouraged many MPs to re-evaluate their loyalties – a process which the Lord Chancellor, Thurlow, had begun as soon as the King had fallen ill. One group, consisting of around thirty MPs and twenty peers, had distanced itself from Pitt and became known (somewhat misleadingly) as 'the Armed Neutrality'. Pitt seems to have appreciated that his delaying tactics had a limited shelf life: the longer he played for time, the longer the King's malady would have lasted and the more the prospects of anything approaching a full recovery would have receded. Thus on 16 December Pitt abandoned his initial plan – to hold things up in the hope that legislation would not be necessary – and embraced the fallback option of moving (without unseemly haste) towards legislation limiting a regent's power.

Although the preliminary skirmishes had gone Pitt's way, the battle was now much more even. On 16 December Fox attempted to re-Whig himself by alleging that Pitt had himself distorted the principles of the Glorious Revolution in his desperation to cling on to power. The prime minister could only retort that Fox was preparing a power grab of his own. The vote at the end of the debate – 268 to 204 in Pitt's favour – provided temporary reassurance to Pitt's ministry while at the same time conveying an unmistakable warning that the balance could easily shift when Parliament reassembled after Christmas. There was at least one favourable symptom; on 15 December Lord Thurlow had finally decided to side with Pitt, closing his address to the Lords by declaring: 'When I forget my King, may God forget me!' Pitt witnessed this nauseating performance, and was reported to have walked away muttering, 'Oh, what a rascal!'[11]

After the Christmas truce, Pitt embarked on the unpleasant but unavoidable groundwork for his new approach, setting out his proposals for a regency in a letter to the Prince of Wales. As so often during the prolonged duel between Pitt and Fox, it is important to avoid judgements which are based on hindsight. If George III had not recovered, Pitt's letter would have had to be regarded as one of the most remarkable documents in British constitutional history. Knowing that he would probably have to abandon politics for the Bar if the King's health was not restored – indeed, having some reason to fear that he would be impeached along with Warren Hastings in that eventuality – Pitt proposed a range of restrictions which amounted to a slur on the character of the Prince of Wales. His powers as regent would be circumscribed in respect of official offices, property and honours: he would not be allowed to grant titles to anyone except members of his own family. The royal household would be controlled by the Queen, rather than the heir to the throne. Left unaided, the prince would probably have fired off a brief reply replete with curses. Instead, he dispatched a letter which had been drafted by Edmund Burke with typical elegance, rejecting Pitt's proposals while observing the formalities of polite society. Pitt replied that, with regret, he must stick to his guns.

If events outside Pitt's control had worked out differently, the 'Foxite' view of this correspondence would have prevailed (i.e. that Pitt had tried to stave off the inevitable for as long as possible regardless of the consti-tutional implications, but that eventually he had to accept the Prince's irrefutable claims). Yet not long after the ink had dried on these letters, Pitt had a new stroke of luck when, on 2 January 1789, the Speaker of the Commons, Charles Cornwall, died. As his replacement, the govern-ment took a calculated risk and nominated an MP who, though not yet a Cabinet member, had been serving as Paymaster of the Forces since 1784 and was also Pitt's cousin. William Grenville was duly elected Speaker of the Commons, by 215 votes to 144. For Pitt and his colleagues, this was a very auspicious indication of parliamentary opinion, with the added bonus that a staunch and very able supporter would be presiding over the crucial debates.

Remarkably, the Opposition decided to follow up this setback by suggesting the establishment of yet another committee. Once again, the King's physicians were to be examined, presumably in the expectation that they would convey doleful tidings. Pitt was more than happy to approve of this step, which hoofed the regency ball into touch once again. The success of his strategy depended heavily on expressions of public support, and these began to emerge, from Scotland as well as many English regions, in the early weeks of 1789. Wealthy backers in London voted to raise £100,000 to pay off Pitt's debts if he was forced out of office. There was even a danger that such addresses could rebound on Pitt and lend credence to the favourite Foxite charge that he was hoping to cash in his personal popularity either by taking effective control of the executive by manipulating the Queen, or even by supplanting the royal family and establishing his own dynasty.

Despite these expressions of support 'out of doors', Pitt was still faced with a parliamentary audience whose loyalties could not be taken for granted. On 16 January 1789 he invited the Commons to vote on the restricted regency which he had set out in his letters to the prince. Given the remarkable nature of these measures, and the uncertainty of the circumstances, the government's victory by 57 votes was a clear indication of the confidence Pitt enjoyed among the political classes, as well as the reservations in the same constituency regarding Fox and (especially) the Prince of Wales.

After this vote it would have been difficult even for a volatile House of Commons to reject a regency bill which embodied the same proposals, but the process was far from being a formality. Fox, who had been forced to seek the health-restoring waters of Bath, continued to prepare for government and warned his followers to disbelieve any positive rumours about the King's health. But in his absence the Opposition lost all sense of discipline; indeed, it seemed that senior figures were anticipating Fox's death and had started to compete for the succession to the Whig throne. When Pitt duly introduced his restrictive bill on 5 February 1789, his cause was helped inadvertently by Burke. In a previous debate, Burke had been called to order for suggesting that Pitt was a contender for the throne, and referring to him as 'the Prince opposite'.[12] Now he followed up some well-founded criticisms of Pitt's policy with an outburst which suggested that he required treatment from Dr Willis: 'But have we forgotten that we are debating relative to a monarch smitten by the hand of Omnipotence? Do we recollect that the Almighty has hurled him from his throne [...]?'[13] Thanks not least to Pitt's shrewd tactics, the Almighty had done no such thing. Within a fortnight of Burke's histrionics, and while the Regency Bill was progressing through the House of Lords, it was announced that the King had entered 'a state of convalescence'.[14]

It was not surprising that George's condition baffled the medical community in 1789; more than two hundred years later, experts were still debating the cause. In the 1960s it was argued that along with his throne he had inherited porphyria, a rare condition which causes temporary bouts of insanity. The evidence, however, was disputed, and indeed the King's symptoms, including extreme excitability followed by lassitude, have been interpreted as evidence of manic depression. While the medical evidence is open to dispute, the political implications were clear; the fact that George recovered in time to prevent his son (who had hoped to be King in all but name) even from taking office as a hamstrung regent was only a final twist to a tale in which Pitt had turned impending disaster into a further strengthening of his position. By keeping his cool while others jumped to serious misjudgements, he had made much of his own luck. His tactics might have caused temporary estrangements in some quarters, but they mainly increased the enmity of people who disliked him already; and the outcome of the Regency Crisis made it less likely that they would be able to hurt him, at least so long as George III's health held up. Even if there was a relapse, Pitt had persuaded Parliament to agree that his eldest son was not a fit and proper person to exercise the full prerogative powers on his behalf. Indeed, the conduct of the prince – which apparently included childish behaviour at the Thanksgiving service held to celebrate the King's recovery – had made the man who had presided over the loss of the North American colonies into something like Lord Bolingbroke's idea of a 'Patriot King'. To some extent at least, the inevitable junkets held to commemorate his deliverance from illness reflected genuine public feeling, as the nation gave a collective national sigh of relief.

For Charles Fox, by contrast, the Regency Crisis had been an unrelieved disaster. While Pitt had been consistently lucky, Fox had been thwarted at every turn, chiefly because of his ill-timed illness. But underlying such unpredictable quirks of fate was an issue which brought his political judgement into question. Before the crisis the Prince of Wales, for all his faults, could be seen as a bankable insurance policy. Now he looked more like an indefinite source of unlimited liability, whose friendship could only be valuable to politicians who had despaired of winning office with dignity. Both of the parliamentary titans were beginning to show signs of failing health; but recent evidence suggested that Fox was failing faster than Pitt. The country was prospering, thanks at least in part to Pitt's policies. In the spring of 1789 Fox badly needed something to turn up – preferably an issue which would restore his reputation as a man of principle. In the summer, events across the English Channel presented him with exactly the kind of opportunity he needed to renew his rivalry with Pitt.

12

The French Revolution and Foreign Relations

I F William Wordsworth thought that it was bliss to be alive on the day when he learned of the outbreak of the French Revolution, Charles Fox was even more enthusiastic. In a letter of 30 July 1789 to Richard Fitzpatrick on the fall of the Bastille, he wrote: 'How much the greatest event it is that ever happened in the world! and how much the best!'

Fox and Wordsworth were not alone. Britain had recently celebrated the hundredth anniversary of the Glorious Revolution of 1688–9, and a very general view was that France was belatedly catching up with its neighbour in rejecting despotism and opting for a constitutional monarchy and parliamentary sovereignty. It was particularly pleasing to Fox that many of the leading figures at the outset of the Revolution were good friends of his whom he had got to know during his many visits to Paris, and who revered him as the very personification of advanced English Whiggery. They included the dukes of Orleans (later known as 'Philippe Égalité') and Lauzun, both of whom were to be executed during the 'Terror', Talleyrand, and especially Lafayette, who was to take charge of Fox's adored young nephew (the third Lord Holland) during his first visit to France in 1791.

The younger Pitt was also pleased to hear about the events in France, though the level of his enthusiasm was several notches lower than that of Fox. On 30 May 1789 he had celebrated his 30th birthday. His reputation as a purposeful, if moderate reformer in domestic matters was firmly established, and Britain's isolation within Europe had ended. In foreign affairs, indeed, Pitt had proved himself to be too hasty when, in an attempt to defend the failing Shelburne government, he had argued that, thanks to Lord North's mismanagement, Britain's 'power and pre-eminence are passed away'.[1]

However, the recognition of Britain's revival was not an unmixed blessing. Indeed, at times Pitt might have thought that there was only one thing worse than being regarded as irrelevant to European politics, and that was being relevant. The main problem for Pitt, as for all his recent predecessors, was France, notwithstanding the Commercial Treaty signed in 1786. Thus the storming of the Bastille in July 1789 must have seemed like a belated birthday present. It looked as if France was entering a period of European irrelevance which would be more deserved and prolonged than Britain's had been, and which could only be ended when it had established a rational system of government along British lines. Indeed, Pitt enjoyed the unusual luxury of feeling genuine sympathy towards France, and would have allowed the export of much-needed supplies of flour had it not been for the restrictions imposed by Britain's Corn Laws.[2] He was reticent in public during the initial stages of the Revolution, but in February 1790 delivered an upbeat parliamentary prophecy:

> The present convulsions in France must, sooner or later, terminate in harmony and regular order; and notwithstanding that the fortunate arrangements of such a situation might make her more formidable, it might also render her less obnoxious as a neighbour.

Pitt went on to exhort MPs 'not to relax their exertions for the strength of the country'.[3] This was entirely consistent with his appraisal of the outlook for France, in which his optimistic expectations had been carefully qualified (a change in the French system *might* make the country 'less obnoxious' in future; a satisfactory outcome could be expected 'sooner or later', rather than immediately). Pitt's oversight was a failure to anticipate a transitional phase in which Revolutionary France might be both 'formidable' *and* 'obnoxious'. This, however, was a mistake common to all the main European decision makers in 1789–90.

While France underwent its preliminary 'convulsions', Pitt found himself dealing with other pressing matters arising from Britain's new prominence in European affairs. In the aftermath of the Dutch crisis he had entered into an alliance with that country. The Dutch, however, also allied themselves to Prussia, and, after some hesitation, Pitt followed suit in August 1788, forming what was somewhat misleadingly known as the Triple Alliance. The British government had good reason to tread carefully, since it was anxious to promote stability in Europe, while Prussia had revisionist inclinations, hoping to extend its territory both East and West. A bankable commitment to Prussia was a considerable risk, since major powers were already engaged in conflict on the periphery of Europe. Russia had declared war on Turkey in 1787, and Austria (Prussia's most obvious rival) had swiftly joined them. This instigated a complex and far-reaching chain of events, including a Danish invasion of Sweden. Sniffing around for territorial gains at Denmark's expense, Prussia threatened to intervene in support of the Swedes. Imaginative British diplomacy helped to defuse the situation.[4]

Another unanticipated repercussion of the war against Turkey was a challenge to Austrian rule over its own territories in the Netherlands, stoked up by the reforms of Emperor Joseph II. In response, supporters of an independent Belgium called on the members of the Triple Alliance for assistance. The Dutch and the Prussians were predictably keen to weaken Austrian influence in Western Europe, but Pitt and his colleagues were much less enthusiastic since an independent Belgium would be vulnerable to French influence once the Revolution had run its course. With the help of the Dutch, Britain persuaded its restless Prussian allies to accept that Austria must be a party to any settlement. Having helped to create a favourable context, Pitt had another stroke of luck in February 1790, when Joseph II died and was succeeded by the less belligerent Leopold II. The new emperor asked the British government to mediate, and in July 1790 Austria and Prussia struck a wide-ranging deal, involving the end of Austrian hostilities against Turkey as well as a pledge that members of the Triple Alliance would help to dampen down the Belgian revolt against Austria.

These controversies are now largely forgotten – certainly in comparison to the French Revolution – but Pitt devoted considerable attention to them, and their very obscurity owes much to the fact that he was able to prevent their escalation. At the time, Pitt's contribution received considerable domestic praise. His reputation at home and abroad was augmented in 1790 by his resolute response to a dispute with Spain, triggered by events which had happened far from home and several months before British policy makers were alerted. In January, news reached London that British trading vessels in Nootka Sound, on the west coast of Vancouver Island, had been challenged by Spanish ships, and that at least one had been seized. The Spanish government justified its action by asserting historic claims to sovereignty over the West Coast of America. Britain had never accepted these claims, based as they were on a papal bull from the time of Christopher Columbus, and the Foreign Secretary, Carmarthen (now advanced in the peerage as Duke of Leeds), demanded the release of detained sailors plus compensation. For good measure, he hinted at military action if Britain's commercial activities continued to be obstructed.

At this point Pitt took a more active role, fearing that Leeds had been unnecessarily provocative. Nevertheless, after new reports of Spanish aggression arrived in London, the Cabinet authorised the dispatch of naval forces to the area. In July 1790 – the month of the satisfactory settlement between Austria and Prussia – Spain agreed to compensation, without resiling from their previous claims to sovereignty. Unimpressed, the British continued to mobilise their ships and obtained promises of support from the Prussians and the Dutch. The Spanish government, by contrast, was unable to recruit any worthwhile allies; even the French, who sounded supportive at first, quickly decided that they were no longer bound by the old 'family compact' between the Bourbon monarchs of France and Spain. By October Spain was ready to come to terms, and Pitt accepted a deal which recognised British freedom to trade and settle on the Pacific Coast, albeit with minimal limitations that allowed Spain to retreat with some dignity. The main point, for Pitt, was that the potential scope for British economic activity had been expanded significantly. It also helped that this had been achieved in a way which would have delighted his father – achieving 'patriotic' goals by convincing potential adversaries that the country was in earnest. George III was delighted, and the success was soon followed by the offer of the Order of the Garter. Pitt insisted that his brother, Lord Chatham, should receive the honour instead.

If Pitt seemed not to have changed in his attitude to insubstantial laurels, it is possible that Nootka Sound turned his head in other respects. The general consensus among Pitt's biographers is that the advantageous resolution of the dispute with Spain, combined with his successful diplomatic engagements with a range of European powers, enticed the prime minister into further activities which exposed the limits of British influence and underlined his own besetting weakness – a tendency to read too much into promising symptoms, amounting to a counting of chickens before the eggs had even been laid. According to Robin Reilly, for example, the combined effect of Pitt's initial successes in foreign policy led to 'a disastrous error of judgement arising from that curious mixture of optimism, obstinacy and arrogance that occasionally robbed him of his natural caution'.[5]

This verdict on Pitt's next major foreign policy initiative seems to be verified by his own reaction to its palpable failure: apparently he took the setback so seriously that he contemplated resignation. Yet the Ochakov crisis of 1791 deserves closer analysis. If it had forced his premature retirement it would have marked a dramatic reversal of fortune, since his narrow but triumphant escape in 1789 was followed by a general election held in the June and July of 1790, which returned a House of Commons more heavily sympathetic towards Pitt than the one elected back in 1784. As the offer of the Garter showed, Pitt could also count on the support of the King with greater certainty than before. Why, then, could this seemingly impregnable position have come near to destruction because of a single mistake?

Even from his limited experience of foreign policy before 1791, Pitt's general approach to such matters was clear. Scholars of international relations would recognise him as a 'realist', placing the perceived interests of his country before any other consideration and overlooking defects in other regimes so long as they posed no tangible threat to those interests. Thus, for example, he offered no assistance to the champions of Belgian independence even though they were enduring ham-fisted intervention from an autocratic Austrian regime. At the same time, however, Pitt can be classed as a 'liberal', or an 'idealist', in that he thought Britain's best interests lay in peaceful commercial relations with other nations. His ideal – no doubt derived from his appreciative reading of Adam Smith – was a world in which economic agents would engage in free competition, to the benefit of all. In this competition national governments would, and should, play a role; but they should not uphold 'artificial' trading monopolies on behalf of their own citizens. As a patriotic Briton, Pitt thought that his country was sure to benefit disproportionally from this arrangement, thanks to the innovative exploitation of its raw materials and the ingenuity of its people. In such circumstances, if Britain took direct political control of overseas territories it would not be doing so in order to exclude more vigorous economic competitors; rather, it would be ensuring what the British considered to be orderly government in those less fortunate places and preventing other countries from monopolising the trade of the territory in question. Instead of fighting amongst themselves, European states should turn their attention to the new markets outside their continent that they could service peacefully.

In 1791, with France thankfully *hors de combat* and Britain on reasonable terms with other major powers, Russia seemed to be the chief remaining obstacle to Pitt's vision. It was seen as generally unfriendly to Britain, and it had achieved considerable success in its war against Turkey. In particular, in 1788 its forces had captured the Black Sea port of Ochakov, situated at the estuaries of the rivers Dnieper and Bug and considered to possess considerable strategic significance. These annexations, if confirmed in a subsequent peace treaty, would increase Russia's chances of capturing the Ottoman capital, Constantinople, in any renewal of the conflict; it would also affect the trade routes of Poland, which was seen by Pitt as a commercial partner of growing importance as well as a possible adherent to the Triple Alliance.

Russian possession of Ochakov would have been unwelcome to Pitt at any time, but in the early part of 1791 he saw a chance of preventing it. Prussia (despite recent flirtations with Russia) now argued that the Triple Alliance could exert pressure to ensure an end to the war without any Russian gains, and argued that this would be an appropriate quid pro quo for its support for Britain's stance regarding Nootka Sound. In

March the Cabinet discussed this proposal, and agreed that ships should be sent to the Baltic and the Black Sea, together with an ultimatum to the Russian empress, Catherine II, to disgorge her conquests. Yet ministers were divided, and the mobilisation of the fleet caused considerable disquiet outside Parliament. In the House of Commons the government won respectable majorities, but failed to produce a convincing argument for action and was in clear danger of defeat if it asked MPs to provide the necessary finance. As Pitt remarked ruefully to the British diplomat Joseph Ewart, his fellow Britons could be 'embarked in a War from motives of passion, but they cannot be made to comprehend a case in which the most valuable interests of the Country are at stake'.[6] Fox and his supporters were understandably keen to capitalise on this evidence that the government was out of step with public opinion. In mid-April Pitt backed down, making very hasty apologies to the Prussians. Catherine the Great was left to dictate her own peace terms to the Ottoman Empire; although these were not especially punitive, they left her in possession of Ochakov. An outcome which Pitt had risked war in order to avoid soon became an accepted fact of international politics.

This was undoubtedly a serious blow for Pitt, but its significance was magnified by his previous record of unblemished success. He had committed himself to war against Russia too far to retreat without serious political embarrassment – but long before Britain's armed forces had travelled beyond the point of no return. He had failed to convince Parliament, the public and some of his closest colleagues that Ochakov was sufficiently important to risk the loss of British lives; but by the same token, this meant that the feeling that he had been forced to abandon important British interests was confined to himself and a handful of associates (notably Leeds). One might say that Pitt contemplated resignation on this issue because to some extent he had believed his own publicity. But in practice, far from being scarred by Ochakov, Pitt remained much as before in his approach to foreign policy, and over-optimism continued to be his greatest failing for the rest of his career as a statesman.

Pitt's blunders over Ochakov – which included a failure to explore the practical ways in which a maritime power like Britain could force the submission of a country like Russia – arose from an assumption that his mastery of the House of Commons could be extended to the international scene as British diplomacy revived. Words, however, were not enough; by 1791 he urgently needed colleagues in whom he could have sufficient confidence to allow him to delegate crucial decisions. In this respect, Ochakov can actually be seen as a positive development in his career. Leeds, who had never enjoyed Pitt's confidence, decided to interpret the incident as one humiliation too far, and resigned. To replace him, Pitt appointed his cousin and near-contemporary William Grenville, who had served as Home Secretary since June 1789 after his brief spell as Speaker of the Commons and had been elevated to the Lords as Baron Grenville in 1790. The new Home Secretary was Henry Dundas, who probably was now Pitt's closest personal friend despite (or perhaps because of) their markedly different characteristics. The ties which had already created a sense of loyalty and respect between this trio were complex, but they ensured a unity of ultimate purpose in the key institutions of government during the unprecedented challenges of the ensuing decade.

In terms of the rivalry between Pitt and Fox, the Ochakov affair was soon obscured by the developing drama in France, but as it receded from public memory it left a mystery which no scholar of the period has been able to unravel. In the summer of 1791 Fox's supporter Robert Adair embarked on a journey to the tsarina's court at St Petersburg. Adair's motives are obscure, but it is well established that he made contact with Russian officials and sent regular reports (largely in cipher) to his Foxite friends back in London. Adair's activities aroused considerable suspicion, and his correspondence was intercepted. In 1797, a letter which Edmund Burke had written to the Duke of Portland was published; it included allegations that Adair had indulged in illegal (if not treasonable) activities, effectively advising the Russian government on the best way to thwart the diplomatic activities of Pitt's government. The story resurfaced in 1821, when Pitt's official biographer Bishop Tomline repeated Burke's allegations. Adair – who by that time had served as an official ambassador to Austria and the Ottoman Empire, in a distinguished career which also included a brief spell as MP for Pitt's old Appleby constituency – challenged Tomline to produce documentary evidence, which was not forthcoming. In fact, at the time Pitt had hinted that an inquiry into the affair might be appropriate, but he had then dropped the subject. The publication of Burke's letter in 1797 jogged the memory of Lord Grenville (by that time Foreign Secretary), but a search for evidence only yielded a recollection that Pitt himself had taken possession of copies of Adair's letters. Grenville did not take the matter further.

The clear implication of this story is that William Pitt had obtained written evidence which strongly suggested that Charles James Fox was complicit in activities which, according to well-informed people, were designed to damage British interests; and yet he never made use of it. To modern observers this gesture is difficult to comprehend. In 2010, the outgoing Labour Chief Secretary of the Treasury, Liam Byrne, left a jokey note to his successor apologising for the fact that 'there is no money left'; and his gallows humour proved to be extremely counterproductive when members of the incoming coalition government exploited it. The Fox–Adair correspondence was potentially far more damaging, providing the basis for potential prosecutions. The obvious question is why Pitt kept the evidence under lock and key. It is unlikely that even so disorganised an individual as Pitt the Younger simply forgot about it; like many clever people, he made no attempt to keep his papers in order, because he had a very organised mind. John Ehrman's forensic account suggests that Pitt kept the matter secret out of a sense of honourable competition with Fox; by implication, he had evidence which might have ruined his opponent but chose not to use this deadly weapon because he did not see this as a fitting end to their rivalry.

Alternatively, Ehrman suggests that Pitt had no wish to revive the debate over Ochakov, which had resulted in such a serious reversal of his fortunes.[7] This seems much more plausible. Pitt might have decided, after his miserable campaign to unseat Fox from Westminster, that he should 'play the ball, rather than the man' in future; but if there really was concrete evidence that Fox had been party to anti-British activities over Ochakov, no one could have doubted the motives of any prime minister who decided to make it public. As it was, the Russian tsarina's admiration for Fox was unhelpful to his radical reputation; although Catherine liked to see herself as an *enlightened* despot, the victims of her regime would be forgiven if they compared it unfavourably to the governing principles of the French *Ancien Régime*, whose overthrow Fox had welcomed so warmly.

Nevertheless, public opinion had seemingly sided with the Opposition over Ochakov. Those in the know, like Burke, might argue that the rights and wrongs of Pitt's policy towards Russia were irrelevant, and that Fox had committed something like treason in allowing Adair to work against that policy; but it was less certain that the political elite as a whole would accept that Fox had instigated Adair's activities, rather than being (at worst) unable to restrain his overzealous colleague. Ultimately it seems best to conclude that when Pitt took possession of the Fox–Adair correspondence he thought that this evidence might be useful to him if, in subsequent years, it ever seemed likely that Fox could force him from office (for example, if George III's health should relapse). In any case, by the time the correspondence fell into Pitt's hands it seemed that Fox's enthusiasm for the French Revolution would be more damaging to the latter's prospects than alleged misdemeanours in relation to Ochakov.

Fox's main problem was a feeling among some of his allies that, far from being 'the greatest event' in world history, the Revolution was a disaster for humanity and an imminent threat to Britain itself. The most eloquent supporter of that view was Edmund Burke, who in November 1790 published a lengthy pamphlet entitled *Reflections on the Revolution in France*. It had an immediate impact, selling 13,000 copies within five weeks. Its central argument was that the Revolution was based on abstract notions of human rights without taking any account of human experience, history or traditions, or of differing local circumstances. In Burke's view, political reform and changes in society were more likely to be beneficial if they were introduced incrementally after careful consideration and a process of trial and error, rather than suddenly and on an unlimited scale, with little or no attempt at checks and balances. In a lyrical and oft-quoted passage, he summed up his view:

> Society is indeed a contract. Subordinate contracts for objects of mere occasional interest may be dissolved at pleasure – but the state ought not to be considered as nothing better than a partnership agreement in a trade of pepper and coffee, calico or tobacco, or some other such

low concern, to be taken up for a little temporary interest, and to be dissolved by the fancy of the parties. It is to be looked on with other reverence; because it is not a partnership in things subservient only to the gross animal existence of a temporary and perishable nature. It is a partnership in all science; a partnership in all art; a partnership in every virtue, and in all perfection. As the ends of such a partnership cannot be obtained in many generations, it becomes a partnership not only between those who are living, but between those who are living, those who are dead, and those who are to be born.[8]

Burke went on to make a series of predictions which were to prove remarkably prescient, though most readers at the time thought them exaggerated and alarmist. These were that the Revolution would lead to anarchy, mass violence, dictatorship and military adventurism.

In the short term, very few people supported Burke's views. He was violently criticised by the Foxites, notably Sheridan and Grey, and Fox himself described the work as in 'very bad taste' and 'favouring Tory principles'.[9] The general view was that Burke had gone 'over the top', and some people began to question his mental stability (which had seemed doubtful enough during the Regency Crisis of 1788–9). A ditty, composed by the poet, William Roscoe, contained the lines:

> Full tilt he ran at all he met,
> And round he dealt his knocks,
> Till with a backhand stroke at last,
> He hit poor CHARLEY FOX.
> Now CHARLEY was of all his friends
> The warmest friend he had;
> So when he dealt this graceless blow
> He deemed the man was mad.[10]

In the House of Commons on 6 May 1791, Fox paid tribute to Burke, saying that he 'was indebted to his right honourable friend for the greater share of the political knowledge he possessed – his political education had been formed under him – his instructions had invariably governed his principles'.[11] Yet he then went on to attack Burke's arguments, quoting out of context earlier opinions of Burke apparently inconsistent with what he now said. Burke leapt to his feet, claiming that

[a] personal attack had been made upon him from a quarter he never could have expected, after a friendship and intimacy of more than twenty-two years [...] He had met with great unfairness from the right honourable gentleman [...] who brought the whole strength and heavy artillery of his own judgement, eloquence and abilities upon him to crush him.[12]

At this point, a badly shaken Fox leaned over to Burke, and said in an audible whisper, 'no loss of friends'. But there was, and Burke refused to have any further dealings with Fox, even declining a deathbed visit from him in 1797.

At the time of this dramatic confrontation Fox, though appalled by the violence of the Revolution in its early stages, regarded these as teething problems rather than the beginning of something even more sinister. His differences with Pitt over the desirability of revolutionary principles did not prevent them from cooperating, in the same month as Fox's final breach with Burke, on his Libel Bill, which was designed to ensure that juries rather than judges would decide the issue in cases concerning the press. This was regarded as a great advance for the freedom of the press. Far from seeming to be on the verge of a 'reactionary' lurch in his outlook, Pitt was prepared to listen to Fox's arguments on questions of conscience, and to honour his father's stand during the Wilkes affair many years earlier.

In fact Pitt still thought that, far from presenting difficulties, the Revolution would turn out to be beneficial to British interests. Although he already disliked Burke for very understandable reasons, like Fox he based his opposition to the *Reflections* on the Tory tendency of its doctrines; as late as 1795, he was still dismissing Burke's arguments as 'rhapsodies [...] in which there is much to admire and nothing to agree with'.[13] In October 1791 he reportedly told Burke that 'we shall go on as we are, until the Day of Judgement'.[14] He was unafraid of sounding equally sanguine in public, using his budget speech of February 1792 to claim that 'unquestionably there never was a time in the history of this country, when, from the situation in Europe, we might more reasonably expect fifteen years of peace, than we may at the present moment.' Two months later, France declared war on Austria, followed almost immediately by a Russian invasion of Poland (which Fox deplored, breaking his budding friendship with Catherine the Great). Pitt's mischief-making allies, the Prussians, lost little time before engaging themselves in both of these conflicts, supporting Austria against France and preparing to help themselves to a second slice of Poland.

Admittedly Pitt had introduced a few qualifications into his budget speech, referring to the impossibility of foolproof predictions in an uncertain world. Nevertheless, his words would have unnerved any superstitious listeners, and those who were more impressed by facts would have found it easy to pinpoint times within recent memory (indeed during Pitt's own premiership) when the state of Europe was far more promising than its condition in February 1792. Pitt obviously saw his 1792 budget as an occasion on which he should 'bury bad news' from abroad, since the economy seemed to be in good health and he wanted to announce cuts in military spending which would allow him to refresh his sinking fund. Nevertheless, the inclusion of the fifteen-year prediction remains one of the most baffling misjudgements of Pitt's career. Even on the most charitable interpretation of his words they only held good for one year, during which time he and Grenville repeatedly stressed that Britain had no intention of interfering in French affairs.

However, much earlier than this Pitt had become conscious of the possibility that the fire in his neighbour's house might spread to his own. After all, Britain was affected by many of the factors which had helped to engender the revolutionary spirit in France. Even in normal times, poor harvests were a regular source of unrest. In Britain the yield was disappointing for three of the four harvests from 1789 to 1792; 1790 was particularly bad. Rioting in such situations was more or less an accepted fact of eighteenth-century British life, so that even the affluent individuals who were charged with the preservation of law and order tended to take a relatively relaxed approach. However, the additional ingredient of political grievances would greatly increase the incendiary potential of these outbreaks; as in France, it could lead people to think that the hunger suffered by themselves and their families was due to political misjudgements by their supposed 'betters' and/or to a defective system of government which should be remedied even at the risk of their own lives. The chance that the French 'contagion' might spread to Britain was enhanced by the publication in two parts (March 1791 and February 1792, virtually coinciding with Pitt's fate-tempting budget speech) of Thomas Paine's *Rights of Man*. This was a classic expression of radical liberalism in accessible prose, sold at an affordable price.

Pitt's response to this perceived threat has divided historians ever since, albeit into very unequal camps. The majority have accused him of turning from a mild 'progressive' into a bloodthirsty 'reactionary' who was happy to preside over a British 'Reign of Terror' despite the radical skeletons in his own cupboard. Others, notably John Ehrman, have acknowledged a change in Pitt's approach to domestic politics with a twinge of regret rather than a howl of anger; the second volume of Ehrman's compendious biography of Pitt was duly entitled *The Reluctant Transition*. The debate has been bedevilled by an understandable tendency among historians to regard the champions of universal suffrage as heroes whose motives should not be subjected to close scrutiny, and to deplore anyone who tried to bar the path towards political equality. In this story Pitt was an obvious villain because he changed sides, having advocated parliamentary reform in the early 1780s and later openly rejected it, even before the French Revolution.

It is in fact highly probable that Pitt was sincere when he argued that he had merely suspended his own support for franchise reform but thought that those who continued to press the case in dangerous times ran a serious risk of destabilising (rather than 'perfecting') the British constitution. It is indeed even possible that, as his eccentric niece Hester Stanhope later reported, Pitt thought Paine to have had the better of his argument with Burke, although he was talking of arguments in the abstract rather than their likely practical impact on Britain in the 1790s.[15] Others felt differently about the contest between Burke and Paine. George III, for example, described the *Reflections* as a book that every gentleman should read – an observation which contrasted sharply with his previous opinion of Burke. This perhaps, was unsurprising since his fellow monarch, Louis XVI, was being reduced to a cipher – brought back to Paris after trying to flee the country in August 1791 and later forced to declare war on behalf of France against the country ruled by his brother-in-law Leopold II.

Thus in the spring of 1792 Pitt was coming under pressure from various influential sources to take some kind of action against British radicals. By the end of May he had done so, after a complex series of events which can still give rise to contrasting interpretations, for in the same month members of the Foxite Opposition were invited to consider the possibility of a major reconstruction of the government, amounting even to the inclusion of their leader in new ministerial arrangements.

On 10 May 1792, Pitt invited Fox's nominal ally the Duke of Portland to Downing Street and presented him with the draft of a Royal Proclamation Against Seditious Writings and Proclamations. This would empower magistrates to hunt down the authors, publishers and propagators of dissident opinions. Portland was strongly supportive of such measures, but quite properly showed the document to colleagues, including Fox, who were likely to take a different view.

This was obviously a calculated move by Pitt, but it seems unnecessary to attribute it to sinister motives. The time had come for the Foxite Opposition to take sides – not because of anything that Pitt had done, but rather because of manoeuvres within its own ranks in response to events in Britain as well as France. In April 1792 a group of aristocratic Foxites had, without Fox's prior agreement, formed a 'Society of the Friends of the People' to press the case for reform. The name of the new body was thought-provoking: who, exactly, were 'the people', and what was the nature of their 'friendship' with privileged politicians like the Eton-educated Charles Grey? Furthermore, the group had chosen to name itself after Jean-Paul Marat's publication *L'Ami du peuple*, which proclaimed Revolution *à l'outrance*, reserving its most ferocious treatment for French reformers whose ideas – though woefully moderate in the contemporary Parisian context – went far beyond the very limited aspirations of the British 'Friends of the People'. In its commitment to radical measures the latter was probably less steadfast than existing groups like the Society for Constitutional Information (originally founded in 1780), and the London Corresponding Society (which held its first meeting in January 1792, just before the appearance of Part II of Paine's *Rights of Man*). But at least it enjoyed parliamentary representation; and Grey promptly brought up the idea of franchise reform at this least propitious of times. He received a predictable reply from Pitt, and his motion went down to inevitable defeat.

A less calculating politician than William Pitt could not have ignored the glaring disunity of the Opposition in its response to the key topic of the day. But the causes of contention among Fox's political friends – the continuing campaign for electoral reform, and attitudes towards the French Revolution – were becoming increasingly disturbing to Pitt himself. There were also practical advantages to be gained if the government put out feelers towards members of the Opposition. According to many historians of the 'Whiggish' school, attempts to divide Fox's followers must, by definition, have been part of a design on Pitt's part to weaken Fox's position. However, the notion of a political realignment was not particularly unsettling for Pitt, who had always tried to hold himself aloof from anything which looked like an organised party; and it was not as if his ministerial ranks were overbrimming with talent. If Portland and those who thought like him agreed with Pitt rather than Fox over the French Revolution – if, indeed, they rivalled George III himself in their hatred of Revolutionary principles – they clearly belonged on the government benches rather than in the same camp as people like Grey.

If Pitt had ever hatched a 'plot' which was chiefly designed to weaken an Opposition which was feeble enough already, it thickened considerably a few days after he had shown Portland the draft proclamation. Lord Chancellor Thurlow had finally overstretched the limits of Pitt's patience on 8 March 1792 by flaunting his support for the slave trade, suggesting that even the compromise position which Pitt had adopted was too radical to contemplate. On 14 May Thurlow went further, attacking the financial policy of his own government. Two days later Pitt sent Thurlow a magnificent letter of dismissal, telling his repellent colleague that he was taking

> the earliest opportunity of acquainting your lordship, that being convinced of the impossibility of his majesty's service being any longer carried on to advantage, while your lordship and myself both remain in our present situations, I have felt it my duty to submit that

opinion to his majesty, humbly requesting his majesty's determination thereupon.[16]

His Majesty, unsurprisingly but grudgingly, sided with Pitt. Thus a very important (and extremely welcome) vacancy had arisen within the government, in the midst of discussions about a more general reconstruction. As it happened, the Opposition ranks included a well-qualified replacement for Thurlow in the shape of Lord Loughborough, who in his previous guise as Alexander Wedderburn had previously served as Attorney General. Loughborough was very eager to join Pitt's government; and if Portland and his closest adherents had followed their inclinations they would also have made themselves available. To reassure any of Fox's followers who suspected him of ulterior motives, Pitt affirmed that there was 'Nothing which could induce him, upon any *personal ground*, to exclude Fox from a share in the government'.[17] When consulted, Fox indicated that he 'was a friend to coalition', but laid down two conditions that Pitt would be unlikely to meet. One was that Pitt should resign his post and consent to serving with Fox under another leader. The second was that George III must be made aware of these initiatives and would have no vetoes or objections to impose. Both an intermediary, the Duke of Leeds (the former Foreign Secretary), and later Pitt himself reported this to the King, and 'predictably found the royal response chilly, with Leeds concluding that the King's "dislike" of Fox remained in full force'.[18]

Despite their increasing alienation from Fox's attitude towards the French Revolution, Portland and his allies felt unable at this time to accept office while their leader was *persona non grata*, so the initiative collapsed. Loughborough did become Lord Chancellor, but not until January 1793.

Thus, far from trying to create divisions in the Opposition ranks for his own purposes, Pitt was merely responding to a schism which existed already. Even so, the instrument which was chosen to help politicians to join the sides which they had already taken in spirit if not in practice – the Royal Proclamation of May 1792, against 'wicked and seditious writings' – stands as an indelible stain on Pitt's record. Under its influence the publisher Richard Phillips was jailed for 18 months; in May 1793 the Winchester-educated lawyer John Frost received the same sentence, as well as being forced to stand in the pillory. The proclamation was obviously directed against Thomas Paine, who had been a friendly correspondent of Edmund Burke when both men had sided with the American rebels but whose subsequent writings had now proved far too persuasive for his own good. At least Paine was luckier than Louis XVI: fleeing to France (with official connivance) before he could be tried for the common law offence of seditious libel – or lynched by members of the public who regarded him as an outlaw – he was found guilty *in absentia* and burned in effigy. Elected to the French National Assembly, Paine spoke against the imposition of the death penalty on Louis XVI; his speech was interrupted more than once by the leading French 'Friend of the People', Marat, and it was only by chance that he escaped 'Revolutionary justice'.[19]

The case of John Frost makes life particularly difficult for those who seek to defend Pitt's integrity, since Frost had cooperated with Pitt in the 1780s, when it was possible to regard campaigns for a more rational electoral system as public-spirited rather than treacherous. After being reported to have exclaimed 'Equality, and No King' during a drunken ale-house argument, Frost accompanied Paine to Paris where, like his friend, he was elected as a deputy to the National Convention. After learning of the allegations against him, the British government encouraged Frost to extend his stay indefinitely, rather than returning to face a trial which would be highly embarrassing for Pitt. It is probably significant that John Ehrman, who extends sympathy towards Pitt wherever possible, mentions Frost only in passing and says nothing about their earlier acquaintance.[20] Certainly if double standards had been made a crime Pitt's guilt would have been more palpable than that of most people who were charged with 'sedition' during these years. If he felt any misgivings about the prosecutions which followed the suspension of long-established liberties, he made sure that he never betrayed them, to the extent of condoning interventions in the judicial process in order to secure the conviction of individuals on trial for their lives. Those who continue to defend Pitt against this weight of evidence can only argue that public opinion in general had become sharply 'reactionary', and that he felt it his duty to reflect this mood to some extent on the assumption that if he resigned he would be replaced by someone who was even less scrupulous.

Pitt's decisions and conduct could be defended more stoutly if the seditious practices proclamation of May 1792 had been issued *after* the appearance of an even more fateful document. In 1791 the Austrians and Prussians had responded to the growing personal threat to Louis XVI by threatening France with retaliation should the French royal family come to any harm. The wily Austrians, however, stipulated that intervention would only take place if all the major European powers joined the enterprise; since they were well aware that Pitt wanted to keep Britain out of any conflict, this amounted to no more than crowd-pleasing rhetoric. However, in July 1792 the Prussian Duke of Brunswick addressed a 'manifesto' to the French people, pledging to restore monarchical rule by military force and threatening that Paris would be razed to the ground 'if a hair of King Louis XVI's head was touched'.[21] The defiant answer was almost instantaneous. In August the Tuileries Palace was stormed and the royal family incarcerated; in the following month, more than a thousand suspected 'counter-revolutionaries' were slaughtered in Paris. Apart from sending the Revolution into a further spiral of depravity, Brunswick had unwittingly encouraged the French people to equate radical ideas with patriotism. Volunteers from all over France flocked to Valmy, a small town halfway between Verdun and Paris, where, under the leadership of Generals Kellermann and Dumouriez, they prepared to make a desperate last stand. Against all expectation, they routed the Prussians, who retreated in disorder back into Germany. The French victory was ascribed to the *élan* of the volunteers, but the decisive factor may well have been the superior skill of the French artillery corps, made up of professional soldiers from the former royal army.[22] The young Goethe, who was with the dejected Prussian troops, tried to cheer them up by declaring 'Here and now begins a new epoch in world history, and you can say that you were there.'[23]

Fox was ecstatic at the French victory, writing to Holland:

You must be almost as much rejoiced [at the Prussians'] flight as I am. No! no public event, not excepting Saratoga and York Town [i.e. the two major British defeats in the American War], ever happened that gave me so much delight. I would not allow myself to believe it for some days for fear of disappointment.[24]

Brunswick's manifesto had also invited French Revolutionary leaders to repay him in the same coin; if he felt justified in imposing a regime by force, they could promise armed assistance to dissident groups around Europe. The only surprise was the delay before the French issued their own edict to this effect; they did not do so until November 1792, but even before this the Revolution had become a general menace rather than an exclusively French problem. King Louis's trial commenced a few weeks later.

By December 1792 the British government faced a new problem, since refugees from France were arriving in their thousands and no one could be certain that all of the migrants were coming in peace. Grenville duly introduced an aliens bill in the House of Lords, the aim of which was to provide for the registration of refugees and which would, in practice, give the government a licence to deport any 'undesirable' elements. It was during the Commons debate on this subject that Edmund Burke, now imagining himself as the prime target for Revolutionary plotters at home and abroad, brandished a dagger, which was part of a much larger consignment ordered by France.

At least Burke had drawn the dagger against France; Pitt, by contrast, had up to this time confined his aggressive gestures to the repression of freethinking members of the British population. There were, though, clear signs that the government would be forced to abandon its ostensible neutrality towards the Revolution itself. Amidst the increasing violence in Paris, Britain had effectively broken off diplomatic relations in August 1792, recalling its own ambassador and denying official accreditation to his counterpart, Chauvelin. Some have seen this as a petty and provocative gesture, but official diplomatic activity at the time revolved around royal courts; the French one had ceased to exist, and it was asking rather a lot of George III to receive the representative of a country which had shown contempt for monarchy. More importantly, it was increasingly difficult to identify an individual who could speak with authority for the faction-ridden French politicians; and in any case, in September 1792 the British government still expected the speedy restoration of full royal authority in France, thanks to the Austro-Prussian intervention. Unofficial contacts with Paris continued, but it is difficult to see how peace could have been maintained even through orthodox channels.

Pitt still hoped for his usual preferred outcome – a general settlement without any territorial changes – but successful mediation was unlikely when any French politician who made conciliatory noises was immediately suspected of treachery. A spectacular example was the career of General Dumouriez, who, having commanded French forces in a successful encounter with the Austrians at Jemappes in November 1792, returned to Paris and tried to save the King from execution. By April 1793 he was a marked man, and after trying to persuade his troops to march against his former Jacobin friends in Paris he defected to the Austrians.

Dumouriez's victory at Jemappes enabled the French to occupy the Austrian Netherlands. As we have seen, the maintenance of Austrian rule in this key area was a major objective for Pitt, since it was regarded as a much better option than independence, which threatened to result in French domination. Now the long-feared French control had been established. As a result, although Fox continued to argue that the government had failed to exhaust its diplomatic resources, conflict was inevitable; from the perspective of Pitt and his colleagues, the execution of the hapless Louis on 21 January 1793 only served as a vivid illustration of the reasons why amicable coexistence between Britain and France was no longer possible. In fact it was France which declared war, on 1 February, after cutting off trade links with Britain and approving an attack on Holland.

On the same day, before the news had been received in London, Pitt explained the situation to MPs, justifying the government's decisions and attacking the 'abominable and detestable principles' of the Revolution before discussing the practical considerations relating to Holland and the Austrian Netherlands.[25] This was an understandable order of debating priorities, not least because it provided Pitt with an opportunity to extol the virtues of the British constitution which, he asserted, was a perfect blend of liberty and stability. By basing his argument on ideological considerations, however, he played into the hands of his enemies, who wanted to portray this as *primarily* a war of opinions, obscuring the extent to which the government regarded it as a new version of the traditional struggle to maintain a satisfactory balance of power in Europe.

That impression was reinforced in Pitt's speech to mark the opening of hostilities, on 12 February:

It now remains to be seen whether, under Providence, the efforts of a free, brave, loyal, and happy people, aided by their allies, will not be successful in checking the progress of a system, the principles of which, if not opposed, threaten the most fatal consequences to the tranquillity of this country, the security of its allies, the good order of every European government, and the happiness of the human race![26]

It did not take the mindset of an Edmund Burke to read this as a declaration that the British would refuse to make peace with France until it had abandoned its Republican experiment and reclaimed its place in the big, happy family of European monarchies.

Fox was shocked that the government had drifted into war with France without making any serious diplomatic effort to avoid it, in particular by attempting to ensure guarantees for the independence of Holland. When war was declared, he made a last-ditch effort to force the government to seek a peaceful settlement before actual hostilities broke out. He secured a parliamentary debate, where he set out a comprehensive case for negotiating about Britain's legitimate concerns directly with France and not associating with the despotic monarchs of Europe in their attempt to suppress the revolution and restore the Bourbons. The House listened to Fox's arguments, but – infected by growing war fever – proceeded to reject his motion by 270 votes to 44. There were well over a hundred Whig MPs, and this showed that Fox had already lost the allegiance of over half of them. A final split in the party now seemed inevitable.

He was unable to prevent Britain from entering the war, but over the following decade Fox distinguished himself by a determined effort to resist government attempts to curb civil liberties. Responding to widespread hysteria – based on virtually no evidence – that an armed uprising was being prepared by British sympathisers of the Jacobins, to be backed by a French invasion, the government introduced a series of repressive measures. These included the suspension of habeas corpus (in 1794), and, in the following year, two acts which tightened the law on treason and clamped down on 'seditious' meetings. The weight of these fell not on dangerous conspirators, who were few and far between, but much more usually on peaceful advocates of electoral and other reforms. These included supporters of the Society of the Friends of the People, and the more working class-based London Corresponding Society, led by Thomas Hardy, a shoemaker. The LCS, which was replicated by similar bodies in a dozen or so English and Scottish towns, put forward six demands for constitutional reforms (which were to be taken up by the Chartist movement four decades later and all but one of which were later incorporated in British law). These were universal male suffrage, the abolition of property qualifications for MPs, equal electoral districts, the payment of MPs, annual parliaments and the secret ballot. Fox did not himself agree with most or all of these, but was appalled that people could be charged with treason merely for advocating them. It was in Scotland that the worst effects of the new legislation were felt, in a series of trials in which severe sentences were handed out. The most notorious of these, in August and September 1793, were of Thomas Muir, a church elder, and the Reverend Thomas Palmer, a Unitarian minister, who were charged, respectively, with treason and sedition. The principal evidence against Palmer was that he had ordered the printing of 1,000 copies of a handbill of which he was not the author. This was 'no more than a complaint against the government for the extravagant war taxation in which the country had been involved, and a claim for universal suffrage and short parliaments'.[27]

The charges against Muir were more wide-ranging. He was accused of 'inciting disaffection by seditious speeches, and of advising the purchase and reading of seditious publications such as Paine's *Rights of Man* and of publicly reading out such seditious writings as the address of the United Irishmen'.[28]

Both men were found guilty and were sentenced, respectively, to seven and 14 years transportation to Australia. In the meantime, they were conveyed to London, put in irons and subjected for three months to hard labour with common criminals in the insanitary conditions of decaying prison hulks. Neither of them was able to return to Britain, and, broken in health, they died miserably, one in France aged 34, and the other aged 55 in the remote Pacific island of Guguan, in the Marianas, then under

Spanish control. Fox vigorously attacked their prosecution, writing to his nephew, Lord Holland, comparing the trials to those of the Committee of Public Safety in Paris:

> I do not think any of the French *soi-disant* proceedings surpass in injustice and contempt of law than those in Scotland [...] Good God! That a man should be sent to Botany Bay for advising another to read Paine's book, or for reading the Irish address to a public meeting![29]

Fox repeatedly raised the plight of Muir and Palmer and other 'Scottish martyrs' in the Commons, as did his friend, Lord Lauderdale in the Lords, to no avail, and pointedly went to the prison hulk to dine with them on the night before they sailed. In London, there were similar trials, but not all of them went the way the authorities intended. In the most famous of these, the famous radical and former clergyman John Horne Tooke and several other defendants, including Thomas Hardy of the LCS, were arraigned. They were charged with high treason, and part of the evidence against them was proposals they had made for electoral reform. Tooke succeeded in obtaining a subpoena against William Pitt, and the prime minister reluctantly admitted, under oath, that the reforms proposed bore a striking resemblance to those he had put forward in his own unsuccessful bill a decade earlier. It took the jury a mere eight minutes to acquit all the defendants. Those in other trials were less fortunate, but in an effort to put these into proportion the historian, John Derry, wrote:

> Pitt and Portland [who became Home Secretary in 1794] did not preside over anything like a reign of terror. Something like a total of 200 prosecutions over a period of ten years hardly merits such a description. Many of the cases ended in acquittal or the charges being dropped and the proceedings being discontinued. The pressure of convention and the weight of public opinion achieved more in damping down radicalism than either the Seditious Meetings Act or the Treasonable Practices Act. With the ascendancy of loyalism and the popular identification of radicalism with Jacobinism, radicals suffered more from the prejudices of the community than from the force of law.[30]

Nevertheless, modern readers are likely to conclude that 200 prosecutions were 200 too many, and it was perhaps only his fame and his membership of the Commons which prevented Fox, who was widely depicted as a traitor, from being prosecuted himself.

13

The Younger Pitt as War Leader

ALTHOUGH Pitt was confident that Britain's involvement in the war against Revolutionary France would be short and successful, he certainly did not welcome the prospect. Indeed, some of his speeches in the early stages of the war read like attempts to reassure himself, as much as his hearers, that he had done everything he could to keep his country out of the conflict.

Even Pitt, with his natural optimism and inability to distinguish between troop numbers on paper and fully trained personnel in the field, knew that Britain could not defeat France without assistance of some kind. The British navy could – and did – provide morale-boosting victories which punctuated the 1790s: 'The Glorious First of June' (1794; this in fact was less than completely 'glorious' because French supply ships reached their destination); Cape St Vincent (1797, against the Spanish fleet); Camperdown in the same year, against the Dutch; and Nelson's great victory over the French at Aboukir Bay ('The Battle of the Nile') in August 1798.

However, confirmation of Britannia's rule over the waves was never likely in itself to bring a continental power to submission; this result would require action on land. Although Britain was hardly short of manpower, raising the kind of force which might match the French *levée en masse* was ruled out by the long-held British suspicion of standing armies. In truth, Pitt had practical reasons to keep military recruitment within limits. A flood of willing recruits to the armed forces would impair economic activity, but it would also bring into being a force which (as in the seventeenth century Civil Wars) might easily fall prey to radical propaganda and become a greater danger to government than the French themselves. Equally, a substantial army animated by loyalty to 'Church and King' might become an instrument of 'reaction', putting the scenes Pitt had witnessed during the Gordon Riots of 1780 comprehensively in the shade. Whether or not Pitt should himself be tarred with the 'reactionary' brush, he certainly cannot be accused of wanting to unleash the atavistic forces of 'Church and King' mobs on British dissidents, as had happened in the Birmingham riots of July 1791, directed mainly against the distinguished scientist and political radical, Joseph Priestley.

There was a good chance that Britain's most effective auxiliaries would come from France's own dissidents – either from faction-ridden Paris or from those provincial areas which had never embraced Revolutionary principles. More likely, France's fighting spirit would be sapped by economic malaise, as war on this scale decimated its trade and turned its paper currency – the *assignat*, introduced in 1789 – into papier mâché. If France did not succumb to the problems which, in Pitt's view, it had brought on itself when it embarked on a revolutionary course, the concerted efforts of other European powers would bring it to its senses. From the perspective of the British government, if France had become a monstrous menace to the peace of Europe, Prussia and Austria had played a considerable part in bringing it into existence. Initially it seemed that these states, goaded into action by a desire to stamp out revolutionary principles and to protect the idea of monarchy as personified by Louis XVI and Marie Antoinette, would overwhelm France. If that had been their motive for aggression against the Revolution in 1792, surely it would have been compounded by Louis's execution in January 1793 and the increasing threat to the life of Marie Antoinette, which had culminated in her own judicial murder that October?

Thus when Pitt finally accepted that war was inevitable, it seemed equally obvious that the Revolution would be defeated. It was just a matter of how quickly it would succumb, and whether the instrument of defeat would be plan A, B or C. Indeed, when historians follow Thomas Babington Macaulay in judging that Pitt proved an unsatisfactory war leader, it is even more tempting than usual to ask whether they – or anyone else – could have fared much better.[1] Plan A failed because by the time that Britain joined the war, support for the French Revolution had become a matter of patriotic resistance to ruthless aggressors. As a result, those who decided to take up arms in defence of the monarchical principle (in places like Toulon or the Vendée) tended to be the most extreme representatives of that view, and thus highly suspect to a British government which was extremely reluctant to endorse a return to the unpalatable status quo which had sparked off the trouble in the first place. To French patriots, of course, such rebels were double-dyed traitors – the sin of taking up arms against the Revolution was compounded by their cooperation with Britain, the traditional national foe.

The British failure to sustain Royalist resistance in Toulon was particularly ominous for anyone hoping for a quick French capitulation. After a siege of three months, the city was forced to surrender to the Revolutionary forces in December 1793 thanks to the inspired tactics of a young Corsican-born artillery captain, Napoleon Bonaparte. However, the episode was not a complete fiasco, since the British were able to destroy or capture 26 French ships of the line – about a third of the country's naval strength. While understandably excited by civil unrest in France as a potential shortcut to victory, Pitt always pinned more faith on plan B – the collapse of the French economy under the twin strains of governmental mismanagement and the demands of war. It was not surprising that Pitt emphasised the economic aspects of warfare, given his ministerial experience and his knowledge of France's plight even before the outbreak of the Revolution. However, the French found the resources to keep on fighting, in defiance of Pitt's regular predictions and the theories of Adam Smith. They might have destroyed the *Ancien Régime*, but the Revolutionaries were able to exploit the old political culture of centralised, arbitrary rule, enabling them to incorporate heavy taxation and outright confiscation in their understanding of the words *liberté, égalité, fraternité*. French armies were perfectly willing to extend this approach to 'liberated' peoples. Thus, in place of Adam Smith's 'invisible hand', France wielded a very tangible iron fist which could make wars of conquest self-financing, if not sources of considerable profit.

Pitt was certainly not oblivious to the potential economic advantages associated with war. Thanks to Britain's naval dominance, he could contemplate the acquisition of distant enemy-controlled territories either to erode hostile trading networks, to enhance Britain's own position, or for the simultaneous satisfaction of both of these desirable ends. Captured French colonies, especially in the West Indies, could also be used as bargaining counters in the ensuing peace negotiations. In this sense, whenever France attracted a new ally Britain's loss in terms of the European 'balance of power' produced potential gains in the wider world. Thus Dutch possessions in South Africa and Ceylon were captured in 1795–6, after Holland itself had fallen under French control. By 1796 France had forced Spain to become an ally rather than an enemy, whereupon Britain promptly annexed the Spanish island of Trinidad, in 1797.

Unfortunately for the British, such conquests could scarcely be regarded as low-hanging fruit. Their forays were not invariably successful, and proved a considerable drain on human resources (even if most of the casualties were claimed by disease rather than combat). Even missions which returned without heavy losses represented major commitments of manpower for many months, during which time they could have been used with greater effect in different theatres. Logistical issues of this kind were, of course, nothing new, and Pitt's father had faced them during his own stewardship of a far-flung British war effort. The difference was that the younger Pitt operated within a much more volatile context of rapidly shifting European alliances and sudden changes of military fortunes. What had been a serious handicap for the elder Pitt was a crippling disadvantage for his son.

The impossibility of rapid communication even between the various courts of Europe was not the only reason why Pitt failed in his attempts to build coalitions capable of defeating the French in practice rather than on paper. If Britain's potential allies had been trustworthy, logistics probably would not have made much difference; in practice, the violent spasm of sympathy exhibited by the rulers of Austria and Prussia in response to the various insults offered to Louis XVI and Marie Antoinette was soon balanced by narrow calculations of national self-interest. For both states, these suggested that Central and Eastern Europe were more important than anything that might happen in the west of the continent, and that, if anything, the primary interest of Austria and Prussia lay in the struggle for supremacy in Germany. This overriding concern was illustrated by Austria's persistent desire to wash its hands of its territories in the Netherlands in exchange for control of the South German Electorate of Bavaria. For both Prussia and Austria, therefore, the priority in the war against France was to avoid overcommitment to either side, in case they turned out to have backed the wrong horse. Meanwhile, they felt relatively free to partition Poland, joining forces with Russia – whose behaviour was even less amenable to accurate prediction given its distance from the main scenes of action and the eccentricities of its autocratic rulers.

Pitt was thus forced to deal with states which, like school bullies, had started a fight in one corner of the European playground and then looked around for someone weaker to pick on. The only recourse, for Pitt, was to bolster anti-French alliances with subsidies (more accurately described as bribes). The first of many disbursements came in 1793, when the British government agreed to provide Piedmont-Sardinia with £150,000 per year. In 1794 Prussia was granted £1.2 million. Along with direct subsidies, Britain underwrote loans, such as the £4.6 million which the Austrians raised in 1795. More than two decades after the first outbreak of hostilities, this 'war of the purse' paid off, but in an important sense it marked a kind of defeat. It certainly was not without risks. Although the British attached conditions to their support, it was difficult to establish (let alone monitor) anything like a system of 'payment by results'; the usual formula was that a certain sum would be granted in return for a specified number of troops, but there was always a danger that countries which were less squeamish than Britain about 'standing armies' would merely use the cash to pay personnel who were never intended for action against the French. Whenever the fortunes of war were turning against Britain, difficulties of this kind became even more acute; the greater the country's need for allies, the less likely the prospects of getting value for money. There was even a possibility that an 'ally' would pocket a subsidy and promptly sue the French for peace. In 1795, indeed, Pitt was working to facilitate a further payment to Prussia right up until news arrived that it had agreed to stop fighting.[2]

By that time Pitt himself was coming under serious pressure to reach an accommodation with France. On 30 December 1794 his friend Wilberforce moved an amendment to the King's Speech, urging the government to negotiate for a settlement 'on such terms as should be deemed just and reasonable'. Although Pitt was deeply upset by Wilberforce's move, the wording of the amendment was a gift for any half-decent debater; the obvious retort was that there was currently no prospect of a 'just and reasonable' settlement, so that an approach to France would merely be an admission of weakness. In the circumstances the margin of Wilberforce's defeat – by 246 to 73 – was surprisingly slender, and a signal to Pitt that he could not take parliamentary support for granted, despite the recent addition of the Portland Whigs to the ministerial ranks.

It was not until July 1794 that Portland and many other leading Whigs girded themselves up finally to sunder their ties with Fox. They drove a hard bargain with Pitt:

[t]he alliance could not have been arranged without Pitt's generous offer of five places in the cabinet, five peerages and one promotion in the peerage, [...] a pension for Burke, two offices in the royal household, the lord lieutenancy of Middlesex, and the promise of the lord lieutenancy of Ireland.[3]

Some of Pitt's supporters criticised him for ceding too much, fearing he would lose control of his own Cabinet, as six of its thirteen Members were now his former political opponents (including Chancellor Loughborough).[4] Pitt was careful to keep the main portfolios in the hands of his own loyalists, and effectively ran an 'inner Cabinet', consisting of himself, his cousin Lord Grenville and Henry Dundas, the Secretary at War, who together took all important decisions. However, the overall ethos of the Pitt government was bound to be affected by the inclusion of colleagues who were generally more 'hawkish' concerning the prosecution of the war and less scrupulous about the methods of repressing domestic dissent. Although Edmund Burke had retired from the Commons in the previous election, he was still a potent influence over Portland and his colleagues, always ready to refresh their commitment to a struggle which could only end when the French had been forced to reaffirm their loyalty to a monarchical system. Portland succeeded in bringing over 62 MPs to the government side, leaving the

Foxites with no more than 55 MPs, a number which was soon to shrink even further. Fox was more affected by the personal loss of so many old friends than by the political damage which their defection had caused, writing to Elizabeth Armitstead that he '[c]ould not help loving the D. of P[ortland], and if with him the D. of D[evonshire] and Ld. Fi[tzwilliam] are to go I never can have any comfort in Politics again.'[5] Although he had lost more than half of his supporters, those who remained with him were fanatically loyal. 'There are only forty of them,' said Lord Thurlow, 'but every one of them was ready to be hanged for Fox.'[6]

While there were advantages in bringing Portland and his friends into the government, there was always a possibility that they would prove just as unhelpful as Pitt's supposed allies in Austria, Prussia and Russia. This made it more difficult for Pitt to act on his more flexible approach to the conflict. He decided to put out feelers towards the French early in 1796, but the new government in Paris (the *Directoire*) dashed his hopes of constructive conversations by demanding the retention of all French conquests (including by this time, crucially, the Austrian Netherlands), while Britain would have to relinquish its gains in Corsica and the West Indies. From Pitt's perspective the *Directoire*'s unreasonable attitude could be regarded as helpful – it certainly lent support to the arguments he had used against Wilberforce's amendment back in December 1794. However, the fact that the government had contemplated negotiations in the first place enraged Edmund Burke, who composed the first of two *Letters on a Regicide Peace*. The letters were published in October 1796 – the month in which the experienced British diplomat (and former Fox ally) the Earl of Malmesbury embarked on more serious talks in Paris.

By that time the war had taken a more promising turn, not least because the Austrians had appointed an energetic commander (the Archduke Charles) and the Russians seemed finally to have decided that the war in the West was worth winning. As a result, while Edmund Burke thought that any deal agreed at this time was bound to be a national humiliation, Malmesbury's instructions were entirely compatible with Pitt's original aims. Broadly speaking, territorial arrangements in Europe would return to their pre-war condition; in particular, the French should give up the Austrian Netherlands and their gains in northern Italy and Germany.

While Britain would return conquered French islands in the West Indies, it would keep Ceylon and the Cape of Good Hope, which had been taken from the Dutch.

Far from being a shameful 'regicide' peace, this, from the British point of view, was a 'realist' proposal based on a recognition that Louis XVI could not be brought back to life and that the absolutist French monarchy had died with him. However, a return to something like the territorial status quo in Europe was never likely to satisfy a post-Revolutionary French government, even if it had exhausted some of its original revolutionary impetus. As it was, negotiations were brought to an end by the arrival of news that Catherine the Great of Russia had died on 17 November 1796. While Catherine's interpretation of Russian interests had made her a suboptimal ally in the war against France, her successor Paul I was even less predictable, and commenced his reign by withdrawing his mother's promise to contribute 60,000 troops to the war effort. Burke had remarked that Malmesbury's diplomatic activities had progressed slowly because he had travelled to Paris 'on his knees'.[7] Malmesbury's return journey was much quicker; the *Directoire* gave him just two days to quit the French capital.

On 30 December 1796, Pitt invited the House of Commons to share his 'deep and poignant regret' that the peace initiative had failed. The government's proposals, he claimed, had been 'dictated by a principle of moderation, of disinterestedness, and earnest desire for peace'.[8] Clearly, then, the breakdown of negotiations could only be the fault of the French; and MPs could be expected to suspend their judgement amid a general howl of patriotic outrage. Nevertheless, some of Pitt's remarks looked curious on close analysis. For example, in the course of a single sentence he denied that Britain had 'nothing to ask for herself', but then made a virtue of the country's willingness 'to surrender a considerable part, nay, almost the whole of her acquisitions'. Britain, it seemed on this showing, would never ask, but was perfectly willing to take. Although the early part of his argument suggested that the present French government was wholly unsuited to constructive discussions, Pitt invited the House to consider the failed talks in the light of 'a dormant negociation [*sic*], capable of being renewed'.[9]

At least Pitt's disappointment at the end of 1796 was mingled with relief, since a French fleet which had been sent to stir up civil unrest in Ireland encountered bad weather and was forced to retreat without effecting a landing. But even this news conveyed a mixed message, since it illustrated both British vulnerability and French audacity. For Pitt things were about to get much worse, both politically and personally.

If they want to present a comprehensible picture, biographers have to impose on their materials a thematic structure which bears little relation to the real experiences of their subjects, who typically had to deal with a variety of issues at once. Some accounts suggest that Pitt the Younger would have been a more successful prime minister if he could have dealt with major issues consecutively – a week devoted exclusively to the economy, say, followed by a fortnight on foreign policy – and that his inability to 'multitask' led to policy mistakes and costly decision-making delays. These criticisms overlook the fact that he was facing unprecedented challenges with very traditional levels of administrative support. In effect, he was trying to oversee both domestic and foreign policy during a world war, with resources which had barely been adequate for less interventionist prime ministers in tranquil times.

In addition to the daily assault from public events, Pitt had a pressing personal issue on his mind in the first weeks of 1797. It is remarkable that while Fox's hyperactive love life seemed to be accepted during his lifetime (and later) as an inevitable corollary of the magnetism he exercised over his male friends, Pitt's only recorded romantic interlude has given rise to considerable speculation. On 20 January 1797 he wrote a letter to Lord Auckland, making it clear that he did not intend to make an offer of marriage to Auckland's daughter, Eleanor. He acknowledged that he had thought about doing so, but on reflection had encountered obstacles which were 'decisive and insurmountable'. In the unfortunate event that Eleanor had experienced similar emotions, he trusted Auckland to break the news gently.[10]

Whatever the state of Eleanor's feelings, Auckland was unwilling to be jilted as Pitt's prospective father-in-law; and Pitt's letter had given him a pretext to continue the correspondence, since the 'decisive and insurmountable' difficulties had not been explained. Auckland guessed that these were financial in nature, and while accepting that there was a problem – he himself was in no position to augment Eleanor's modest inheritance – he argued that money should not be allowed to 'affect the ultimate result'. Pitt had to undertake the 'trying but indispensable duty' of writing again, to put an end to Auckland's hopes. Again, however, he declined to give a detailed explanation of his irrevocable decision.[11]

Inevitably, Pitt's biographers have tried to compensate for his reticence by canvassing various reasons for his rejection of matrimony. It has even been suggested that these related to 'sexual incapacity or deviation' rather than his bank balance. Pitt, in other words, was gay, although 'he suppressed his desires well enough to leave no positive evidence of the fact'.[12] This style of argument could easily be used to support a very different conclusion – that Pitt was a raging heterosexual who 'suppressed his desires well enough to leave no positive evidence of the fact'. Equally, he might not have felt much physical attraction of any kind. This, indeed, is what the 'evidence' (such as it is) suggests, and William Hague alights on this as the main reason why Pitt did not marry Eleanor Eden.[13] But this implies that physical desire was a crucial factor among the reasons for marriage among representatives of Pitt's social class. Pitt's immediate family includes two examples which suggest different impulses: his own father only tied the knot on the day after his 46th birthday, when he married someone he had known well for two decades, and in 1783, at the age of 26, his brother John (the second and last Earl of Chatham) embarked on a marriage which lasted almost forty years but produced no children.

The most likely explanation of this abortive intervention by Cupid was advanced by Pitt himself, in a reported conversation years after the event. To William Hague, his remarks 'sound like the arguments of a man making excuses rather than one reluctantly abandoning a passionate love'.[14] Quite so: but if 'passionate love' was not necessarily the motivating factor of eighteenth-century marriages, the arguments sound much less like excuses. What Pitt was trying to explain was why, having found Eleanor Eden's company sufficiently congenial to raise the possibility of a marriage proposal, he decided not to ask her to become a permanent fixture in his life. When thinking of a wife primarily as a partner in a shared project whose central aim was continued and if possible increased political success, Pitt must have considered whether Eleanor Eden fitted his requirements as completely as his mother, who had proved indispensable to his father in so many ways. The comparison could be seen as flattering to Eleanor as a person, but distinctly unhelpful to the prospect of marriage. In Pitt's reported words to his niece, Lady Hester Stanhope, 'she was not a woman to be left at will when business might require it' – that is, if they got married he would find it difficult to persuade Eleanor that his job would always take priority over their own relationship. In case this explanation had been too opaque for his listeners, Pitt attempted to summarise it with clichés – 'he sacrificed his feelings to a sense of public duty', and 'for my King's and the country's sake, I must remain a single man.' He also referred to Eleanor's irritating family, singling out her mother for criticism (although, on the basis of the correspondence of January 1797, Pitt could be forgiven for baulking at the prospect of connecting himself so closely with Eleanor's *father*).

Dismissing the idea that the pressure of 'business' was a key consideration for Pitt, Hague argues that 'hard-working as he was, it is clear that Pitt had sufficient time to enjoy friendships and recreations if he wanted to.'[15] Yet, as suggested above, Pitt worked in a way which combined a laser-like focus on crucial matters with a brutal disregard for secondary considerations, a trait which often rebounded on him when the business which he had consigned to the 'secondary' category turned out to be more important than he had thought. His desk was a chaos of unanswered letters from correspondents who had reason to consider their business as urgent. If he had been a creature of routine, he would have kept at least a modicum of control over his personal finances – and thus, ironically, would have been in a better position in at least one respect to contemplate marriage. But for Pitt, the prospect of marriage threatened to introduce a jarring element of order into his essentially anarchical approach to his official duties – the same approach which, occasionally, enabled him to carve out some breathing space in which to 'enjoy friendships and recreations'.

The carefree dalliance with Auckland and his family in the winter of 1796 was untypical. Normally Pitt tried to combine 'friendships and recreations' with business, most frequently in the company of Henry Dundas, with whom he seems to have spent considerable time alone and drinking copiously (without giving rise to speculation that the very happily married Dundas was an object of his romantic interest). By January 1797 Pitt had been prime minister for more than thirteen years and had developed a style of decision making on the basis of what was essentially a bachelor's lifestyle. In any case, if he needed reassurance, he could always call on the same person who had performed this service for his father: Lady Chatham, who was still very much alive in 1797. A comparison of the letters which passed between the elder and younger Pitt and the former Hester Grenville is highly instructive. The elder tended to report things like 'Everything is going well, and I can't wait to see you so I can tell you about it,' while the son's version was 'In case you haven't heard by now, I have done pretty well.' Pitt the Younger and his mother did see each other occasionally after he became prime minister, but they certainly did not exert themselves to ensure regular meetings. The younger Pitt seemed to like things this way, feeling that his mother would be more than satisfied if she could hear reports which signified that he had lived up to the expectations of both of his parents. If anything, physical propinquity might reduce the effect of stories heard at second hand. If Pitt felt this way about his mother, he was unlikely to suppose that marriage would help him through his various trials. In other words, although it took him a long time to admit it to himself, the elder Pitt was not emotionally self-sufficient. At least partly because of his training, his son never seemed to need validation from any external source; and, as such, there were no obvious gains to set against the perceived disadvantages of abandoning his established lifestyle.

Pitt had only just extricated himself from this personal embarrassment when he was confronted with a political problem which threatened to destroy his strategy as a war leader. The French intention to take the war to the British Isles, signalled by the abortive expedition to Bantry Bay, was given further confirmation on 22 February 1797, when an assorted body of around a thousand men landed near Fishguard in Pembrokeshire. Although they were quickly rounded up by local volunteers, this new evidence of British vulnerability triggered a financial panic, resulting in the speedy passage of the Bank Restriction Act, which meant that banknotes could no longer be redeemed into gold at their face value. Pitt has rightly been praised for taking prompt action which ensured that Britain preserved its reputation for financial probity. Nevertheless, his regular predictions of French military collapse had relied heavily on the enemy's resort to a currency based on paper notes – the *assignat* – and now Britain had been forced to adopt an approach which, while very different in the details, could easily be compared in its essentials.

As Pitt hastened to shore up one indispensable prop to Britain's war effort, the other one suddenly seemed on the verge of giving way in spectacular fashion. Discontent had been growing for some time among naval personnel, whose pay had not advanced in line with the importance of the service (indeed, it had not increased for more than a century). On 15 April 1797 the Channel Fleet disobeyed an order to set sail. The initial negotiations for a settlement were amicable, and the government authorised concessions. However, the deal was not implemented immediately, and the seamen began to suspect that they would be double-crossed. By the time that Pitt brought in a bill to authorise a pay increase, the mutiny in the Channel Fleet had erupted again, this time spreading to other naval forces including part of the North Sea Fleet anchored at the Nore in the Thames Estuary. In contrast to the other mutineers, the crews at the Nore issued more far-reaching demands relating to naval discipline and the appointment of officers. While all of the mutineers had displayed a disconcerting degree of coordination, those at the Nore were prepared to use their skills to blockade London, and even exchanged fire with troops onshore at Tilbury. There were concerns that the contagion would spread from the navy to the army, raising the prospect that Britain would be wracked by internal conflict at a time when its defences against external aggressors were seriously weakened.

Although some commentators, including John Ehrman, have used this episode to insinuate that Pitt was justified in his fears of revolutionary ideology (especially when, as in this case, the rebel ranks included numerous Irishmen), the most notable feature of the 1797 mutinies is the reluctance of sailors on whom British security depended to take full advantage of their bargaining power, and to accept a settlement which ensured that their services would continue to be taken for granted.[16] Having been woken one night by the sound of gunfire from Tilbury, Pitt decided that the time for talking was over. Legislation was introduced which extended the death penalty to anyone who offered assistance to mutineers. By the end of June 1797 more than twenty ringleaders had been hanged, and the government had resumed control of the fleet.

Thus when confronted with dissent either at sea or on land, Pitt had shown once again that he was prepared to be ruthless once he perceived that a line had been crossed. If he had been prepared to send radical propagandists to their deaths when Britain's security was not directly at stake, he would not hesitate to authorise drastic measures against mutineers in the circumstances of May 1797. At that time, an attack from the Dutch navy was confidently expected, and Britain had been left without continental allies after the Austrian agreement at Leoben on 18 April to a provisional treaty with France. This agreement proved that the French general, Bonaparte, was as adept at diplomacy as he had already begun to prove himself as a military commander. The terms, later confirmed by the Treaty of Campo Formio, officially transferred the Austrian Netherlands to French control. Not only was Britain now bereft of effective allies in its struggle against France, but it had already lost the key objective of ensuring that the government of the Netherlands was kept out of hostile hands. To make matters even worse for Pitt, earlier in April he had persuaded George III that Britain should make a new effort to secure a negotiated peace with France. For the British, it was important that a deal should not be secured without proper consultation with its remaining allies; but before negotiations could begin, the country's crucial ally, Austria, had shown far less sensitivity about a separate peace and accepted Bonaparte's terms.

Taken together, these successive developments added up to a heavy indictment of Pitt's government – comparable, perhaps, to Lord North's loss of the North American colonies. A war which he had initially regarded as likely to prove beneficial for Britain had turned into an expensive – indeed, potentially ruinous – endeavour. Although Pitt had managed to avert a financial disaster, the run on the banks had undermined his reputation for economic acumen, and he could only maintain his much-vaunted sinking fund by means of additional taxation (following a 'loyalty loan' which had been announced in December 1796). The conflict had exposed Britain's limitations as a military and diplomatic European power and now made it look vulnerable to invasion. Even when the British navy was obeying orders, enemy forces were able to evade it and either effect a landing or come close to a descent on Ireland, which could easily have triggered a civil war in that volatile country.

Pitt was a proud man who might once have thought seriously about abandoning politics, but by now he was engaged too deeply to contemplate an alternative career. However, at some point in the early months of 1797 it seems that he hatched a plan which offered a temporary escape from the crushing pressures of office. According to his official biographer and close confidant, Pretyman, he discussed with the King the possibility of resigning in favour of Henry Addington, in the hope that the French would be more willing to make peace with a new prime minister. When Pretyman's wife expressed astonishment that Addington should be considered, Pitt's brother-in-law Edward Eliot assured her that the arrangement would only be temporary, and that the stand-in prime minister would be acting 'under the direction of Mr Pitt'.[17]

This story is too astonishing to have been invented by Pretyman, whose biography of Pitt has generally been treated as a masterpiece of non-revelation. If true, it testifies to Pitt's desperation during this most testing of years – desperation, that is, to try anything that might secure a viable peace agreement short of giving up the reality (as opposed to the appearance) of his own power. The veracity of the story, indeed, is supported by events after 1801, when Pitt did indeed resign in favour of Addington and acted in accordance with the original script while Addington, not satisfied with the role of supporting actor, evidently now aspired to a starring role. For the time being, at least, the plan was shelved. But by the end of September 1797 Pitt might have wished that he had carried it out. The reported discussion between Mrs Pretyman and Edward Eliot illustrates the continued importance of the latter in Pitt's life as a poignant reminder of his sister Harriot and of Cambridge days, a continuing link with friends like Wilberforce, and also as a privileged recipient of the prime minister's most intimate political thoughts. Whether or not Eliot's health was fatally undermined by Harriot's death in 1786, his subsequent career was blighted by illness and he died on 20 September 1797, aged 39.

In Edward Eliot's final hours, Lord Malmesbury, who had been selected once again to undertake negotiations with France, was sent packing by his hosts for a second time. If Britain was suffering the consequences of the prolonged conflict, in France there had been definite signs of war fatigue, combined with a swing in public opinion towards a restored monarchy in elections of March/April 1797. The five-member *Directoire* included politicians who either favoured a return to constitutional monarchy, or at least the establishment of a regime that offered the kind of stability which, for Pitt, was a precondition for peace. The result of the elections turned out to be a devastating blow for the moderates, since it suggested that France was polarised between radicals and reactionaries. The radicals were still in the ascendancy, particularly within the army, and on 4 September 1797 they carried out a coup which removed the moderates, along with senior army officers who had been in contact with the British. For the winning faction, this was not a moment to make peace with the country which had been backing their opponents, even though Pitt had offered terms which seemed recklessly generous even to his closest colleagues.

While he was being buffeted by these unpalatable tidings, Pitt's state of mind was the subject of varying reports. During the mutinies, the First Lord of the Admiralty, Lord Spencer, felt compelled at an early hour to visit Downing Street and wake the prime minister. To Spencer's amazement, having digested the disconcerting news Pitt fell asleep almost immediately.[18] But after the personal and political setbacks of September 1798 Pitt complained of headaches and stomach problems. He even looked seriously into the possibility of bribing the *Directoire* to the conference table, having been told that its members would allow Britain to keep some of its overseas acquisitions if the price was right. At least on 11 October there was something tangible to celebrate: a naval victory over the Dutch at the Battle of Camperdown. When Britain had entered the war, not even the most pessimistic observer would have expected that, after five years of struggle, the Dutch would be dangerous enemies rather than allies. Rather than turning the tide of war against the French, the battle merely confirmed that the British still had sufficient resources to continue the conflict, in one way or another. In short, by October 1797 Pitt the Younger was having to derive the strength to sustain the struggle from occasional crumbs of comfort.

14

Union and Resignation

O N 10 November 1797 Pitt provided the House of Commons with a lengthy explanation of the failure of his latest peace initiative. He closed with a rousing declaration that Britons were 'determined to stand or fall by the laws, liberties, and religion of our country.'[1] His audience responded with a spontaneous rendition of 'Britons Strike Home'. Pitt was still capable of defending his record as a war leader with considerable aplomb; and, with the parliamentary balance now heavily tilted in his favour, those who sought to subject it to critical scrutiny had a near-impossible task.

Pitt's dominance of the Commons was apparently assured in November 1797, since his main rival was no longer attending the House. By the summer of that year Fox's following had dwindled, perhaps to as little as 25 MPs, as his supporters decided to give up the unequal struggle. A deliberate 'secession' from Parliament, as a means of protesting against a government which was riding roughshod over the will of the people, had been recommended by Lord Rockingham at one stage during the American War; Fox had strongly criticised this idea at the time, but by 1797 it seemed more persuasive. Fox spent more and more time at St Ann's Hill, immersed in his books and garden and sublimely happy with his beloved Liz. Some of his friends, however, looked upon Fox, despite his 46 years and his portly and untidy appearance, as an eligible husband for a wealthy heiress. One of these, apparently, was the banker Thomas

Coutts, the father of three daughters, two of whom were unmarried. One of these, Fanny, aged 22, took a shine to Fox, and asked him to send her a lock of his hair. Fox good-naturedly agreed, not regarding it as a matter of any significance. Elizabeth, however, more worldly-wise than Charles, interpreted it as a marriage proposal, was extremely upset, and offered to give him up so that, with the help of a large dowry, his future would be finally assured and he could start a family with a much younger wife. Fox was horrified at Elizabeth's reaction; he wrote a long letter to her assuring her that his whole happiness was dependent on her, and that theirs was a lifelong union. So Fanny Coutts did not get the lock of hair, and consoled herself by marrying the widowed Marquess of Bute, who was in his early fifties but ended up outliving Fox and producing two children with Fox's former admirer.[2]

Prompted by this episode, Fox determined to marry Elizabeth. She agreed, but, wishing to avoid a scandal, insisted that the marriage should remain secret. On 28 September 1795, in the remote village of Wyton in Huntingdonshire, they were married, in the presence only of Elizabeth's maid and the parish clerk, who acted as witnesses. Fox appeared in the register as 'Charles J. Fox of the parish of Chertsey in the county of Surrey', his bride as 'Elizabeth B. Cane, of this parish', where she had been living for the previous few weeks to establish a residency qualification. Cane was her birth name, and no mention was made of a previous marriage, if it ever existed, with a Mr Armitstead.

Unlike Pitt, Fox could at least contemplate entry to the holy state of wedlock without serious financial worries. By 1793 his debts had reached mountainous proportions, and some of his friends got together with the object of raising a fund which would not only pay off all his debts, but would also provide him with an annuity which would give him a reasonable income for the rest of his life.[3] They hoped to raise enough to provide him with an annual income of £2,000 – a very comfortable nest egg considering that as recently as 1770 Oliver Goldsmith had written that a village parson would be considered 'passing rich' on £40 per year. William Adam, who 14 years earlier had fought a duel with Fox but was now party manager of the Whigs, was deputed to solicit subscriptions, with a suggested minimum of £100, though Sheridan, himself perpetually in debt, could only manage £25. The initial objective was to raise £55,000, but this was later raised to £65,000, which was eventually reached after the Duke of Bedford and other grandees had dipped more deeply into their pockets. They had little doubt that Fox would not hesitate to accept their largesse. On a previous occasion when a whip-round had been organised, a potential contributor, thinking that Fox would be greatly embarrassed, asked how the recipient would take it. 'Take it? Take it?' Sir George Selwyn, an old friend but severe critic had replied. 'Why, quarterly, to be sure.'[4] Fox never completely overcame his gambling addiction, but it was now greatly moderated, and, having settled down in quasi-marital bliss with Mrs Armitstead, he had sobered up and his acute financial difficulties were at an end.

While Fox could find compensations in his semi-rural retreat, whether or not Pitt had bungled Britain's previous war effort he was now beginning to benefit from a growing sense that national survival was at stake, and that criticism of the minister was tantamount to aiding the enemy. The radical poet Samuel Taylor Coleridge provided a vivid illustration of the process of polarisation at this time. In response to Pitt's policy towards the Vendée, Coleridge had written his eclogue 'Fire, Famine and Slaughter', a re-enactment of the opening scene of *Macbeth* in which the personified scourges of humanity announce that they have been unleashed by someone whose name is too diabolical (or dangerous, even to them) to spell out, although they helpfully reveal that it consists of four letters. In gratitude, 'Fire' promises that, far from deserting Pitt, she will 'Cling to him everlastingly' (i.e. that Pitt will burn in hell). By April 1798 the danger to Britain's security had forced Coleridge to reconsider his position – a dilemma which found eloquent expression in a new poem, 'Fears in Solitude'. After this epiphany Coleridge continued to criticise Pitt, but instead presented him as an inadequate champion of a just cause rather than as an 'apostate' who gloried in human suffering.

Pitt's knowledge of classical literature should have alerted him to the possibility that his posthumous reputation would be permanently blighted by brilliant antagonists like Coleridge. However, far from trying to propitiate his literary contemporaries Pitt flung an inkpot in their faces by agreeing in 1790 to the appointment of Henry Pye (1744–1813) to the post of Poet Laureate. A versifier whose productions have not passed the test of time, Pye's only recommendation for this position was his service as a Pittite MP from 1784 to 1790. His most noteworthy contribution to the canon of British literature was a prose work of 1808 entitled *Summary of the Duties of a Justice of the Peace out of Sessions*. This tract was inspired by Pye's experience as a magistrate for Westminster, a position he had taken up when he retired from the House of Commons.

In the early months of 1798, there seemed to be a bizarre logic behind Pitt's determination to restrict government patronage to poets who could also turn their hands to law enforcement. This was the period in which his 'reign of terror' was most productive, at least in terms of arrests. More than fifty dissidents were rounded up in Margate, Manchester, Leicester and London. In April the Duke of Norfolk was sacked as Lord Lieutenant of the West Riding of Yorkshire and from his position as a colonel in the militia for toasting 'Our Sovereign's Health, the Majesty of the People' at a birthday celebration for Fox, whom he compared favourably to George Washington. In the following month Fox showed his solidarity by delivering a similar toast at a meeting of the Whig Club. Pitt has been praised for his own restrained reaction to Fox's defiance, but he probably would have favoured prosecution if there had been a good chance of conviction, and he suggested that his rival should be sent to the Tower if he repeated the provocation.[5] Finally Pitt wrote to the King, humbly proposing '[t]he propriety of directing tomorrow that Mr Fox's name should be erased from the list of Privy Councillors.'[6] As Pitt no doubt expected, George took considerable pleasure in complying, striking out Fox's name with his own hand.

The government's action against dissidents, however distinguished, coincided with growing concern for Britain's security. In April 1798 Pitt had told his colleague Lord Camden '[t]he general zeal and spirit of the country is everything that we can wish for.' Yet on 25 May he invited the Commons to rush through legislation to facilitate recruitment to the navy, referring to 'the present alarming state of the country'.[7] The contrasting judgements can be explained by reference to Ireland, where Camden was serving as Lord Lieutenant. In the spring of 1798 the French fleet based at Toulon was clearly preparing for a major expedition, and Pitt was convinced that, of several possible destinations, it was preparing for a descent on Ireland. The previous French attempt to foment existing tensions there (1796) was still fresh in his mind, along with a realisation that it had come perilously close to success. The looming threat of a new French mission to bring the war to Britain's backyard explains the renewed crackdown on potential 'fifth columnists', culminating in a further suspension of habeas corpus after a perfunctory debate. At the same time, Pitt supported Canning's idea to produce a journal (the *Anti-Jacobin*) which added new venom into the propaganda war by means of slurs, squibs and poems whose literary qualities rarely surpassed the standard of undergraduate pranksters. It was the cue for the ex-radical Coleridge, whose youthful offences had not been forgotten by the *Anti-Jacobin*s, to testify to the depth of his patriotism: 'O native Britain! O my Mother Isle! / How shouldst thou prove aught else but dear and holy.'[8]

On 25 May 1798, during the parliamentary debate on naval recruitment, the state of Pitt's own mind was revealed. In answer to Pitt's motion, George Tierney, leading for the Opposition in Fox's absence, raised objections not to the substance of the government's proposals but rather to 'the precipitate manner' in which it was asking Parliament to act. With the recent precedent of the suspension of habeas corpus clearly in mind, Tierney suggested that the present measure was part of a more general design of ministers who were 'hostile to the liberty of the subject'. Pitt retorted that he was at a loss to understand Tierney's position unless it arose 'from a desire to obstruct the defence of his country'. Prompted by Tierney, Speaker Addington asked Pitt to clarify these remarks. Pitt merely took the opportunity to restate his charges, and appealed to 'the judgement of the House'.[9]

Although the published record of the debate conveys an impression that Pitt was under a degree of self-control, the attack on Tierney suggests that he had forgotten how to behave as prime minister of a country which was blessed with (imperfect) representative institutions. He was under severe stress and his health was poor, but his conduct also suggests intoxication – either by liquor, or the sense of his own power. For whatever reason, he was clearly inspired by the dangerous feeling that he could say whatever he liked in the House of Commons and get away with it, hence his appeal to the 'judgement of the House' when challenged by Speaker Addington (who, of course, was not only his long-standing friend but also the person he had earmarked as his preferred successor as prime minister).

Since 'the judgement of the House' at that time was unlikely to be impartial, Tierney decided to appeal to a court of arbitration which was even less likely to record a rational verdict, and challenged Pitt to a duel. Pitt was not the first prime minister to be asked to submit himself to trial by combat; his one-time mentor Lord Shelburne had accepted a similar challenge in 1780. But when one takes account of his own analysis of Britain's peril in May 1798 – and of his view that he was indispensable in the cause of national salvation – his deliberate provocation of Tierney seems all the more astonishing, and is deserving of far more censure than the 'boys will be boys' style of rebuke which his biographers have tended to deliver. Having been challenged, Pitt resigned himself to the possibility of death with characteristic sangfroid. His second was Dudley Ryder, a junior minister and fellow Cambridge graduate. Tierney's assistant was George Walpole, who had fought with distinction in the West Indies before becoming a Foxite MP. Despite being the grandson of a prime minister, Walpole had joined the army as a cornet, the lowest rank available for commissioned officers. William Pitt the Elder had never progressed beyond that stage, but George Walpole had gone on to serve (albeit temporarily) as a major general. If Pitt had fought his duel in the hope that the affair would somehow vindicate his attempt to impugn the Opposition's patriotism, he had lost before a shot was fired on Putney Heath.

No injuries were sustained during the duel itself; although the odds strongly favoured the slender Pitt over the corpulent Tierney, the antagonists both missed with their first shots, whereupon the prime minister fired in the air. Subsequently Pitt treated Tierney with a little more respect, but the episode threatened a new breach in his relations with Wilberforce, who was horrified (not least because it had taken place on a Sunday), and Pitt had to exercise considerable diplomacy to persuade his friend to drop a proposed parliamentary motion condemning duels. A few days later the prime minister was incapacitated by an illness which had probably affected (though it could hardly excuse) his conduct towards Tierney, and did not attend Parliament again until the end of June. However, there could be no respite from the demands imposed on a wartime premier. Even on the day of the duel, Pitt was corresponding with Camden about a possible solution to the problems in Ireland. It had transpired that the Toulon fleet was destined for Egypt rather than Ireland, but civil unrest was already brewing and the United Irishmen, who had managed to draw support from both sides of the sectarian divide, were in close contact with the French. In the first half of 1798 some key figures in the movement, including Lord Edward Fitzgerald, were arrested and martial law was declared. Fitzgerald, who was Fox's greatly beloved cousin and another descendant of Charles II, died of wounds he received when resisting arrest. In desperation, the United Irishmen took to arms even though promised French support had yet to arrive. By the end of June the rebellion was effectively over, and hundreds of captured rebels were put to death by the local authorities. When the French troops did arrive their attempt to rekindle resistance was rapidly repulsed, although some did manage to disembark. The ship carrying the rebel leader Wolfe Tone was intercepted and surrendered; Tone himself was quickly tried and sentenced to hang, but he died either by suicide or from the effects of torture.

Pitt's favoured solution to the problem of Ireland was a full legislative Union, and once he had recovered from his illness he devoted considerable attention to this idea. By the end of the year he had secured Cabinet approval, and, crucially on such a key constitutional question, the support of the King. In January 1799 he offered the House of Commons a vision of Ireland's future which illustrates the influence of Enlightenment ideas on his own approach to political, economic and social questions. He was willing to trot out the stereotyped English view of the Irish to the extent of referring to their 'want of intelligence or, in other words, their ignorance'. But this was not due to some kind of genetic imperfection; Pitt attributed it to the distribution of property in Ireland and to 'the rancour which bigotry engenders and superstition rears and cherishes'.[10] Prejudiced Protestants who were not listening very attentively might have interpreted this as just another version of the obligatory attack on Catholicism. But it is more easily read as a condemnation of both sides of the religious divide in Ireland, adding a charge of 'bigotry' against hard-line Protestants to the standard equation of Catholicism with 'superstition'. If anything, Pitt's criticism of 'the state of property' in Ireland implied that his sympathies lay on the Catholic side. Whether or not one credits the report that Pitt secretly sympathised with the arguments of Thomas Paine, the sentiments expressed in his speech of 23 January 1799 can be reconciled with the ideas of United Irishmen like Wolfe Tone, who had recently been repressed by Pitt's allies in Dublin as if they had been common criminals.

Initially the proposed Union met significant opposition in Ireland, but Pitt and his colleagues were well aware of a relevant precedent – the legislative Union with Scotland, facilitated in 1707 after protracted negotiations and a generous allocation of money, titles and the like to smooth the process. Pitt's defenders have argued that the word 'corruption' should be used with caution in relation to dealings with the Irish Parliament, but it seems fairly clear that in this instance Pitt was ready to employ methods of persuasion which, throughout his career, he had been trying to root out when he uncovered them within the machinery of English governance. By the same token, however, he had been prepared to resort to outright bribery if that would bring the European war to an end; and in that ongoing context the inducements offered to members of the Irish Parliament possibly deserve a less value-laden noun than 'corruption'. It was, perhaps, not the most promising basis on which to realise Pitt's idealistic plans for Ireland's future; but Pitt himself recognised that the constructive work would take time, and it is not his fault that his successors tended to ignore Ireland until that country forced itself onto their consciousness.

The Act of Union had passed all its parliamentary stages by August 1800, and a new Parliament of Great Britain and Ireland (with 100 Irish MPs) was scheduled to meet in January 1801. However, Pitt's idea of an Irish settlement was incomplete. The Roman Catholic Relief Act passed by the Westminster Parliament in 1791 was subsequently adopted by the Irish legislature, removing most of the civil disabilities imposed on Catholics. Catholics were no longer disqualified from voting on religious grounds (although, as in the rest of Britain, the Irish franchise was restricted in other respects); they could serve on juries; and they could hold a range of offices, including university posts and certain commissions within the armed forces. To a considerable extent, therefore, 'Catholic Emancipation' had been achieved, at least insofar as discrimination had affected the civil rights of the middle and upper classes. However, Catholics were not allowed to sit in Parliament in Ireland or at Westminster.

When the Portland Whigs entered a coalition with Pitt in 1794, one of their number, Lord Fitzwilliam, had been sent to Ireland as Lord Lieutenant. Fitzwilliam was determined to complete the process of 'emancipation' and thought that he had secured Pitt's approval. It is possible that he misinterpreted Pitt's support for the *principle* of emancipation as a signal to embark on the process without delay, but it seems more likely that he chose to ignore reasonably clear instructions to tread carefully and to consult closely with London. As it was, once he had arrived in Ireland Fitzwilliam made no attempt to douse expectations of reform, and began to replace officials who enjoyed Pitt's trust with his own supporters. Pitt reacted quickly, securing Portland's agreement to Fitzwilliam's peremptory recall. The prime minister was probably actuated by resentment at Fitzwilliam's insubordinate conduct, rather than being influenced by George III's views on emancipation, which were emphatically negative. George, indeed, expressed the view that this matter lay 'beyond the decision of any Cabinet of Ministers': that is, it concerned the Royal prerogative and his coronation oath.[11] He was, in short, reserving the right to exercise a veto on any future proposal of emancipation.

Possibly by 1800 Pitt had forgotten this clear statement of intent; indeed, he might never have attended to it, since he felt that Fitzwilliam had jumped the gun on emancipation and only needed to know that, for whatever reason, the King would be on his side if Fitzwilliam's dismissal caused trouble with the Portland Whigs. However, Pitt believed that emancipation was essential to cement the Act of Union, and for good reasons. The main purpose of that legislation, after all, was to enhance the security of Britain as a whole. Given the grievous economic inequalities in Ireland which clearly reflected religious divisions, it was never likely that poor Catholics would feel much enthusiasm for the Union. But their more affluent co-religionists could be brought fully on board if the last vestiges of legal discrimination were being removed thanks to the formal association with Britain. In effect, Pitt was proposing to exploit the union with Ireland in order to facilitate a reform which he considered desirable for the whole of Britain. The key test for those wishing to hold office, he thought, was no longer religious affiliation but rather loyalty to the Crown. For someone with Pitt's secular outlook, this was the only kind of oath which made any kind of sense. He was, in short, hoping to build the case for a change which he believed desirable in itself on the plea of necessity – a concession designed to reconcile Irish Catholics to the idea of the Union would remove the remnants of discrimination against citizens in the rest of Britain (including Protestant dissenters) who refused to conform to the established Anglican Church.

Like most plans which turn out to be 'too clever by half', Pitt's proposed reform included some minor features which were intended to mollify its likely opponents. However, whether or not Pitt remembered George III's unequivocal warnings from 1795, he must have expected some trouble from that quarter. His response showed that, whatever changes he had undergone since becoming the King's first minister back in 1783, he remained at heart a constitutional innovator, if not consciously radical. Arguably, in fact, despite all of the familiar evidence which suggests that Pitt underwent a 'reluctant transformation' as a result of his confrontation with revolutionary France, in terms of the British system of government he was much *more* radical in 1801 than he had been in the early days when he championed limited changes in the electoral system.

Pitt, it seems, did not try very hard to change George's mind by means of personal interviews. This might have been because the prime minister was too busy with other matters, but more likely he knew that George was not amenable to rational persuasion. The latter explanation suggests that Pitt *did* remember George's objections, but that he expected them to be overcome when he was confronted by a Cabinet which was united in favour of emancipation. In constitutional terms, this would have served as vivid confirmation of what Pitt seemed to be assuming already – that is, that the King should be treated as little more than a glorified rubber stamp in a legislative process which was now controlled by the ministers who dominated a supine Parliament. The implications were certainly much more dramatic than those of the Fox–North India Bill, which Pitt had denounced in such lurid terms.

Unfortunately for Pitt's projected constitutional coup, even at the outset the Cabinet was not unanimous. This was made abundantly clear to George in September 1800, when Pitt sent a letter to the Lord Chancellor, Loughborough, an opponent of Catholic Emancipation who happened to have taken a holiday at the same resort (Weymouth) as the royal personage and promptly betrayed the prime minister's confidence. The time needed to build a Cabinet consensus only allowed the differences between senior ministers to widen; Portland swung from initial support to mild opposition, while even Pitt's brother, Lord Chatham, lined up against him. However, the main opponents – Loughborough, Chatham and the King's long-standing ally, the first Lord Liverpool (Charles Jenkinson) – were absent from a Cabinet meeting called by Pitt on 25 January 1801. Although the majority of ministers in attendance supported Pitt, they urged him to win the King's assent. George, however, was not in an assenting mood: at his levee on 28 January he approached Dundas and declared 'in a loud voice and agitated Manner' that 'I shall look on every Man as my personal enemy, who proposes [emancipation] to me.'[12]

George, in short, had launched a reprise of his role in the downfall of the Fox–North coalition, to the extent of plagiarising the old script. The difference between this situation and the dramatic events of 1783 was that, to some extent at least, the King had used the Indian issue as a pretext for using his influence to destroy a government whose leading figure, Fox, was already anathema to him. In January 1801 he felt so strongly about the issue of emancipation, and the deeper constitutional implications of Pitt's initiative, that he was prepared, if necessary, to break with individuals who, if not exactly his 'friends', had certainly proved useful to him for nearly two decades. Pitt responded to the King's challenge in a letter which rehearsed the case for emancipation and offered George some time to reconsider his own position, but affirmed that he would resign if the measure was not adopted in due course 'with your Majesty's full concurrence, and with the whole weight of Government.'[13] The letter closed with a request for a period of silence on George's part – that he should desist from branding the supporters of emancipation as his enemies. This part of the correspondence is, frankly, baffling. If, as seems highly probable if not proven, Pitt had given at least tacit approval to the use of the King's name as a means of destroying the Fox–North coalition, it would have been hypocritical for him to protest against the use of the same tactic when he was its main intended victim. On the other hand, Pitt might have been thinking of the future of the fledgling Union, rather than his own position; certainly he believed that the whole project, which seemed so essential to Britain's security, would be placed in jeopardy if the King continued to speak out in a way which suggested that emancipation could never be enacted while he remained on the throne, whether or not Pitt happened to be in office when the time came to revisit the question.

Pitt's letter reads like the work of a plate-spinner who has finally dug too deeply into the crockery cabinet. He was trying to express a willingness to resign without making this seem like an attempt to blackmail the King, and the best way to achieve this was to persuade George of the case for emancipation; but the letter would not have been written if Pitt had felt any confidence that rational argument would do the trick. As a result, the composition of the letter was akin to the exercises in classical literature at which Pitt had excelled since early childhood; although the style of expression was exemplary, there was never any chance that it would produce any positive effect. The reply that Pitt received the next day had also been composed with considerable care, but its central message was much easier to convey. From George's perspective, the only thing that mattered was his coronation oath to uphold the established order in Church and State. Since Catholic Emancipation would destroy this constitutional arrangement, he could never agree to it. He would be happy for Pitt to remain as his chief minister, provided that he gave up the obnoxious idea. In reality George was just going through the verbal motions; he had already begun preparations for a change of ministry.[14]

Catholic Emancipation, in short, had given the King the chance to reassert his constitutional position after a prolonged war which had led ministers to suppose that George would never try to overturn their decisions. Presumably George would have been able to tolerate this treatment if the war had been going well under ministerial direction. However, by 1801 the prospects of eventual victory seemed bleak. The diplomatic isolation and strategic vulnerability of 1797–8 had been replaced by renewed confidence in a system of alliances in which the absence of Prussia seemed to be outweighed by the adhesion of Russia. However, this 'second coalition' was, if anything, less productive than the first one. While Napoleon's Egyptian adventure kept him away from the European theatre, France's opponents prospered. As before, though, relations between the supposed allies were bedevilled by mutual misunderstandings and suspicions which proved more potent than Pitt's financial inducements. A Russian incursion via Switzerland foundered due to the lack of Austrian support at the crucial moment. Britain's main military contribution to this effort – an attempted invasion of Holland in August 1799, under George's second son Frederick – ended in the ignominious withdrawal of inadequate forces, earning its commander-in-chief an unwanted immortality as 'The Grand Old Duke of York'. From George III's perspective, the Duke of York, a fairly efficient soldier rather than the hapless figure portrayed in the nursery rhyme, had been given an impossible job by ministers who had denied the King any meaningful role in the planning of military operations.

In January 1800 the Cabinet had treated with contempt a letter from the new First Consul of France, Napoleon Bonaparte, which was either a sincere invitation to peace talks, a propaganda ploy, or a mixture of both. Pitt, indeed, had interpreted the message as a symptom of French weakness, and in a speech to the Commons the following month he portrayed Bonaparte as an adventurer who owed his power entirely to military success. If anything, Pitt showed more antipathy towards the First Consul than to any of the previous Revolutionary leaders.[15] It seemed that France had undergone the kind of constitutional developments envisaged by Pitt's favourite classical authorities – an initial period of anarchy, replaced by the oligarchy of the *Directoire*, lapsing into Bonaparte's 'tyranny'. Under Napoleon, France itself might have found a degree of stability; but while his power lasted, Pitt's objective of a peace which gave Britain 'security' seemed unattainable.

Pitt was answered by a speaker who began by apologising for his poor recent record of attendance in the House. Charles Fox embarked on a review of the war to date, emphasising the failure of Pitt's regular predictions of imminent French collapse in the face of financial exhaustion. He made no attempt to justify the Revolutionaries, whose conduct had not lived up to his initial expectations. However, he argued that even at their worst they were merely repeating the crimes of the Bourbon monarchy – and Britain had never made the nature of that regime a reason for maintaining a state of war when there had been any prospect of a lasting peace settlement. As for the Napoleonic regime, his parliamentary colleagues claimed to despise the idea of a military dictatorship, but they made no complaint about the enforcement of a similar system in Ireland. He claimed that ministers were keeping up the war because they could not as yet be sure of Napoleon's intentions, and that they had placed him in 'a state of probation'. As such, the war must continue, on a kind of autopilot; or, as Fox put it, the conflict had entered a kind of 'pause':

> Put yourselves – oh! that you would put yourselves – in the field of battle, and learn to judge of the sort of horrors that you excite [...] if a man were present now at a field of slaughter, and to enquire for what they were fighting: 'Fighting!' would be the answer; 'they are not fighting, they are *pausing*.' 'Why is that man expiring? Why is that other writhing with agony? What means this implacable fury?' The answer must be: 'You are quite wrong, Sir, you deceive yourself. – They are not fighting – Do not disturb them – they are merely *pausing*! – This man is not expiring with agony – that man is not dead – he is only pausing! Lord help you, Sir! They are not angry with one another; they have now no cause of quarrel – but their country thinks that there should be a pause.'[16]

Fox had delivered his speech in the full knowledge that there was no chance of influencing the vote; and he duly lost, by 265 to 64. But his knowledge that he was bound to end up on the losing side of this debate only adds lustre to his speech. No one could possibly accuse him of opportunism; if anything, his eloquence on that occasion was more likely to land him in more trouble. It was easy to pick holes in his argument. He overlooked the possibility that Bonaparte himself might be seeking nothing more than a 'pause' to gather his strength for a new struggle in which he would ensure that many more Britons would die 'writhing with agony'. But the speech showed that, in the course of his secession from Parliament, Fox had undergone a 'conversion' similar to the one experienced by Wilberforce in the late 1780s; he was now a humanitarian first, and only secondly a politician. In that speech, delivered on 3 February 1800, Fox attained a standard of oratory which Pitt could never match. He was always more impressive than Pitt in his ability to rouse the emotions of his listeners, but Pitt usually got the better of him by presenting his argument in a more logical order. On that occasion, Fox managed to combine the best of Pitt and Fox. Even if the 'rational' case for peace was flawed, it was organised to best effect; and the emotive finale was powerful enough to make anyone who disagreed with the preceding argument forgetful of the flaws. Yet although Pitt was a connoisseur of rhetoric, he was not going to be swayed by speeches. By the time of the crisis over emancipation he would have accepted the need for serious peace talks, whether or not Fox had stuck to his decision to stay away from Parliament. Apart from the unpromising military outlook, the unstable Russian Czar Paul I was now decidedly hostile and had organised a League of Armed Neutrality, incorporating Prussia as well as the Baltic States, to defy Britain's policy of disrupting trade with France. The domestic scene was darkened once again by poor harvests and the threat of famine, forcing the government to introduce legislation to limit the consumption of wheat. Significantly, a royal proclamation on this subject was printed before the King had been given a chance to read its contents.[17] The favourable reaction to George's recovery from illness in 1789 was a distant memory. An assassination attempt at the Theatre Royal, Drury Lane, in May 1800, seemed to evoke as much public sympathy for the (deranged) assailant as for his intended victim.

As Pitt contemplated the task of persuading the King to endorse yet another round of peace talks, he was conscious of diminished royal support, the strong reservations of Grenville and Dundas, and alarming symptoms of discontent within the populace as a whole. On his own (accurate) estimation of Napoleon, there could be no lasting peace with France; it would, at best, provide Britain with a much-needed respite. To a man who was himself in need of respite, the task of justifying this step was hardly appetising. Back in 1797, Pitt had flirted with the idea of engineering the succession of Henry Addington in his place, with the intention of remaining as a 'back-seat driver' or, perhaps, of retaking the steering wheel once Addington had performed his sacrificial role as the man who had presided over an unsatisfactory peace. If even a rational political operator like Pitt had considered this a plausible plan in 1797, in the early weeks of 1801 it must have seemed blindingly obvious. The initial idea was based on an assumption that Britain would be better placed to make peace under a new prime minister, and this calculation was even more relevant in 1801 after Pitt had shown that France's new regime was even less trustworthy than its predecessors. In addition, back in 1797 Pitt could have accused himself of abandoning a monarch who had come to regard him as a trusted partner. By contrast, in 1801 Pitt had good reason to expect that George would positively welcome a new prime minister.

The fact that Pitt thought of resigning in 1797, but failed to act on his idea for more than three years, could lend support to the notion that the crisis over Catholic Emancipation merely provided him with a convenient excuse to secure the retirement for which he had been longing. However, the Catholic question was far more than a pretext; the prime minister who hankered after 'security' in his dealings with France had come to feel that the Union with Ireland was essential to the same end, and that this had only been secured by means of promises, however imprecise, that remaining civil disabilities would be removed. If Catholic Emancipation had just been a pretext, Pitt would have resigned as soon as George III threatened to muster his forces against it. As it was, he hesitated, seeking alternative ways out of the impasse before asking on 3 February 'to be released, as soon as possible, from his present situation'.[18] Even then, he tried to dissuade George from allowing his name to be used as a means of whipping up opposition to emancipation. In his reply, the King indulged himself in the pretence that the idea had never crossed his mind. He was in a celebratory mood; the mere suggestion of his disapprobation had seen off Charles Fox in 1783, and it was still potent enough to unseat Billy Pitt. When he described the duty of finding a new prime minister as 'unpleasant', he probably allowed himself the rare luxury of a grin.

15

The Addington Interlude

H ENRY Addington had hesitated when the King had offered him the premiership, but was strongly encouraged by Pitt to take it on. The King said to him: 'Lay your hand upon your heart, and ask yourself where I am to turn for support if you do not stand by me.'[1] When Addington finally agreed, George III embraced him, exclaiming: 'My dear Addington, you have saved your country.'[2]

The King's effusive welcome said a great deal about the strength of his opposition to Catholic Emancipation, and the depth of his disillusion with Pitt. In other circumstances his identification of Addington as a national saviour might have been taken as a symptom of recurring madness. Addington was to be the first 'middle-class' PM; all his predecessors had been aristocrats or gentry. The more aristocratic members of Parliament, including many of Fox's supporters, had condescended to him, giving him the contemptuous nickname of 'the Doctor' in mock tribute to his father's profession. Addington had been elected to Parliament in 1784 and had made little public impact, being only an occasional, hesitant and dull speaker, but he had an amiable disposition and soon made many friends, particularly among the country gentry. Nevertheless, when Pitt proposed him as Speaker in June 1789 many MPs were shocked that a more distinguished Member had not been proposed and put up a rival candidate, Sir Gilbert Elliot, to oppose him. Despite the intervention of government whips, Addington only prevailed by 215 votes to 142.

Addington proved totally satisfactory from Pitt's point of view, and in fact had dinner every week in the Speaker's House with Pitt, Grenville and Dundas and gave them invaluable advice on parliamentary tactics. Yet in the Chair he was studiously fair, particularly to the Foxite Opposition, and eventually became widely popular. This did not mean, however, that he was regarded as a natural successor to Pitt – hence Mrs Pretyman's astonishment in 1797 when she heard that Addington was being lined up for the position (see Chapter Thirteen). There was certainly no evidence that he would be more successful as a war leader than Pitt had been. Far from 'saving his country', Addington was not even saving George from having to appoint Fox, whose parliamentary support was much diminished since the defection of the Portland Whigs.

The widespread consternation at this sudden political upheaval was increased by Pitt's continuation in office while the new national saviour put together his ministerial team. Indeed, he delivered yet another budget speech, on 18 February, which announced significant new government borrowing and increased duties, to add to a system of revenue-raising which had already been augmented in 1798 by an income tax. This was a very sombre statement, but it attracted no critical comment in the Chamber. To add to the sense of unreality, Pitt and the King seemed on better personal terms than ever. Possibly George was trying to make sure that the fallen minister would continue to support the government, but a few days later it was clear that the King's malady had returned. Far from enjoying some respite from his crushing workload, Pitt was as busy as ever and under added strain thanks to the uncertainty of the situation. Once again the country faced the prospect of a regency, but whereas it could be assumed in 1788–9 that the Prince of Wales would instal Fox as prime minister, this time round he would be confronted with several possibilities – all of them problematic. Luckily, the King spared his son from this dilemma by recovering on 3 March 1801. One of the first products of his returning sanity was a message to Pitt, which blamed him for the relapse. Clearly accepting George's self-diagnosis, Pitt replied with a promise never to raise the issue of Catholic Emancipation again and to oppose it if it were put forward by anyone else. As William Hague has pointed out, this was a costless concession on Pitt's part, since he knew that emancipation could never be implemented while the King was in good health.[3] At the same time, Pitt's pledge kicked the issue which had caused his resignation into very long grass. This meant that he could resume the reins which he had only just relinquished, and many of his former colleagues (including even Portland, who had disagreed with him over emancipation) urged him to throw Addington over and stay in office.

Addington, indeed, was having considerable trouble forming a government. He had assumed that he would take over the great majority of Pitt's ministers, but this was not to be; only four of the ten members of the Cabinet decided to carry on. The greatest loss was Lord Grenville, previously holding the joint posts of Foreign Secretary and Leader of the House of Lords. He was a fervent supporter of Catholic Emancipation, and had dissented from Pitt's promise not to raise the question during George III's lifetime. As Addington regarded himself to be bound by the same pledge, Grenville refused to serve under him. Other former ministers, including George Canning, were ultra-loyal to Pitt, and refused to serve under anyone else. Canning spitefully circulated a ditty he had composed:

> Pitt is to Addington,
> As London is to Paddington.

The most extreme case was that of George Rose, who had been Pitt's Secretary to the Treasury for 17 years. He was heard to remark that he would 'as soon assent to the prostitution of his daughter as to remain in office'.[4]

Even in 1797 Pitt had considered that Addington might just be a temporary stopgap; now it looked as if he could be kept on the substitute's bench. The Doctor, though, had other ideas. Apart from personal ambition and pride, he had been a close confidant of the King during the crisis over emancipation and was therefore well aware that George's differences with Pitt extended far beyond this single issue. He could thus discount the King's apparent regret at losing Pitt's services as nothing more than an understandable emotional spasm which was unlikely to last. Once it was over, George would probably feel as glad to be rid of Pitt as he was to be free from Fox in 1783. Armed with this knowledge, Addington dashed

Pitt's hopes by constructing a Cabinet which included some of his personal friends but also featured established figures as well as younger politicians who would later make a considerable mark. The Duke of Portland remained as Home Secretary, but after three months was transferred to the Lord Presidency of the Council. The most interesting newcomer was Lord Hawkesbury as Foreign Secretary, who 11 years later, as the second Earl of Liverpool, became prime minister and subsequently served for almost 15 years, the third-longest tenancy after Walpole and Pitt. Also in the government was another future premier, Spencer Perceval (who was to be assassinated in the House of Commons in 1812), as solicitor general, and Hawkesbury's father, the first Earl of Liverpool, as President of the Board of Trade. Previously known as Charles Jenkinson, Liverpool had, along with John Robinson, been one of the most prominent of the 'King's Friends'.

Watching these tortuous developments from his semi-detached vantage point, Fox had sensed that the appearance of change was likely to be deceptive, calling the idea of an Addington ministry 'a mere juggle'.[5] When it seemed that Pitt had truly received his comeuppance he was deliriously happy and welcomed Addington's appointment, even though he despised the Doctor. He ended his 'secession' from Parliament and decided to fight the next general election, due in 1802, although he had previously considered giving up his seat at Westminster. A number of his constituents had expressed displeasure at his absenteeism, and Sheridan had been manoeuvring to take over the seat. The overall result of the election was a large working majority for Addington. Fox wrote to his nephew, Lord Holland, giving his own estimate of the new membership of the House, as 'Pittites 58, Grenvillites 36, Foxites 69 and all the rest Ministerial'.[6]

The Grenvillite group consisted of the followers and family connections of the three sons of George Grenville, who had been prime minister in 1763–5, and who was the brother-in-law of the elder Pitt. The eldest was the third Earl Temple, who had been instrumental in evicting Fox from office in 1783 and who was now the first Marquess of Buckingham, but who had had been relatively inactive in politics since his precipitate resignation in December 1783, after only three days as Home Secretary. The second, Thomas Grenville, was a long-time MP who had always been a great admirer of Fox. The youngest, Lord (William) Grenville, was by far the most able of the three, and, as we have seen, worked closely with Pitt as Foreign Secretary, although he gradually lost confidence in Pitt's strategy, which he regarded as being opportunistic and lacking in focus.

During his absence from Parliament, Fox had started work on what was to become his only book, a study of the reign of his great-great uncle, James II. He took great trouble over the work, consulting many historians and burying himself in family papers and other archives. It was intended to be a major exposition of the Whig interpretation of history, and Fox did not fail to discern parallels between the growing despotism of his ancestor and the actions of the current monarch, George III. Yet he made depressingly slow progress in his work and began to wonder whether he was really cut out to be an author. On his return to Parliament, he was for a time a strangely hesitant and rather lonely figure. He constantly sought advice from his followers, especially Charles Grey. Despite his earlier liaison with Georgiana, Duchess of Devonshire, who bore him an illegitimate daughter who was brought up by his parents and passed off as his much younger sister, Grey had become a devoted family man. He and his wife had 16 children, and as Grey grew older he became increasingly reluctant to leave his idyllic estate in Northumberland, Howick Hall, to attend to his parliamentary duties. Fox, who was equally reluctant to make the much shorter journey from St Ann's Hill, fully understood, but bombarded Grey with plaintive letters urging his attendance and asking for advice. Then, one day in 1802, he was pleasantly surprised to receive a formal approach from Tom Grenville, on behalf of himself and his two brothers, offering to combine their forces in opposition to the Addington government. A tentative agreement was reached, with lingering suspicions on both sides, but these were gradually dispersed and an increasingly warm collaboration began. Fox became more and more impressed by William Grenville's honesty and steadfastness, and Grenville, who had always been an admirer of Fox's talents, easily succumbed to his charm. Within a very few months the seeds of a future partnership were effectively sown.

Addington's primary aim was to negotiate an armistice with France, and this took almost exactly a year. The Treaty of Amiens was signed on 25 March 1802, ending war with France, Spain and Holland. The terms which Addington's negotiators had been able to obtain were, perhaps, marginally inferior to those which Pitt had rejected during the earlier abortive negotiations of 1796 and 1797, but in the meantime Britain's continental allies had been decisively defeated in the War of the Second Coalition. In these circumstances, Addington drove as hard a bargain as could realistically be expected. Under the terms agreed, all the conquered French and Dutch colonies were returned, with the exception of Ceylon, while the island of Malta was to be handed back to its historic custodians, the Knights of St John. Britain was to keep Trinidad, while the French would withdraw from Naples and give up their claim to the Ionian islands. Nobody in London thought these terms were glorious, but they were grudgingly accepted, with Pitt (who privately regretted the return of the Cape Colony to the Dutch) enthusiastically endorsing them in public, and they were carried with large majorities in both Houses of Parliament. In the country as a whole, the response was more positive, and Addington gained greatly in popularity as the man who had finally brought peace after ten dispiriting years of conflict.

Having been cut off for ten years from the delights of the French capital, large numbers of Whig aristocrats arranged visits to Paris as soon as the peace treaty was ratified. It was no surprise that Charles Fox was among them, though he was in less of a hurry than many of his colleagues. He was determined to take Elizabeth with him, and, to avoid her being snubbed by other British visitors, insisted on publicising their marriage, which during the previous seven years had been unknown even to his closest relatives. Not everybody was happy at his disclosure – Lady Bessborough, the sister of the notorious Georgiana and herself the former mistress of Sheridan, was quoted as saying, 'The odd thing is that people who were shock'd at the immorality of his having a mistress are still more so at that mistress having been his wife so long.'[7]

Mr and Mrs Fox, with their secretary, John Trotter, left St Ann's Hill for Dover on 29 July 1802 and made the three-hour crossing to Calais by packet boat, but instead of heading straight to Paris spent the next month making a leisurely tour of Flanders and the Netherlands (both under French control), savouring their cultural delights. They finally arrived in Paris on 19 August, where they were joined by the Hollands,

Richard Fitzpatrick, Lord Robert Spencer, Thomas Erskine, James Hare and other leading Whigs. Fox insisted on staying at the Hotel Richelieu, which was within walking distance of the Bibliothèque Nationale, to which he repaired every morning to study the archives of the court established by the exiled James II at Saint-Germain-en-Laye, generously financed by his cousin, Louis XIV. Fox was made much of by his many Parisian friends, notably including Talleyrand, now Foreign Minister to Napoleon Bonaparte, who had made himself First Consul in his coup of the 18th Brumaire (9 November 1799). Talleyrand had been fortunate to survive the Terror, from which he had fled to England in 1792, and had been befriended by Fox before being expelled from the country by Pitt and seeking refuge in the United States, where he had remained until 1796. Fox's other great friend, the Marquis de Lafayette, had also returned from exile and was living peaceably under Napoleon, though he refused to take any official post as he disapproved of the First Consul's dictatorial ways. Both Talleyrand and Lafayette entertained Fox and his friends royally, and introduced them to many leading figures of the Revolution. Fox was well known in France for his anti-war views and generally sympathetic attitude to the Revolution, and he created quite a stir when he and Elizabeth attended a performance of Racine's play, *Phèdre*. His secretary, John Trotter, recorded the scene in his journal with no little pride:

> Every eye was fixed on him, and every tongue resounded Fox! Fox! The whole audience stood up, and the applause was universal. He alone [...] was embarrassed [...] So unwilling was Mr Fox to receive the applause as personal, that he could not be persuaded upon to stand forward [...] No man had ever less vanity.[8]

Other witnesses corroborated Fox's modesty, but when Trotter proceeded to recount that Bonaparte was also present but received an ovation 'much inferior to that bestowed on Mr Fox', the suspicion arises that the devoted secretary's hero worship of his employer may have got the better of him.[9]

The highlight of Fox's visit was expected to be a meeting with Napoleon, but Fox did not want to seem to be paying court to the new French ruler. His hesitation was probably wise. One afternoon, when he and his party were visiting the Louvre, Bonaparte drove by in a carriage drawn by eight horses and accompanied by Mameluke guards. Most of his friends flocked to the window to see the First Consul go by, but Fox was reluctant to abandon his perusal of one of his favourite pictures, Raphael's *Transfiguration*, and appeared to agree with a comment by his wife: 'Considering Buonoparte [sic] was a republican, he seemed very fond of state and show.'[10]

On 2 September the two men finally met at a reception, at which Fox and Elizabeth were formally presented to the First Consul, who made a carefully prepared speech in which he made laudatory remarks about Fox. The latter recorded in his journal: 'Long talk with Bony he talked almost all, was presented to Mme. Liked her very much.'[11] In fact, Elizabeth had made a remarkable impression on Napoleon, and when his will was published in 1822 it was revealed that he had left her a lock of his hair.[12] The conversation had not, otherwise, gone well, according to Lady Bessborough, who overheard much that was said. She reported that

> Buonaparte [sic] also talked a good deal […] but in much too Princely a style, and seeming to dislike any difference of Opinion, he was startled and seem'd surpris'd and displeas'd at Mr Fox answering rather abruptly to his lamentations on the necessity of keeping up a great Military establishment, un grand etablissement Militaire est toujours odieux et doit l'être, car tout Gouvernement qui n'existe que par la force est *oppresif* et mauvais. (Mr F. told Sir Robert that he spoke bad French to soften it; that he meant *Tyranique*, but thought it too harsh to say).[13]

The following day over dinner, the two men tried to get on better terms, as described by L. M. Mitchell:

> Clearly irritated, Napoleon returned once again to the defence of a large standing army, and went on to claim that the press in England had too much liberty, particularly in reference to commenting on himself. When Fox retorted that the freedom of the press was a necessary evil, and that in England people did not mind being abused in the NewsPapers, he answer'd, 'C'est tout autre chose ici'. Later Fox was

to find himself defending Pitt against Bonaparte's accusations that the English prime minister was behind a plot to have him blown up by an 'Infernal Machine'. In two encounters, Fox and Napoleon had found almost no common ground. At a final meeting on 7 October, not even the question of the slave trade could bring them wholeheartedly together. Both agreed that its abolition was desirable, but Napoleon then went on to dwell on the 'difficulties' of putting such a policy into execution.[14]

Fox was undoubtedly somewhat disillusioned by these encounters. It became clear to him that Napoleon was no sort of Whig, and he was shocked by the monarchical airs which he was already adopting. Nevertheless, he did not abandon his conviction that his intentions were peaceable. He believed that Napoleon, having established his primacy by his military prowess, now needed a long period of peace to legitimise his rule. On his return to England, on 17 November, he wrote to Lord Lauderdale, saying:

> As to War I can only say that my opinion is clearly that it will *not* be. I can tell you my reason for this opinion in two sentences. 1st. I am sure that Bonaparte will do everything he can to avoid it. 2nd. that, low as my opinion is of our Ministry, I cannot believe them quite so foolish as to force him to it, without one motive either of ambition or interest to incite them.[15]

Fox's visit to France did no good to his reputation. He was pictured as fraternising with the recent (and probable future) enemy, and a vicious cartoon was published by Gillray entitled *Introduction of Citizen Volpone and his Suite, at Paris*, in which Fox and his companions were shown fawning in front of Napoleon. The British embassy kept a close eye on Fox's movements, and one of its officials reported to the Foreign Office that

> the English Opposition Party here [...] seem to be exerting all their Industry to do their Country and its Government every possible Mischief, as it is natural to infer from their associating with several

of the worst Class of His Majesty's Subjects who are here, such as the O'Connors, Corbett etc.[16]

Arthur O'Connor, a United Irishman, had been tried for treason in 1798, but had been acquitted after Fox and other leading Whigs had given character evidence on his behalf. One of his co-defendants, a priest, was hanged.[17] O'Connor was then rearrested on another charge, but was released when he promised to live abroad. Fox dined with him several times in Paris, and when challenged about this replied that, though he disagreed with O'Connor's views, he had been a good friend, and that there was no reason to turn his back on him when he had fallen on hard times.

Pitt was never likely to seize the opportunity of refreshing his distant memories of Paris, even if he had been a more enthusiastic traveller. The loss of office had been a financial blow as well as a psychological shock, and he no longer had any excuse to ignore his chronic indebtedness. The King tried to present him with a parting gift of £30,000, more than four times the annual income he had received for his governmental duties, but although the offer was made with considerable discretion, Pitt was bound to guess the source of such a prodigious sum and when he learned about it he turned it down. A whip-round among his closest friends produced nearly £12,000 – an amount which he asked his executors to repay in his will – but this was not nearly enough to spare him the pain of relinquishing his Holwood estate, which was heavily mortgaged and which was sold for £15,000. Thankfully Pitt still had a country residence – Walmer Castle, the Tudor fortress on the Kentish coast which he occupied as Lord Warden of the Cinque Ports, a post which the King had given him in 1792 on the death of its previous holder, Lord North. This allowed him to indulge his inherited rage for 'improvements', a task in which he was joined after 1803 by his niece, the mercurial Lady Hester Stanhope, who had previously lived with Pitt's mother and now took on the role of hostess as well as instigating changes to the gardens at Walmer. But although his household expenses were brought under a semblance of control, Pitt still had to pay for property in London.

In theory, Pitt could have transformed his financial situation by returning to the legal profession, where he would have been inundated with well-paid work. However, the very factor which would have netted him a fortune – his former political eminence – was now an insuperable obstacle, since the acceptance of lucrative legal retainers would have contradicted his pose as an incorruptible public servant. In any case, he had good reason to suspect that his days at Downing Street were not over. In May 1802, a banquet was held in London to celebrate Pitt's 44th birthday. The indefatigable Canning produced (under a pseudonym) a poem in his honour, which closed with the thought that

> if again the rude whirlwind should rise!
> The dawning of peace should fresh darkness deform,
> The regrets of the good, and the fears of the wise,
> Shall turn to the Pilot that weather'd the storm.

By Canning's standards, this was a subtle piece of cajolery. In May 1802, it was difficult to detect any 'fresh darkness' descending on the European scene; this, indeed, was two months before Charles Fox felt sufficiently safe to embark on his trip to the territory of Britain's former enemy. Canning, it seems, thought that the Treaty of Amiens would mark a pause, rather than a genuine peace; and Pitt had good reason to share that view. After all, his declared war aim had been 'security', and he had spoken in terms which suggested that this could never be found while Napoleon Bonaparte controlled the destiny of France. Despite his official departure from office, he had been in close contact with Addington throughout the process which led up to the Treaty of Amiens. Whatever the true extent of his influence, evidently he had not objected to terms which he, if he had remained as prime minister, would have found it difficult to accept. In order to satisfy his sense of personal integrity, he had defended those terms in Parliament, even though this caused consternation to his political friends. However, he had ensured that the responsibility for the Treaty of Amiens lay elsewhere; and he could rely on those friends to attribute his support for the terms to his overdeveloped feelings of honour. By May 1802, in short, Pitt could calculate that if peace could be sustained without dishonour to Britain, he would be credited for his role in the right quarters and could return to government at a time of his choosing, in a position which might seem secondary but would in fact allow him to resume his dominance. But if the peace broke down, it would not just be Canning who clamoured for the restoration of 'the Pilot that weather'd the storm'.

As it was, relations with Addington were strained on occasion during 1802. For example, in February Pitt was offended by a report that his successor had been insufficiently robust in defending his record after a critical speech by his old duelling partner, Tierney. However, in June, after the general election which reinforced Addington's parliamentary position, the two men held a harmonious meeting, and Pitt was asked for advice on the ensuing King's Speech.

Pitt was ill for most of the second half of the year, and it was even thought that his life might be in danger. In November he accepted medical advice to spend several weeks at Bath in the hope of curing his familiar digestive complaint. Here he was visited by his old colleague George Rose, who succeeded where more excitable followers like Canning had failed. Rose persuaded him that he was beginning to jeopardise his reputation through his public declarations of support for Addington. He had discharged his duty by helping the Doctor through the initial months of his administration, but after the general election Addington should have been in a position to stand on his own two feet, and Pitt was effectively helping to shield him from justified criticism. Rather than turning to all-out opposition – which would have seemed indecorous at this stage – Pitt should gradually withdraw from the tutelary role which was no longer necessary.

Pitt's ill health made it easy for him to obey Rose's advice to stay away from Parliament. But Rose had also counselled him to stop offering advice behind the scenes. This, apparently, was the decisive stroke. Once Pitt was liberated from any residual sense of responsibility for the government's actions, he began to find fault with almost everything it (and its allies in the press) said or did. In particular, Pitt was roused to anger by Addington's budget of 8 December 1802, regarding some of its proposals as a frontal attack on the principles he had followed as Chancellor. By Christmas, his mood was as 'bilious' as his stomach; but still he would not commit himself to open criticism of a government which was in part his own creation (and which now included one of his most promising disciples, Viscount Castlereagh).

The flaw in Rose's idea of a graceful retreat from open support of Addington to something more like 'armed neutrality' was that Pitt's attitude was the subject of constant speculation, and everyone would notice the change. In the early part of 1803 Addington suggested various ways in which Pitt could return to office without resuming his place as prime minister – including the idea that both men would serve under the nominal leadership of Pitt's own brother, Chatham, who evidently had still not proved his unsuitability for such a role. When this gambit failed (for understandable reasons), Addington resorted to a plan which would make Pitt prime minister while he continued to serve in a junior capacity. On the face of it, this made it look as if Addington was waving a white flag – an interpretation supported by William Hague, among others.[18] However, Addington's supposed surrender included a stipulation that Lord Grenville, who had felt no reason for restraint in his criticisms of the ministry, should be excluded from office. Pitt's ill-advised concession to the King over Catholic Emancipation made it difficult for him to cooperate with Grenville; but family ties, as well as underlying mutual respect, made it inevitable that the cousins should at least talk things over before Pitt agreed to Addington's proposal. Grenville duly paid a visit to Walmer Castle and told Pitt not to resume his post unless the King joined members of the current ministry in soliciting his services. It would be surprising if Pitt had not already reached the same conclusion, since George had not relented in his support for Addington and, as Pitt had good reason to know, his life would be very difficult if he returned to Downing Street without the King's support. Hague argues that Pitt's refusal of Addington's offer shows that 'he would rather have the support of the Grenvillites, who had once been his colleagues, than that of the Addingtonians, whom he was coming to despise.'[19] More likely, apart from the natural inclination to side with his cousin even against a long-standing family friend (all other things being equal), Pitt recognised that the circumstances of April 1803 offered him the chance to rebalance the British constitution, in favour of its representative institutions. On 10 April 1803 he told Addington that he would resume the office of prime minister only on the terms suggested by Grenville: an invitation would have to be extended by the King, and Pitt could submit for consideration a list of ministers which could include some of his former colleagues, as well as members of Addington's team.

Addington gave the impression of being satisfied with these terms – a reflection, no doubt, of his sense of inferiority in Pitt's presence. Privately, though, he realised that he was unlikely to win the consent of his Cabinet colleagues, let alone the agreement of the King, who had not been informed of the negotiations. On 12 April he sent a sheepish letter to Pitt, ruling out the possibility of wholesale changes but clearly hoping that the latter would still consider joining the government. From Pitt's perspective, it would be profitless to persevere with these negotiations. However, it was possible that the abortive talks would be reported to the King in a way which would damage the prospects of his returning to office. Accordingly, Pitt wrote an account of the negotiations from his own point of view and demanded that the whole correspondence should be shown to the King. Whether or not Addington provided George with all of the written testimony, the result was predictable: with his characteristic blend of insight and hyperbole, the King chose to interpret the incident as an assault on his constitutional position, and laid most of the blame on Pitt. The upshot was that Pitt retired, hurt, to Walmer, while Addington remained in Downing Street. There was one ministerial change, to the position of Treasurer of the Navy, which proved Addington's ability to attract support from the Foxite Opposition. However, since the new office holder was George Tierney, whom Pitt had recently accused of wishing to 'obstruct the defence of the country', the appointment was certainly not calculated to mollify the ex-premier.

For observers of the international scene, these inelegant manoeuvres seemed discreditable to all the parties concerned, since by April 1803 it was clear that the Treaty of Amiens would not hold. Napoleon fulminated against the savage personal attacks of the London press, and complained that Britain was in breach of the treaty because it had not surrendered the island of Malta to the neutral custody of its former rulers, the Order of the Knights of St John. In isolation, these causes of complaint would have justified Bonaparte's claim that Britain had never been seriously interested in a peace settlement.[20] But if the British were breaking the treaty, they had ample evidence that Napoleon had negotiated in bad faith. After Amiens, French influence was extended in Germany, Italy, the Netherlands and (especially) Switzerland, and it seemed increasingly likely that Britain would be excluded completely from European trade. Yet Napoleon's ambitions were not confined to Europe; his forces occupied Louisiana in North America, and it was obvious that he had not abandoned his designs on Egypt. It was this threat which had induced Addington to make his ill-advised overture to Pitt, who, even if he had not masterminded a military victory over France, had at least ensured the maintenance of British economic strength since 1793. Whatever his limitations, Addington was unafraid to commit his country to war, which he did on 17 May 1803.

Six days later, Pitt expressed support for the war in a speech which, though imperfectly reported, was considered by well-qualified observers to be one of his best. However, while attempting to rally the country in resistance to Napoleon, Pitt was careful not to express wholehearted confidence in the Addington government, and he subjected his successor's budget of June 1803 to merciless critical scrutiny. In the autumn of 1803 it was strongly rumoured that France would attempt an invasion, which meant that Pitt had good reason to take his duties as Lord Warden of the Cinque Ports very seriously. On his own admission, Pitt was unsuited to military matters; but his appointment as Lord Warden had placed him in what seemed likely to be the front line of national defence, and his concentration on these duties rather than parliamentary skirmishes for the rest of 1803 was entirely consistent with his ideal of public service. He organised three battalions of volunteers and accepted the role of colonel in the Royal Trinity House Volunteers Artillery, which was charged with vital defensive duties on the Thames.

When he returned to the Commons, on 9 December 1803, Pitt was thus furnished with new insights into the state of Britain's defences, which his supporters judged to be inadequate thanks to the government's complacency after the Treaty of Amiens. Even so, Pitt was reluctant to come out in open opposition to Addington, still hoping to receive from the government and the King a summons which would give him a free hand when he formed his next administration. His obedience to constitutional niceties had by this time overtaxed the patience of Lord Grenville, who told Pitt on 31 January 1804 that the Addington government was 'manifestly incapable of carrying on the public business', and that the only alternative was a new ministry which incorporated all of the politicians whose abilities fitted them for service at a time of national crisis.[21]

Grenville clearly did not think that Addington deserved a place in a 'ministry of all the talents', and Pitt hoped that the Doctor could be bought off with a peerage and the Speakership of the House of Lords. A much greater problem was presented by Grenville's idea of people who should be *included* – in particular, Charles James Fox. In recent debates, Fox and Pitt had occasionally found themselves on the same side, but there had been no attempt at a personal rapprochement; and while Pitt could agree unreservedly that Fox would merit a prominent place in a government which contained the most talented politicians of the day, it took a considerable leap of imagination to see Fox as a constructive coadjutor in steeling the country for a renewal of hostilities with France. In this respect, the deepening affinity between Grenvillites and Foxites was hardly more improbable than the Fox–North partnership of old. Since the fall of the Fox–North coalition Grenville and Fox had agreed on Catholic Emancipation, but on nothing else of significance. As we have seen, Pitt felt the same way about emancipation, but this was singularly unhelpful since, unlike Fox or Grenville, he had promised George III that he would do his best to prevent the issue being considered. Pitt would have been forgiven for thinking that Grenville and his followers had allowed themselves to fall under spells cast by 'the magician's wand'. Indeed, now that Fox had recognised Addington's inadequacies he had joined his followers in all-out opposition to the ministry, while Pitt could be accused of being 'willing to wound, and yet afraid to strike'.[22]

In short, although cooperation with Grenville and Fox offered easily the best way of securing Addington's resignation in the near future, this course of action presented Pitt with very awkward dilemmas. Far from solving these difficulties, a successful campaign against Addington was likely to make them more acute. In asking George III for permission to construct a 'ministry of all the talents', Pitt would be inviting him to accept the removal of a prime minister who still enjoyed his confidence and affection, and the installation in high office of somebody he had loathed for most of his adult life. At one time, the King's devotion to Pitt had been even greater than his new-found Addingtonian addiction. Even in those happier days, Pitt could not have been certain of convincing George to let bygones be bygones where Fox was concerned. Since then, the act of expelling Fox from the Privy Council had provided the King with one of the few moments of genuine satisfaction in his public life. Even if Pitt succeeded in convincing George that Fox was trustworthy after all, he would have to confront the problem of finding a suitable role for his rival. It would be difficult for Pitt to give Fox a post which measured up to his personal 'talents' without making a mockery of his own insistence that he would only return to office as a prime minister with unchallenged authority.

Pitt continued to delude himself that he might be called back to his rightful position once the Cabinet and the King had decided that there was no alternative. In the real world, however, he was faced with two stark alternatives: to act in accordance with his exalted notion of personal integrity even if this entailed a risk of national defeat under inadequate leadership, or to join with Fox and Grenville in forcing a change of government on the assumption that any alternative to Addington's administration – even if Pitt turned out to be the only proven 'talent' who was able to serve within a new ministry – would be more likely to pilot the country through the fresh storms which it was about to encounter. Another calculation which he could not ignore was the state of the King's health. In March 1804 George suffered a recurrence of his 'malady' which proved temporary once again, but since he had now entered the second half of his seventh decade there was every chance that there would be no recovery from a further attack, precipitating the regency which was unlikely to help Pitt's political prospects.

Ultimately, and by a supreme irony, it was Fox who furnished Pitt with a means of escape from his dilemma. On 23 April 1804 Fox introduced a motion on the state of the nation's defences, arguing that this question should be examined by a committee of the whole House. Pitt spoke in support of the motion. When an Addingtonian MP tried to raise memories of the Fox–North coalition, Fox was able to deny that he had known in advance that Pitt would speak in favour of the motion, and to claim that 'we fully concur in one particular opinion; we are perfectly agreed as to the weakness and incapacity of the present ministers.'[23] The government prevailed in that vote by 256 to 204; on 25 April, in a division on the militia, Pitt returned to the attack and succeeded in reducing Addington's majority to 37.

Pitt, of course, had first-hand knowledge of a government which had lingered on in the face of decisive defeats in the House of Commons. But confidence in the Addington ministry was evaporating, at a time of national emergency. In 1783, Pitt had held his own in Commons debates, virtually unaided; so at least it could be claimed at that time that governmental defeats were merely a matter of arithmetic. In April 1804 Addington and his colleagues were comprehensively outgunned by the various Opposition factions – they might be able to win the votes, but only thanks to the support of MPs whose default position was loyalty to the government in being. In these circumstances, a victory by just 37 votes on a crucial question was tantamount to a decisive defeat. On 29 April 1804, ministers accepted the inevitable, and the Addington interlude was brought to an end.

16

Return and Death

P ITT did not attend the 1802 birthday celebrations which George
Canning had devised to remind the world of his hero's personal integrity and political pre-eminence, although apparently he seemed gratified
by accounts of the event. However, even the star-struck Canning had to
present Pitt's achievements as essentially defensive in nature, referring in
'the Pilot that weathered the storm' to 'dangers by wisdom repelled', and
asking the former premier to accept 'the thanks of a people thy firmness
has sav'd'. This was very different from the record of glorious colonial
conquest associated with Pitt's father. In his anxiety to embellish Pitt's real
record, Canning overlooked what was arguably his greatest achievement –
the thwarting of French ambitions to dominate Europe as a whole. It was
due to Pitt that Britain was 'one kingdom preserv'd amid the wreck of the
world'; but, by the same token, that meant that he had failed to prevent the
rest of the world from being wrecked. Whatever he thought of Canning's
final version, Pitt would surely have been disconcerted by the first draft
of the song which alluded to 'thy hopeless retirement'.[1]

While Canning's idolatry arose from a sincere conviction that Pitt was
the greatest British politician of his age and thus by far the best-equipped
leader for any future challenges, a more apposite title for his song would
have been 'The Pilot who made the best of a bad job'. Enthusiasts like
Canning undoubtedly played some part in convincing Pitt that he should
regain his place at the controls, but they were pushing at an unfastened

door; Pitt had plenty of unfinished business. Far from living up to his father's example, it was arguable whether at the time of his resignation in 1801 Britain was better placed than he had found it. According to Pitt's script, Addington would step aside without a struggle when it was time to end his retirement, but in practice the process had been messy, even undignified, and as a result some of his natural allies now regarded Pitt as untrustworthy, while others (including even Canning) doubted his resolution.

The only way to satisfy Pitt's sense of destiny was to lead his country to outright victory, rather than acquiescing in a peace which tacitly recognised his inability to build a successful coalition against France. However, when Pitt was asked to form a government on 30 April 1804 his first challenge was to recruit a ministerial team which could offer him the necessary domestic support. Given an unrestricted choice, Pitt's problem was not a lack of talent at his disposal but rather an overabundance of well-qualified candidates for office. For various reasons, he had held his reservations concerning the Addington ministry in check while the supporters of Grenville and Fox led the attack. It would be absurd to deny that these auxiliaries deserved significant representation in a new government – a sense of honour, as well as parliamentary calculation, made it impossible for Pitt to ignore their claims. But the hope of a free hand over ministerial appointments encouraged Pitt to sketch out a 'dream team' which included Fox as Foreign Secretary, Grenville as Lord President of the Council and Charles Grey as Secretary at War. He was prepared to forgive old embarrassments and give a place to Lord Fitzwilliam (though not, obviously, anything connected with Ireland).[2]

However, the construction of the new Cabinet depended crucially on the King's attitude. Back in 1783, George had pestered Pitt to take office because he regarded him as his only defence against the hated Fox. However, he had never shown the level of personal affection for Pitt which he clearly felt with regard to Addington; and now the former had forced him to accept his favourite's resignation, thanks to an unholy parliamentary alliance with Fox. To put it mildly, it was unlikely that George would accept his demands without a considerable show of resistance.

On 2 May 1804 Pitt wrote to the King, essentially arguing for a genuine 'ministry of all the talents' which would incorporate Fox as well as Grenville. In his reply, George made disparaging remarks about Grenville and refused to contemplate Fox's inclusion. Pitt requested a private audience with the King, during which he again pressed the case for a broad-based government. Sensing he had gone too far, George withdrew his veto on Grenville, and agreed that while Fox could not be Foreign Secretary as Pitt had hoped, he could serve as an ambassador (perhaps to Russia, which would have been a rich irony given Fox's ambiguous dealings during the Ochakov affair).

Presumably Fox had assumed that Pitt would make only a token attempt (at best) to argue on his behalf. Certainly he did not think that the King could be persuaded to waive his veto, and in that expectation he made it known that he would not object if any of his supporters agreed to join Pitt's government. This gesture is usually taken as testimony to Fox's generosity of spirit; Pitt himself apparently 'expressed [...] great pleasure at Mr Fox's conduct.'[3] But that seasoned gambler could easily have guessed that his gesture would make little difference. The King's health was sufficiently shaky at the time to deter any Foxite who was tempted to earn the displeasure of the Prince of Wales party by joining Pitt. The prospect of preferment at the hands of a new monarch certainly seems to have proved too tasty for Tierney, who had agreed to serve under Addington but declined Pitt's offer to continue as Treasurer of the Navy.[4] In effect, by allowing his friends to join the government if they so wished, Fox was offering people who had continued to follow him despite all the disappointments and desertions of the past two decades a free licence to emulate the treachery of the Portland Whigs. It was not in Fox's nature to resort to emotional blackmail; but on this occasion, at least, it was quite unnecessary to do so.

In this respect, the ministerial reconstruction of April/May 1804, which on paper provided a final opportunity to combine the talents of the political titans of the age, provides a vivid illustration of the contrasting personalities and approaches to politics of Fox and Pitt. Both men could inspire levels of admiration which made their followers act against their rational self-interest. However, they exercised this fascination in very different ways. For Fox's disciples, political allegiance also entailed membership of a social milieu in which play was at least as important as principle. To be Fox's follower, one also had to be his friend; and to act or speak against him entailed ostracism from a charmed circle. This is why, when Edmund Burke made a public display of his differences with Fox over the French Revolution, both men emphasised the social as well as the political consequences of their dispute. By 1804, personal animosity towards Pitt was regarded by Fox and his followers as a key motivation for their continued engagement in politics. Thus at this time Fox's correspondence was marked by disparaging comments about his rival, who was 'a mean, low-minded dog', and 'a mean rascal'.[5] Pitt's admiring biographer Lord Stanhope was probably going a bit too far when he commented that 'I doubt whether in the whole course of Pitt's most private correspondence there can be found a single expression about Fox inconsistent with the personal respect which eminent men owe to one another.'[6] From Pitt's letters (and his conduct after 1784) it was usually easy enough to infer a degree of contempt for Fox's public character – and he did not need to spell this out because he could take it for granted that most of his colleagues shared his opinion. The language was different, but the sentiment was the same.

As he struggled to put together a new government in May 1804 Pitt's ill-feeling was directed towards Grenville rather than Fox. Having cooperated so closely in the campaign to unseat Addington, Grenville considered himself under obligation to Fox. In his conversations with Pitt, Grenville had shown a strong commitment to the idea of an inclusive government; however, it was difficult for the most optimistic observer to expect either the present King or his successor to accept a government which included both of the parliamentary titans. Failing this, when the nation's security was under threat it could be argued that a government of 'two talents' (Pitt and Grenville) would be preferable to an administration which depended on Pitt alone. Grenville, however, was deaf to this argument, and used the exclusion of Fox as a pretext to spurn Pitt's invitation. He might not have found the prospect enticing in any case, since it was unlikely that he retained any appetite for an arrangement which would, essentially, reunite the team which had come under increasing strain thanks to the repeated false dawns and frustrations in the years before 1801. Pitt's response was highly characteristic. According to the Lord Chancellor, Eldon, who had acted as an intermediary between George and Pitt, the latter exclaimed that 'he would teach that proud man [i.e. Grenville] that, in the service and with the confidence of the King, he could do without him, though he thought his health such that it might cost him his life.'[7]

Whether or not Eldon's memory was coloured by hindsight, Pitt's reported remark proved uncannily accurate. It is unlikely that any alternative government would have served the country better than Pitt's second administration in the unpropitious circumstances of 1804–6; but it is possible that the prime minister himself would have lived longer if his parliamentary position had been stronger. Like the 'mince-pie' government, Pitt's new team was a makeshift affair, with the advantage that this time he was free from a malevolent interloper like Chancellor Thurlow. The Cabinet was a mixture of Pitt's personal followers (like Lord Harrowby, the former Dudley Ryder who served as Foreign Secretary until he injured his head falling down the departmental staircase) and some survivors from Addington's government. The latter group included people (like Lord Hawkesbury and Lord Castlereagh) whom Pitt held in high regard, as well as his brother, the second Earl of Chatham, who thus contrived to hold continuous Cabinet rank for a decade without showing noticeable ability. The fact remained, however, that Pitt had helped to force Addington out of office; and his most eloquent supporter in the Commons, George Canning, wasted no opportunity of exhibiting his contempt for the Addingtonians. Pitt himself turned a cold shoulder to Addington until January 1805, when he suddenly decided to invite his former friend to join the Cabinet as Lord President of the Council.

Probably Pitt calculated that a reconciliation with Addington would strengthen his parliamentary position to some extent, at the cost of nothing more than a subsidiary ministerial role and a peerage for his former friend. Unfortunately, Pitt's original mistake of lining Addington up for promotion beyond his abilities had left a lasting impact on his protégé, who now regarded himself as a major political player with an independent following, whereas in truth his personal supporters were mainly those who clung to him in the hope that he could still be a power broker with sufficient leverage to secure them ill-deserved offices (and official salaries).

Foremost among the Addingtonian place-seekers was Robert Hobart, an undistinguished figure who was promoted to the Cabinet as Chancellor of the Duchy of Lancaster, and ennobled as Lord Buckinghamshire.

It is difficult to convict William Pitt of many obvious mistakes, but in his dealings with Addington and Buckinghamshire his personal and political failings were brought together with a quasi-classical symmetry that might have inspired a tragic poet. In 1799 Buckinghamshire had married none other than Eleanor Eden, the jilted heroine of Pitt's single venture into the world of romance. Far from being an innocuous presence, Addington (the newly dubbed Lord Sidmouth) saw fit to throw his weight around in a way which caused Pitt considerable trouble. In particular, Sidmouth was keen to follow through on an inquiry into the Navy Office, which threatened to undermine the position of Pitt's friend Henry Dundas. During his time as prime minister, Sidmouth had actually given Dundas a peerage (making him Viscount Melville) without consulting Pitt, who chose to regard this as a personal slight despite the award being a recognition of Melville's political influence in Scotland rather than a token of affection.

At regular intervals during the 1790s Melville had pestered Pitt to let him lay down his office of Secretary at War, because his exhausting duties conflicted with his family life. Pitt, however, had insisted that he should stick to his task. When Pitt returned to office in 1804 Melville agreed to join him, in the crucial role of First Lord of the Admiralty. Contrary to the view that Melville was a spent force, he immediately set about the task of reviving morale in the dockyards, which had slumped under the heavy-handed regime of his predecessor, Lord St Vincent.[8] It was St Vincent (an Addingtonian appointee) who had instigated the inquiry into naval affairs, and thus it was perhaps not coincidental that this should have brought Melville under suspicion. At any time in the eighteenth century, such an inquiry would have yielded evidence that government officials had abused their positions to augment (or establish) their fortunes to some extent, since they were allowed to treat money allocated to the armed forces as their own until it had to be spent. Charles James Fox would probably never have entered the House of Commons if he had not benefited from the industrial-scale corruption of his father, Henry; even the offences alleged against Melville were nothing like the proven abuses of the Fox family, although Melville had certainly not been as self-denying as Pitt's father Lord Chatham, who had famously refused to take advantage of funds entrusted to him as Paymaster of the Forces.

While the Addingtonians could prosecute their personal vendetta against Melville without seeming to be guilty of double standards, the Foxite Opposition was more vulnerable to this charge. However, to Fox himself the opportunity for embarrassing the new government seemed too good to miss. When Melville's nephew, Secretary at War William Dundas, accused Fox of hypocrisy, he cheerfully admitted that his own fortunes might have been based on corrupt practices, and that he had frittered away these ill-gotten gains through gambling; however, none of this had been illegal at the time in question. By contrast, the regulations regarding naval finances had been tightened in 1785 (i.e. during Pitt's early years in office, which had been devoted to the general eradication of corrupt government practices). In other words, while the Fox family could escape scot-free, Dundas stood in danger of being hoisted by his own petard, since he had been a member of Pitt's reforming government.[9]

Instead of defending Melville, Pitt argued that the charges against his colleague should be examined by a select committee. The speech was judged to be poor by Pitt's standards and was hardly calculated to appease independent MPs, who tended to be sympathetic to any campaign to root out corruption. However, it looked as if the government would prevail – until Pitt's old friend Wilberforce spoke forcefully against Melville. Wilberforce had allowed himself to be duped into taking sides in an old-fashioned faction-fight, thanks to his moralistic distaste for the worldly Melville and (probably) more than a hint of personal resentment against a man whose company Pitt clearly (and understandably) now preferred. The ensuing vote, in a packed House, was a tie: 216 in favour of censure, 216 against. The Speaker – Abbott, an Addingtonian – duly cast his vote in favour of the motion. Melville duly resigned, and advised Pitt to remove him from the Privy Council in the hope of staving off at least some of the inevitable trouble to come. Eventually, rather than facing a normal criminal charge (as his tormentors would have preferred), Melville earned the dubious distinction of being the last British politician to suffer impeachment and to be tried in the House of Lords. The verdict was consistent with the implicit line taken in Pitt's ill-fated speech of April 1805: Melville was cleared on all charges, and deemed at worst to be guilty of inadequate supervision of his underlings. By the time of his acquittal, Pitt was dead.

Although Wilberforce, with characteristic ethical dexterity, was able to acquit himself of any role in hastening Pitt's demise, the Melville affair and its repercussions placed an additional burden on a prime minister whose health was already fading. After the tied vote of April 1805, with Foxites baying for Pitt's resignation, he reportedly shed tears which he tried to conceal, and a group of supporters formed a protective shield as he left the chamber. In the following month, Pitt faced searching questions about irregularities in his own financial dealings, which (predictably) arose from an attempt to maintain the government's lines of credit rather than to restore a semblance of order to his horribly ill-managed accounts. According to taste, this episode could be hailed as a vindication of the British system, in which no individual should be immune from inquiry – or as an indictment of the spirit of the party, which allowed petty proceedings to take place against a minister who was playing a crucial role in a battle for national survival. However, it can be argued that 'the Pilot who weathered the storm' was now reaping a whirlwind of his own making, since Pitt had successfully traded on his sea-green incorruptibility and had demonstrated a pronounced streak of vindictiveness during his protracted struggle to evict Fox from Parliament after the 1784 election.

Although the Addingtonians had been instrumental in Melville's downfall, Pitt was determined not to let them capitalise on their triumph. He insisted that Melville should be replaced by Sir Charles Middleton, a long-standing member of the Admiralty Board who had worked closely with his predecessor. Middleton (who now became Lord Barham) was also a veteran opponent of the slave trade, unlike Sidmouth, who added this to an enviable record of being on the wrong side of moral arguments. Sidmouth protested vehemently that the first vacancy in the Cabinet should have been filled by one of his own acolytes; Pitt decided that this was not the best time to part with another senior minister, and talked Sidmouth out of resignation. By late June 1805, however, Pitt had become so infuriated by continued attempts to persecute Melville that he signified his refusal to promote any of Sidmouth's most prominent supporters (including his brother, Hiley) to ministerial office. Addington again offered to resign, and despite a last-ditch attempt by the King to keep Pitt in harness with his new favourite, this time the breach was irreparable.

On the face of it, Pitt's short-lived dalliance with the Addingtonians was an avoidable mistake. Some of Pitt's younger political friends thought that the government's parliamentary position, though undoubtedly uncomfortable, could have been sustained without the adhesion of these unsavoury allies. Indeed, Pitt did prevail in a series of fairly closely contested votes on the most ambitious legislation of his second term, the Additional Forces Bill, introduced in June 1803, which was designed to improve on Addington's attempt to ensure a proper balance between volunteers for home defence (the militia) and those who were available for service overseas. However, when it seemed that the bill might be defeated Pitt was forced to dust down his old argument – that a ministry could lose even a division on a key piece of legislation yet still remain in office – since the King was the ultimate arbiter of such matters. However, unlike the situation in 1784 Pitt could no longer be sure that, if push came to shove, King George would sustain him in office; the increasingly complicated parliamentary situation, in which old enemies were now cooperating and former friends were at loggerheads, meant that it suddenly seemed possible that George might contemplate a government which excluded *both* of his twin tormentors, Fox and Pitt.

Realising that the card which he had played so well in the 1780s had diminished in value, in July 1804 Pitt had embarked on an audacious bid to reconcile the King with the Prince of Wales. If this initiative had succeeded, it could have triggered 'nothing less than a coalition of all the bitterest enemies of the previous quarter of the century, and a coming together of almost the whole political establishment'.[10] Unfortunately for Pitt, the result was only a slight easing in relations between George and his heir, combined with an emphatic confirmation of the royal anathema against Fox. If the King was grateful to Pitt for this gesture, the emotion was short-lived. In January 1805 George refused to appoint Pitt's old friend Pretyman (currently Bishop of Lincoln) as Archbishop of Canterbury. It was obvious that the agnostic Pitt regarded this as a crucial test of his patronage powers rather than a profound theological dispute, but the old-fashioned King would not budge from his view that the position was to go to the Bishop of Norwich, Charles Manners-Sutton, in accordance with a previous agreement.

The feeling that he could no longer count on the King evidently helps to explain why Pitt asked the royal favourite, Addington, to join his government at around this time. On the same logic, however, Pitt would only try to keep Addington within the fold for as long as he remained an asset rather than becoming a nuisance. By the summer of 1805 Sidmouth had moved from the positive category to the negative; and Pitt duly decided to let him resign. In the interim, however, many of Pitt's supporters were at best dumbfounded, and in some instances alienated, by his rapprochement with Sidmouth. Whether due to lack of time, failing health, excessive confidence in his personal judgement or some combination of these factors, in his second spell as prime minister Pitt tended, at best, to *rationalise* his decisions to others rather than discussing them before they were taken. His old habit of taking supporters too much for granted was even more marked after 1804; several important parliamentary patrons deserted him for reasons which could have been addressed if he had given even token signs of interest in their concerns. If Pitt was reported accurately as having labelled Grenville 'that proud man', it would have been unusually appropriate to retort that 'it takes one to know one', especially since Pitt's ancestors had not been devoid of pride and his own mother had been a Grenville.

In fact, although Pitt had declared initially that he could 'do without' Grenville, by September 1805 he had changed his mind and made one last effort to persuade the King that the government should be reconstructed on a broader basis. George's opinion was unchanged – except that he now seemed to dislike Grenville as much as Fox. As recently as May, the Opposition had reminded the King of his reasons for excluding their leaders by bringing forward a motion on the toxic issue of Catholic Emancipation. As well as confirming George's view that Fox and his associates were intent on destroying the constitution, the ensuing vote gave the impression that Pitt had no need to appease them. Despite having been forced to defend his own previous record on the subject, Pitt had succeeded in defeating the motion by 336 votes to 124 – a margin which suggested that, with or without Sidmouth's support (or indeed the positive backing of the King), his parliamentary position was stable enough to keep him in office, at least while the war seemed to be going well.

Thus throughout his second spell as prime minister Pitt enjoyed enough support to convince him that he could undertake the country's essential business – but without ever feeling the margin of comfort which would allow him to ride out any serious setbacks in the war against Napoleon. Any attempt to compare Pitt's performance in his second ministry with the period between 1784 and 1801 would be inadequate unless it recognised the prime minister's changing estimation of Britain's most formidable neighbour, France. When he first came to office he was optimistic that recent hostility could be replaced by amicable relations, cemented by trade agreements. Reluctantly drawn into war by the expansionist tendencies of Revolutionary France, he remained confident that its unstable and erratic governments would eventually succumb to internal feuding or their gross infringements of the financial gospels as revealed by Adam Smith. The emergence of Napoleon Bonaparte as First Consul in 1799 shattered his optimistic (even complacent) outlook. In an aide-memoire on Napoleon, probably composed in 1803, Pitt wrote that 'I see various and opposite qualities – all the great and all the little passions unfavourable to public tranquillity – united in the breast of one man.'[11] In the early stages of the war with France, Pitt had been hesitant about the necessity for 'regime change'; he would make peace with *any* French government, provided that the deal offered a good prospect of stability and security for Europe. However, his private analysis of Napoleon's character suggested that there was no chance of a lasting peace with an individual whose legitimacy depended on the kudos associated with successful aggression.

When Pitt returned to office in 1804 the renewed war against Napoleonic France had resumed the basic pattern of the earlier contest. On the European mainland, there was no chance that Britain could resist French military power, unless it won wholehearted cooperation from the other significant states (Austria, Russia and Prussia) who tended to be disunited or even openly hostile to Britain. Nevertheless, it was easy to assume on the basis of experience since 1793 that the prowess of the

British navy could guarantee the country's security against any probable combination of the other European powers, and especially if it only had the French to deal with.

The conduct of the Opposition after Pitt returned to office suggests that they retained this confidence in British security, despite the advent of Napoleon. They continued to snipe at Pitt, despite evidence that Napoleon was mustering his naval forces for an attack on Britain. The British navy was able to blockade European ports, but there was always a chance that Napoleon's ships could break out and disembark a formidable force on British territory. The danger to Britain was obviously greatest while Napoleon had no powerful continental enemies to distract him from his preparations. In the early months of 1804 Britain had no effective allies on the continent, so Napoleon was able to commit more than 100,000 men to the projected invasion, and in July 1803 the French First Consul had even been able to occupy George III's hereditary electorate of Hanover. Whatever the Opposition might think, the government took the new invasion threat seriously. After a meeting attended by Pitt and other senior ministers in October 1804 a series of circular defensive forts, known as Martello towers, was constructed along the southern and eastern coasts of England. Ironically, the British had borrowed the idea from Napoleon's native Corsica.[12]

Pitt had no intention of confining himself to defensive measures. He continued to hope for a grand alliance of the European powers against France, and perfected earlier ideas for a system of collective security which would also draw in smaller states on a continent which would be restored to its previous rulers once the Napoleonic nightmare was over. From this perspective his first aggressive move seemed counter-intuitive. In September 1804 ministers authorised an attack on a convoy carrying an estimated £2 million of gold bullion to Spain. There was considerable loss of life on the Spanish side, and before the end of the year the country had declared war on Britain. In his defence, Pitt argued with considerable justification that this had been a pre-emptive strike, since Spain was likely to side with France in any case.

Remarkably, a buccaneering exploit of exactly this kind had been proposed by Pitt's father during the Seven Years' War (as mentioned in

Chapter Five). However, it was unlikely to be appreciated by jittery MPs who, understandably, continued to focus on Britain's isolation. In his attempt to remedy this crucial problem, Pitt found an unexpected ally in Napoleon himself. On 18 May 1804, the same day that Pitt finalised his new government, the Senate in Paris proclaimed Napoleon as emperor of the French. After winning approval of this decision through a referendum – the favourite device of demagogues – Napoleon was crowned at Notre Dame, with the assistance of the Pope, on 2 December. Previously, Napoleon had ordered the arrest and execution of the Duc D'Enghien, a member of the former royal family who was accused of working in the British interest. These events horrified the young Russian tsar, Alexander I, and made him more susceptible to British diplomatic advances despite persisting tensions between the two countries, particularly over the future of the island of Malta.

Britain's first emergence from isolation was a treaty with Sweden, signed in December 1804. After painstaking negotiations Russia agreed to an alliance in April 1805; Austria followed suit in August, forming a Third Coalition against France. The remaining piece of the jigsaw was Prussia, which preferred to wait on events to see which side would offer the highest price, with a particular penchant for King George's hereditary domain of Hanover, currently occupied by the French. Nevertheless, in October 1805 Pitt despatched Lord Harrowby (now recovered from his Foreign Office tumble) in the hope of coaxing the Prussians into the coalition with a subsidy of £2.5 million. In fact, the new threat from Austria forced Napoleon to end his occupation of Hanover, making the British bait of hard cash seem more attractive than the hypothetical territorial gains offered by the French. However, the emperor's tactical retreat was a distinctly mixed blessing; using his habitual tactic of concentrating his main forces at the crucial point of action, Napoleon routed the Austrians, who surrendered at Ulm on 19 October to a force which included most of the French soldiers who had been earmarked for the invasion of England.

Pitt heard rumours of this disaster on 2 November, and they were confirmed the following day. News of naval engagements travelled more slowly, and it was not until 7 November that Pitt learned of Lord Nelson's crushing victory over the combined French and Spanish fleets at Cape

Trafalgar. But less than a month later Napoleon once again demonstrated his tactical mastery with an overwhelming defeat of the Austrians and Russians at Austerlitz (in what is now the Czech Republic).

The public response to Trafalgar showed that Pitt was still regarded as a focal point for national resistance. On 9 November an enthusiastic crowd pulled his carriage to the Guildhall, where the Lord Mayor hailed him as 'the Saviour of Europe'. In response, Pitt disclaimed any personal achievement and avoided any premature professions of European salvation: 'England has saved herself by her exertions, and will, as I trust, save Europe by her example.'[13] Better than anyone present at the Lord Mayor's Banquet, he knew that Trafalgar had merely confirmed the existing presumption that Britain could repel invaders. Even that reassurance had come at a heavy cost; Pitt was deeply affected by the death of Nelson at the pinnacle of his glory. The outcome of Ulm, however, underlined France's domination of the continent under its seemingly invincible leader. At least the Austrians had kept on fighting, despite Napoleon's occupation of Vienna. But Austerlitz put paid to their resistance, and on 4 December they accepted a truce leading to the Treaty of Pressburg, signed on 26 December.

Just after the Battle of Austerlitz took place, but almost a month before the result was officially confirmed in London, Pitt had been persuaded to leave the capital for Bath in search of better health. In his prime he could have taken the sharply contrasting emotions evoked by Ulm and Trafalgar in his stride, but by the last few weeks of 1805 these momentous events represented a roller-coaster ride for a vehicle which was no longer roadworthy. There were occasional bouts of buoyancy – notably in October 1805, when the Third Coalition had been agreed and Pitt could revert to his habitual practice of calculating the size of allied forces on the basis of promises rather than actualities. But after Pitt's return to office numerous observers were struck by the extent to which the Pilot had been weathered by the storm. He looked emaciated, with a sallow countenance and a persistent cough – symptoms which were acclaimed by his more unsavoury opponents as signs that the hated minister was on his last legs.

Pitt was still at Bath when the early reports of Austerlitz were confirmed. As New Year's presents go, this left something to be desired. It was accompanied soon afterwards by tidings that, far from uniting with

Britain to resist Napoleon's hegemony, the Prussians had struck a deal which gave them the prized plum of Hanover as their reward for inactivity. In a letter of 10 January Lord Auckland was only exaggerating slightly when he wrote that 'We are engaged in a war of boundless expense, some peril, and incalculable duration. Our continental influence and interests are lost and undone.'[14]

On the previous day Pitt had left Bath for London to prepare for a parliamentary session which Auckland expected 'to bring forward a conflict of parties beyond what has happened in our times.'[15] As William Hague has argued, it seems unduly melodramatic to conclude that Pitt was killed by Austerlitz, since his final decline had begun even before he learned of the previous coalition defeat, at Ulm.[16] However, apart from the task of rallying parliamentarians once again for another round in the 'Consuming Struggle' with Napoleon, Pitt was now faced with the utter ruin of the project that had inspired his first spell in government, which had been based on an expectation of rising prosperity for Britain and free trade in a peaceful Europe. Instead, his country was sinking deeper into debt, not least because the asking price for allies had risen exponentially since Napoleon had taken complete control of France's military operations. Subsidies which would once have bought an entire coalition were now required to secure the services of a single state. The William Pitt of 1784, young and unbowed by experience, might have relished a challenge which, if surmounted, would have marked an achievement to rank alongside his father's legend. But the Pitt of January 1806 had run through all of his mental and physical resources.

On 11 January Pitt arrived at Bowling Green House, which he had rented since 1804. This fairly modest but picturesque residence on Putney Heath was very close to the scene of his exchange of fire with George Tierney in May 1796. Now Pitt was engaged with a far more deadly duellist. Despite the obvious medical prescription of complete rest, Pitt continued to receive some of his colleagues and to discuss the military and diplomatic situation. By the time Parliament opened again, on 21 January 1806, he was unable to retain more than a few morsels of food, and his doctors had accepted that they could do no more to help him. Various diagnoses have been suggested posthumously, ranging from bowel cancer to a peptic ulcer; whatever the precise malady, Pitt's chances of recovery could not have been improved by his daily dosage of stress and alcoholic beverages. On 22 January he was told that death was near, and received the news calmly. To his considerable credit, he rejected Pretyman's attempts to administer the sacrament, and although he agreed to join in a prayer he managed to joke that the exercise would be pointless since he had 'neglected prayer too much to allow him to hope'.[17] This did not prevent his Anglican eulogists from pretending, after his death, that he had always been as pious as Wilberforce himself.

After making his will, William Pitt died at 4.30 a.m. on 23 January. There are various reports of random phrases uttered in his final delirium, including parliamentary interjections ('Hear! Hear!') and expressions of hope that he would soon receive news from Harrowby at the Prussian court. It is quite possible that he said these things, since he had been a member of the House of Commons for the whole of his adult life and the policies of Prussia had been a constant preoccupation since 1804. The 'last words' attributed to Pitt – 'Oh, my country! How I leave my country!' – are a different matter. As we have seen, he left 'his country' in a similar state to the one which he had taken over when he returned to office; and although the international scene was bleak, he knew that Britain had plenty of fight left in it. By contrast, it is credible that on arrival in London after his final journey he told his attendants to 'Roll up' a map of Europe because 'it will not be needed these next ten years': as a parting piece of advice to his successors it proved unduly pessimistic, but for someone who was well aware that he would not be alive to witness much of the ensuing decade it was a pardonable exaggeration.

The 'Oh, my country!' story is so improbable that it is tempting to accept the alternative version, in which Pitt's dying words were an expression of interest in devouring 'one of Bellamy's meat pies'. But given Pitt's intolerance of any nourishment in his last days, this story (apparently related to Benjamin Disraeli many years later by a parliamentary attendant) is almost equally dubious. Whatever he might have said in his final throes, William Pitt was indisputably dead, worn out by the pressures of office at 46. At the same age, his illustrious father had still been awaiting his first Cabinet appointment.

17

Fox's 'Last Hurrah' ...
and Final Disappointment

WITHIN days of Pitt's death two motions were put to the House
of Commons, one proposing a state funeral and the erection of a
monument 'to that excellent statesman', the other that Pitt's debts should
be discharged at the public expense.[1] Fox had no difficulty in warmly supporting the second proposal, claiming that 'Never in my life did I give a vote
with more satisfaction.'[2] His attitude perhaps reflected the generosity of so
many of his friends in paying off his own much larger and more ill-begotten
debts. He drew the line, however, in approving any motion which described
Pitt as an 'excellent statesman'. To support this, he thought, would reveal
himself as a most consummate hypocrite. He began his speech with the
words 'I do not know, Sir, that I ever rose to address the House in the
performance of my public duty with more pain than I do at this moment.'[3]

He went on to credit Pitt with 'great qualities in no ordinary degree [...] in
private life and great qualities in points connected with his administration',
and conceded that he had shown disinterestedness of a very high order
in financial matters and the distribution of patronage.[4] Yet, he continued:

> I must say that the country at present is reduced to the most danger-
> ous and alarming situation – a situation which might call for anything
> than honours to be conferred upon him, who had the direction of the
> measures which brought it to this state.[5]

Lord Grenville had begged Fox not to make this speech, warning that it would damage his popularity, and that proved to be the case. Yet 88 MPs, not all of them Foxites, joined him in voting against the motion, whose supporters numbered 258.

It was fortunate for both Fox and Grenville that they were able to smooth over this disagreement. Pitt's death had left George III at a loss to decide whom to appoint as prime minister. He summoned the surviving members of the Cabinet and invited them to choose amongst themselves who Pitt's successor should be. But they failed to agree and, at the suggestion of Lord Portland, the most senior member of the Cabinet, sent a message to the King, saying that, in their view, only Lord Grenville had the necessary experience and authority to fill the role. The King invited Grenville to form a government, but he was unenthusiastic, saying that if he did he would want it to be 'a government of all the talents', including the most able men from all the parties and factions represented in Parliament. The King accepted this condition, saying specifically that there would be 'no exclusions', clearly implying that he would not continue to blackball Fox. His second daughter, Princess Augusta, was later to write:

> At the period of Fox's return to power the King [...] showed for several days considerable uneasiness of mind. A cloud seemed to overhang his spirits. On his return one day from London the cloud was evidently removed, and His Majesty, on entering the room where the Queen and Princess Augusta were, said he had news to tell them. 'I have taken Mr Fox for my minister, and on the whole am satisfied with the arrangement.'[6]

With a single exception, it was the first time Fox had been received in the royal closet since 1783, and the King said:

> 'Mr Fox, I little felt you and I should ever meet again in this place. But I have no desire to look back at past grievances, and you may rest assured that I shall never remind you of them.' Fox bowed, and replied: 'My deeds and not my words shall commend me to Your Majesty.'[7]

Grenville did, indeed, intend Fox to play a central role in his government, appointing him for the third time as Foreign Secretary and doubling this up with the Leadership of the House of Commons. Yet he did not succeed in his aim of uniting *all* the 'talents'. The leading Foxites and Grenvillites duly secured most of the senior Cabinet portfolios, but then Addington, newly transferred to the House of Lords as Viscount Sidmouth, demanded that he and his leading supporters should also be included. This was not universally popular, but Grenville reluctantly agreed. The Pittites, notably George Canning, angrily refused to serve with the Addingtonians, which meant that several of the more able potential recruits were left out. Beyond the Cabinet there were also a substantial number of places to be filled – junior ministers, promotions in the peerage, pensions and sinecures of every description. As the Foxites in particular had been shut out from such opportunities for two decades, there were a large number of applicants, many of whom were inevitably disappointed. Among these was Fox's glamorous aunt, Sarah, once coveted by the King and a widow since the death of her second husband, George Napier, in 1804. Three of her sons were army officers (all of whom were to end up as generals), and she applied to Fox for promotions or pensions on their behalf. But Fox had no shortage of other claimants, and perhaps felt that Sarah had already received her due by the pension of £800 a year which the King had awarded her (for old times' sake?) the previous year.

Despite the absence of the Pittites, the new government appeared to be very strong, at least on paper, and very Whiggish in its composition. The Chancellor of the Exchequer was the 26-year-old Lord Henry Petty, son of Shelburne, who had died the previous year, and Earl Fitzwilliam, the nephew and of heir of Rockingham, was Lord President of the Council. The Home Secretary was Earl Spencer, while Charles Grey was First Lord of the Admiralty. The leading Whig lawyer, Sir Thomas Erskine, was made a peer and became Lord Chancellor, while Lord Auckland, the father of Lady Eleanor Eden, was President of the Board of Trade. More junior offices were filled by Tom Grenville, Sheridan, General Richard Fitzpatrick and George Tierney, who had fought the duel with Pitt, while Sidmouth was shunted into the more ceremonial role of Lord Privy Seal.

Fox, now in his fifty-eighth year, embarked on his resumed ministerial career with some reluctance, as he explained in a letter to his favourite cousin, the former Lady Susan Fox-Strangways, now Lady Susan O'Brien:

> You are quite right in surmising that my new situation will not add to my happiness, except in the case (which I fear is far from a probable one) of my being able to do some great good. What I owe to the Publick and to a set of Political Friends whose attachment to me has been exemplary left me no choice about taking an opportunity which has been so long waited for.[8]

He had many misgivings, but despite his now chronic ill health girded himself for the task ahead. He and Elizabeth left their idyll at St Ann's Hill and moved into a house lent to them by the Duke of Bedford, in Stable Yard, adjacent to St James's Palace and just across the Park from Downing Street and the Houses of Parliament. Here he spent long days attending meetings and receiving numerous visitors before sitting down in the evenings to work on state papers. Elizabeth acted as his 'gatekeeper', and exerted herself to ensure that he led as orderly a life as possible. There were, however, constant worries and afflictions, including, not least, the death in March 1806 of Georgiana, Duchess of Devonshire, 'his constant and cherished friend since her childhood'.[9]

He set himself two overriding aims. One was the abolition of the slave trade, first proposed by William Wilberforce 14 years earlier and strongly backed by eloquent speeches from both himself and Pitt. There were high hopes in 1792 that Wilberforce's motion calling for 'immediate' abolition would be carried, but Henry Dundas (later Lord Melville) put forward a compromise amendment calling for the process to be gradual, which was carried by 193 votes to 125. Predictably, this meant that no progress at all was made. Wilberforce persisted in presenting his motion virtually every year, but Pitt's ardour weakened, and he failed to carry it through during his nearly nineteen years in office. Fox now agreed with a very ready Grenville that the time had come to make a decisive push. On Fox's other objective – a permanent peace with France – Grenville, who was deeply suspicious of Napoleon's intentions, was far more sceptical, but he agreed that Fox should make the attempt. An event which occurred soon after he assumed office seemed to augur good chances of success: a stranger called at the Foreign Office and demanded to see Fox, saying he had to communicate something of the greatest importance which he could only disclose to Fox in person. Fox granted an interview, and it transpired that the caller was a French émigré who

> confided in him that he was about to slip across to Paris to assassinate Napoleon. Everything was ready, he said: a house had been hired in Passy from which the attempt could be made with assured success and without risk.[10]

The visitor had assumed that Fox, famous for his love of liberty, would be delighted at the prospect of killing a tyrant, particularly one who was waging war against his own country. It was a gross misreading of Fox's character, to whom, in the words of Eric Eyck, 'Nothing was more repugnant [...] than the principle that the end sanctifies the means. It disgusted him to think that his noble cause might be stained by murder.'[11]

Fox ordered the immediate arrest of his visitor, and sent a communication to Talleyrand, telling him of the attempt which had been planned. Talleyrand's reply began: 'I have placed your Excellency's letter in the hands of His Majesty. His first words after reading it were: "I recognise here the principles of honour and virtue which have always distinguished Mr Fox."'[12]

Napoleon, who had crowned himself emperor in 1804, insisted that his intentions were pacific, referring to the conflict between the two nations as unprofitable, according to Eyck, who added, 'Fox at once seized on this and declared himself ready to enter into negotiations for a sure and lasting peace.'[13]

After exchanging further friendly letters with Talleyrand, Fox unwisely agreed that Lord Yarmouth (later the third Marquess of Hertford) should be the main British negotiator. Yarmouth, a Tory MP, had been stranded in France when the Peace of Amiens broke down and thus had the advantage of being already on the spot, so the peace talks could start without delay. Meanwhile, Fox turned his attention to the slavery issue, and quickly established that Wilberforce would still be the key figure. As we have seen, Wilberforce shared Fox's opposition to the war against France as well as sharing his view of the slavery issue, but although he had drifted away from Pitt he never became a 'Foxite'.

Wilberforce had enjoyed a rare success in July 1804, when he had persuaded Pitt to use an Order in Council to ban the slave trade in Dutch Guiana (modern Surinam), which had been captured by British troops. The Order had, not, however, been issued until September 1805, and had still not been presented for parliamentary approval by the time of Pitt's death in January 1806. Fox now hastened to secure its passage, and it was soon approved by large majorities in both Houses. Then, on 10 June 1806, in his last speech in the House of Commons, he moved a resolution calling for the general abolition of the slave trade. It was a short but eloquent speech (see Appendix II), in which he paid great tribute to Wilberforce and even to Pitt, of whom he said that his 'talents have always so justly been entitled to admiration, and whose eloquence was never more powerfully displayed on any occasion, than in opposition to this trade'.[15]

Fox had rarely praised Pitt during his lifetime, and had once written to Wilberforce complaining that Pitt, though personally strongly in favour of abolition, had never made a serious attempt to unite his government behind the cause.[16] Perhaps he now invoked his name in the (apparently successful) hope of encouraging the still substantial number of Pittite MPs to vote in favour of his motion. His own commitment had never been doubted, and its strength was revealed in what were nearly his very last words uttered in the Commons:

> So fully am I impressed with the vast importance and necessity of attaining what will be the object of my motion this day, that if, during the almost forty years that I have now had the honour of a seat in parliament, I had been so fortunate as to accomplish that, and that only, I should think I had done enough, and could retire from public life with comfort, and conscious satisfaction, that I had done my duty.[17]

The House responded to his words by voting overwhelmingly in favour of his motion, by 114 votes to 15, while the Lords approved a similar motion moved by Lord Grenville by 41 votes to 30. The way was open to abolition, which was duly effected by the 1807 Abolition of the Slave Trade Act; the Act received Royal Assent on 25 March, having been approved in the House of Commons by 283 votes to 16. Less than a year later the United States Congress passed a similar bill. In neither country, however, was slavery itself abolished by these acts; Wilberforce and his friends hoped that a further bill would soon be passed bringing this into effect, but the Grenville government was very shortly afterwards dismissed by George III, to be succeeded by a series of six Tory administrations – under Portland, Spencer Perceval, Lord Liverpool, George Canning, Lord Goderich and the Duke of Wellington – none of which were reforming governments, and it was only in 1830 that a Whig government came to power, led by Charles Grey (by then the Second Earl Grey). For two years it was dominated by the struggle to push through the 'great' Reform Act of 1832, but soon after, in 1833, it passed the Slavery Abolition Act, which abolished slavery throughout the British Empire. The Americans had to wait another 32 years until the 13th Amendment to the US Constitution was carried by Abraham Lincoln in 1865.

The 1807 Act was vigorously enforced, principally by the establishment of the West Africa Squadron of the Royal Navy, which was authorised to intercept any vessels, of whatever nationality, that attempted the Atlantic crossing. According to Admiralty records, between 1808 and 1860 they seized approximately 1,600 slave ships and freed 150,000 Africans who were aboard.[18] Its passage was deservedly seen as a great tribute to Fox (and also Grenville), though it was also seen as something of a rebuke to Pitt. In his otherwise admiring biography, William Hague describes the issue as 'his greatest failure'. Hague writes:

> The sincerity of his opposition to this dreadful trade was all too plain, but so is the fact that he lost the energy, focus and will to pursue the matter to a successful conclusion in the early 1800s. The fact that abolition was so speedily secured by Grenville and Fox so soon after Pitt's death suggests that he too could have secured it if he had marshalled his forces to do so. The fact is that by 1805, weighed down by the conduct of the war and deeply troubled by domestic controversies, Pitt was a spent force as a reformer.[19]

If Fox had attained the first of his two major objectives in returning to office after more than twenty years in the wilderness, the second was to elude him. Despite Talleyrand's evident goodwill, and his personal judgement that a generous peace settlement would be in France's best interest as well as Britain's, he was unable to mitigate the expansionist instincts of Napoleon. Fox's effective aim was to restore the situation envisaged by the Treaty of Amiens but to ensure that this time the provisions of that treaty were actually carried out by both sides. Napoleon, however, was now making additional territorial demands, notably that his forces, already in control of Naples, where he had installed his brother, Joseph Bonaparte, as King, should now also occupy Sicily. Fox, who had appointed his own brother, General Henry Edward Fox, as commander-in-chief of the British forces in the Mediterranean, based in the Sicilian port of Messina, was appalled. He was even more shocked by the French attitude towards Hanover. Still ruled by George III as Elector, it had been occupied by French troops during the war but had been handed over to Prussia in exchange for two small provinces in south Germany, Bayreuth and Anspach, which had been ruled by the Prussian Hohenzollern dynasty for the best part of five hundred years. These Napoleon now transferred to his ally, Bavaria. British negotiators demanded that France should ensure the withdrawal of the Prussian troops and the return of the Electorate to King George; the French response was, in effect, that this was none of their business and that it was a matter for negotiation between Britain and Prussia. Fox described this transaction to the House of Commons as '[a]n outrage, unprecedented in the history of the worst measures of the worst times of Europe.'[20]

The negotiations with Talleyrand were going from bad to worse, and it dawned on Fox and Grenville that Yarmouth was far from being an ideal negotiator. A drunken playboy, he was completely lacking in diplomatic gifts and was easily hoodwinked by the wily Talleyrand. Fox wanted to send Holland to replace or supplement him, with plenipotentiary powers, but his nephew, concerned by Fox's by now rapidly deteriorating health, insisted that his rightful place was by his uncle's side. So Grenville sent Lauderdale instead, who, while more sober than Yarmouth, proved not much of an improvement as a negotiator. When Lauderdale arrived in

Paris, he encountered a very hostile environment, which he reported back to London, and it was clear that peace was obtainable, if at all, only on the most humiliating terms. This was something that even Fox was not prepared to contemplate, and he sadly reflected:

> The manner in which the French fly from their word [...] disheartens me [...] They are playing a false game; and in that case it would be very imprudent to make any concessions which [...] could be thought inconsistent with our honour, or could furnish our allies with a plausible pretence for suspecting, reproaching or deserting us.[21]

Although desultory negotiations continued for some time, it was now clear to Fox that his bid for peace had failed. This was a devastating blow to him as it placed doubt not only on his recent judgements, but even on his confident claims throughout the 1790s that an honourable peace was there for the taking. Despite his success over the slave trade, and his later claim that he 'die[d] happy', it is clear that he was deeply disappointed.

When Fox took office in February 1806 he was far from being a well man. For the previous four years he had been intermittently ill, and in December 1805 had been incapacitated for several days by the disease which was eventually to kill him – dropsy. Having little faith in doctors, Fox did not seek any treatment, and two months later felt well enough to join the new government. But from March onwards his condition began slowly to deteriorate, though on 21 May his devoted aunt, Lady Sarah Napier, sent a relatively reassuring report to her (and Fox's) cousin, Susan:

> I saw C. Fox for *one hour* that he came of a Sunday to see me, and happy was I to *see* that his dropsy & water in the chest, and Lord knows what of his liver etc., etc. is all fabricated. *He is very very anxious* & very much worried, but he sleeps well if he *can* get to bed by 12; if not he lies awake and *thinks*, & owns that it w*ears* him. He is also billious [*sic*] with heat & worry, & he chose to *frisk* to B[uckingham] House in silk stockings out of *respect*, and so got a pain in his bowells [*sic*].[22]

About this time, it was suggested to Fox that in order to ease the pressure on himself he should give up his seat in the House of Commons and join the Lords. He discussed this with his nephew, and concluded: 'The peerage, to be sure, seems the natural way, but [...] I have an oath in Heaven against it; I will not close my politicks in this foolish way.'[23]

He managed to function reasonably effectively and to attend to his ministerial duties until early July, but then had to take to a wheelchair and eventually to his bed. Later that month it was decided that he should be moved to St Ann's Hill, so that what were now assumed to be his last days could be spent in his and Elizabeth's family home. But halfway there it became clear that the journey was too much for him, and he was dropped off at Chiswick House, the suburban London home of the Duke of Devonshire. Here his great friend Georgiana had died a few months earlier, and – by a strange quirk of fate – his father, Henry Fox, had been born there more than a hundred years earlier, in 1705. Fox remained at Chiswick House until his death in mid-September. Here Elizabeth and his nephew, Lord Holland, were constantly at his bedside, while his secretary, John Trotter, spent several hours each day reading to him from his favourite classical (and sometimes modern) authors. His daughter, Harriet Willoughby, then aged 21 or 22, was also there for much of the time, and many of his oldest friends and political associates hastened to pay a final visit. He was in great pain and had to submit on several occasions to the primitive practice of 'tapping', by which large quantities of water were drawn from his chest. It was to no avail and – greatly to the alarm of Lord Holland, who shared his uncle's tolerant but unbelieving religious views – Elizabeth arranged for a priest to be called to say prayers. Holland need not have worried; the priest was extremely discreet and made no attempt to prompt a deathbed conversion, and Fox smilingly acquiesced to please his fervently Christian wife. He died at 5.45 p.m. on 13 September 1806, his last words, addressed to his wife, according to John Trotter, being 'I die happy, I pity you.' Elizabeth, however, claimed to have distinguished several further words, 'It don't signify, my dearest, dearest Liz.' As these words, sometimes abbreviated to 'It don't sigs', frequently appeared in his letters to her whenever he was conveying bad news, it seems probable that she heard right. Holland wrote immediately to the Prince of Wales to inform him of the passing of his friend, saying:

> Indeed if one had not known it before, his last hours would have convinced us that the ruling passion of his heart was affection and tenderness for her. She has the consolation of knowing that he died with that sentiment & the comforting reflection that her society formed the happiness of his life for years & that her care prolonged it.[24]

In 1827 Pitt's devoted follower George Canning died in the same room as Fox, having reached the top of the 'greasy pole' and served as prime minister for just four months.

Fox died at the age of 57 years and eight months; his widow survived him for nearly thirty-six years, dying three days ahead of her 92nd birthday, on 8 July 1842, at St Ann's Hill, where she had become known for her good works, including the founding of a village school. The Grenville government did not last for very long after the decease of its most illustrious member. Fox had hoped that he would be succeeded as Foreign Secretary by his nephew, but Grenville, probably wisely, chose Charles Grey (now known as Lord Howick, following his father's creation as the first Earl Grey) instead. Grey also took over Fox's role as Leader of the Commons. But within six months the government fell foul of the incorrigible monarch, who turned them out of office when they refused to give him an assurance that they would not again raise the issue of Catholic Emancipation. Grenville, whose premiership had lasted a mere year and 42 days, became leader of the Whig Party, a post he held for another 12 years, with Grey as his deputy. The 'talents' ministry was succeeded by a purely Tory administration, led by the Duke of Portland, who 25 years earlier had headed a predominantly Whig government (the Fox–North coalition). It was to be another 23 years before the Whigs returned to power, when Grey (now the second Earl) became prime minister in 1830.

Unlike Pitt, Fox was not awarded a state funeral, but he was also buried in Westminster Abbey, in the heart of his constituency. His grieving friends exerted themselves to ensure that the crowd of admirers was at least equal to that at Pitt's funeral just six months earlier, and the occasion was undoubtedly a great deal more emotional. He was laid to rest just a few feet from his great rival. An impressive monument was later erected, featuring a statue by the sculptor Sir John Westmacott depicting Fox with a weeping African slave kneeling at his feet. Their proximity in death led Sir Walter Scott to write a rather maudlin ode, entitled 'Patriotism: Nelson, Pitt, Fox'. Its final stanzas read:

> With more than mortal powers endow'd,
> How high they soared above the crowd!
> Theirs was no common party race,
> Jostling by dark intrigue for place;
> Like fabled gods, their mighty war
> Shook realms and nations in its jar;
> Beneath each banner proud to stand,
> Look'd up the noblest in the land,
> Till through the British world were known
> The names of PITT and FOX alone ...
>
> Drop upon Fox's grave the tear,
> 'Twill trickle to his rival's bier.
> O'er PITT's the mournful requiem sound,
> And FOX's shall the notes rebound.
> The solemn echo seems to cry,
> 'Here let their discord with them die.
> Speak not for those a separate doom
> Whom fate made Brothers in the tomb;
> But search the land of living men,
> Where wilt thou find their like agen?'[25]

18

The Long Aftermath

I T is easy enough to caricature and contrast the qualities of Fox and Pitt. One was rotund, impulsive, spontaneous, gregarious, amorous and extrovert. Total time in Cabinet office: one year, seven months. Clearly a 'loser'. The other was thin, calculating, cool-headed, introverted, secretive and apparently asexual. Total time in Cabinet office: 19 years, six months (nearly nineteen of these years as prime minister). Equally clearly a 'winner'. What they had gloriously in common was their skill as orators, where each outperformed their contemporaries. Their styles were very different: Fox's speeches were mostly extemporised, though he was capable of making carefully crafted speeches, full of facts and statistics as well as brilliant argumentation, as he showed when he introduced his India Bill in 1783. Pitt's orations were almost always meticulously prepared, and depended for their effect mainly on the coolly logical way in which he built up his argument and his generous use of sarcasm, as in his speech opposing the formation of the Fox–North coalition on 21 February 1781 (see Appendix I). He and Fox must have clashed on hundreds of occasions during the twenty-five or so years that they faced each other across the House of Commons. Both had their triumphs and occasional disasters, but the oratorical honours were more or less even over the years. There were many occasions on which they both highly distinguished themselves, which might perhaps be qualified as 'score-draws'. Less frequent were the 'no-score draws', when neither of them shone. One perceptive witness, the merchant banker Sir Francis Baring, who was an MP for several years, was quoted as saying, in 1806, that Fox 'had flashes of genius that were beyond Mr Pitt', but that 'over a period of two to three years [...] Mr Pitt had the ascendancy.'[1]

The contestation did not end with their deaths; instead, it was carried on by their followers for at least several decades afterwards. The next six governments were led by disciples of Pitt, and the two following ones by those of Fox, and each of them claimed the mantle of their hero. The first prime minister not to be personally linked to either one of them was Sir Robert Peel (PM in 1834–5 and 1841–6), who had served his ministerial apprenticeship in governments impregnated with Pittite views. The direct link was restored when Lord Aberdeen became prime minister in 1852; Pitt and his colleague Henry Dundas had been Aberdeen's guardians. The chief cheerleader for Fox was, of course, his beloved nephew, the third Lord Holland. With his formidable wife, formerly Lady Elizabeth Webster, who had left her more elderly first husband to become Holland's mistress and later his wife, he presided over the most famous of Whig salons, at Holland House. This became a veritable shrine to Charles Fox. Its centrepiece was a marble bust of Fox, generally regarded as being the masterwork of Joseph Nollekens, reputedly the most fashionable – and certainly the most skilled – sculptor practising in London, though he was of Belgian origin. Several hundred copies of the bust were made, which ended up decorating the houses and gardens of Whig notables throughout the country. Nollekens went on to make a similar bust of Pitt, taken from his death mask, as Pitt had refused before his death to sit for the artist. This was also copied many times, and served the same function in Tory households. Holland sold the rights to Fox's unfinished work on James II for the remarkably high sum of 4,525 guineas, and it was published in 1808 under the title *A History of the Early Part of the Reign of James II*, by the Right Hon. Charles James Fox. Priced £1. 16s., it was not a success. Although running to 276 pages, with a further 400 of appendices and endpapers, it was but a fragment of the intended work, going up only to the year 1685 and the rebellion and execution of the Duke of Monmouth, who was, of course, Fox's distant cousin. It did little to keep Fox's memory green, unlike two ambitious ventures of

Lord John Russell, Peel's successor as prime minister in 1846–52 and again in 1865–6. His three-volume *Life and Times of Charles James Fox* (1859–66), and four-volume *Memorials and Correspondence of Charles James Fox* (1853–7) are works of genuine scholarship, though highly biased in Fox's favour. They sold large numbers of copies and were extremely influential. Since then there have been many other biographies, few of which are at all objective. Of those which are, the best are those by John Derry (1972), Stanley Ayling (1991) and, especially, L. G. Mitchell (1992), which is beyond praise.

What was it that Fox actually succeeded in bequeathing to posterity? Certainly he did not leave a large body of legislation. The only bill he succeeded in carrying was his Libel Act of 1792, which increased the powers of juries in deciding cases relating to the press. He was already dead when the Slave Trade Abolition Act was passed in 1807, but no one doubted the crucial role he had played in bringing this about. He was leader of his party for a quarter of a century, longer than anyone in British history, even Robert Walpole (who, however, was prime minister throughout his 21 years as leader of the Whigs). Fox inspired great devotion among his followers and periodically dazzled them with his oratorical triumphs, but he failed to give them strong and consistent leadership on a day-to-day basis and showed poor political judgement on crucial occasions such as the Regency Crisis of 1788–9. Moreover, Fox had little interest in (or knowledge of) economic affairs, and, unlike Pitt, completely ignored the arguments of Adam Smith, whose great work, *The Wealth of Nations*, had been published in 1776. This led him to take a frankly obscurantist view of Pitt's unsuccessful attempt to introduce a customs union with Ireland in 1785, and his free trade treaty with France in 1787. Consequently, the Whigs remained for several years tied to much more backward-looking policies than their Tory opponents. For long periods in the late 1790s and after, he became disheartened and bored with politics, but he was unable either to galvanise himself into action or to make way for an alternative leader (perhaps Sheridan?). This might have been due to hubris, a justified estimate of the abilities of his potential successors, or perhaps down to his very strong family loyalties. He saw himself as having taken over the baton from his father, but whom should he pass it on to? In an extraordinary letter to his nephew, in 1793, referring to his illegitimate (deaf and dumb) son, Harry Fox, he wrote:

> Poor Harry, tho' an excellent Boy from his misfortune is not what I can look forward to with much satisfaction so when I have a mind to build castles and look forward to distant times I must think of you and only you.[2]

But the third Lord Holland, an amiable and easy-going man, though utterly devoted to his uncle and all his causes, was essentially a lightweight figure; Fox may have sensed this, and, though he wanted Holland to succeed him, have been in no hurry to stand aside.

Fox's career was of course blighted by George III's unconstitutional action in turning him, Portland and North out of office in 1783, and keeping him out for almost twenty-three years. Had he not done so, Fox seemed set for a long period as Foreign Secretary and the de facto head of government, with a serious possibility of eventually replacing Portland in the premiership. He justifiably blamed George and Pitt for this disaster and nursed a grievance against them for the rest of his life, believing that George was bent on imposing a personal despotism and that Pitt had behaved both dishonourably and dishonestly. His party shared his abhorrence at their action, and – with very few exceptions – stuck loyally to him throughout the next decade. The aftermath of the French Revolution, however, strained these loyalties to their limit, and first Burke and then the Portlandites split off and rallied to Pitt's government. Yet Fox was wrong to place the entire blame for his downfall on the King and Pitt. His actual (and perceived) character faults had also contributed to his discomfiture. His father's overindulgence to him in his childhood has a lot to answer for. He was raised to believe that instant self-gratification was his birthright, and it is hardly an exaggeration to argue that he never really grew up until he reached the verge of middle age. His uncontrollable urge to gamble with money which he did not have was only the most conspicuous of the failings which may have contributed to his downfall. John Cannon argues in his brilliant study of the overthrow of the Portland government that it was only the widespread unpopularity of Fox which allowed George and Pitt to get away with their coup and its retrospective justification by the 1784 election. He writes:

> It is not easy to explain why a man, so attractive in his private circle, should have been so distrusted by the public at large [...] Paragraph after paragraph [in the public press, which was overwhelmingly pro-George and pro-Pitt], it is true, dwelt on his debts, his love affairs, and reminded readers that his father had once been called 'the public defaulter of unaccounted millions'. The accusation of 'Cromwell' was particularly effective. It was reported to be the 'received notion among the inferiors in Yorkshire' that Fox was 'attempting to dethrone the King and make himself an Oliver Cromwell'. In Lancashire the name of Fox was said to be 'most universally execrated', and in Gloucestershire 'the Good Women and the Mob' exclaimed against him.[3]

The contrast with the perceived upright character of both George and Pitt was sufficient to induce a substantial swing against the Whigs when the voters went to the polls in 1784. All might not have been lost to Fox; he had several subsequent chances of entering the government under Pitt, but he always declined on the principled grounds that this would exonerate Pitt for his unconstitutional behaviour in 1783. A less charitable interpretation is that his refusal was due to damaged *amour propre*. Had he accepted, it might have led to many years in a senior ministerial post, with great influence and the opportunity to introduce important reforms close to his heart. Possibly, however, he might have choked at the bit and impulsively resigned, as he did from the Rockingham government in 1782.

Despite Fox's great political disappointments, he never became a morose or resentful man. He retained his vitality almost to the end, and his genius for friendship, and was happy in his domestic life and his intellectual pursuits. With his death perished all memory of his faults and shortcomings. What persisted was a vision of a heroic fighter on behalf of a range of progressive causes, some of them markedly more radical than his actual beliefs. Apart from his commitment to peace and a civilised conduct of international relations, these included, notably, the severe limitation of the powers of the Crown, the supremacy of Parliament and the defence and expansion of civil liberties. In the fullness of time, all these objectives were largely achieved, with the monarchy reduced to a largely ceremonial role, a democratised Parliament, and civil liberties enshrined in a series of Acts culminating in the Human Rights Act 1998. Nearly all of these reforms were either implemented by the Whigs or inspired by his example (or their successor Liberal and Labour Parties), though Benjamin Disraeli also played a role. Perhaps Fox wasn't a 'loser' after all.

Pitt has also been well served by his biographers, although the first major study (by his former tutor Bishop Tomline) was generally regarded as a flop – Lord Rosebery (himself the author of a more successful study in 1891) thought that 'there is no drearier book in all biography.'[4] Pitt's relative Earl Stanhope produced a four-volume study (1861–2) which was surprisingly balanced and included transcripts of original documents; it remains one of the best sources on Pitt. The naval historian John Holland Rose published two volumes on Pitt, *William Pitt and National Revival* and *William Pitt and the Great War* (both 1911), along with a volume of essays on Pitt and Napoleon (1912); these books also contained useful primary material. Yet scholarship on this subject is dominated by the gargantuan three-volume biography by the late John Ehrman – *The Years of Acclaim* (1969), *The Reluctant Transition* (1983) and *The Consuming Struggle* (1996) – which overall occupied almost as many years of researching and writing as Pitt's political career. It would seem churlish to find fault with such a magnificent feat of scholarship, but the book is not always a page-turner and despite its length devotes little attention to the relationship between Pitt and Fox. It has certainly provided a rich source of material for the authors of more 'user-friendly' biographies, including Michael Duffy (2000) and Michael Turner (2003). In 2004 the former Conservative Party leader, William Hague, produced his own substantial study, which was strongly sympathetic without sparing criticism and proved that the author was a highly talented biographer in addition to being a skilled politician and a sparkling public speaker.

To his admirers, Fox was a potentially great prime minister who was denied his proper place by monarchical machinations. While Pitt had plenty of time to show his fitness for the highest offices, the various biographies show that his career can also be regarded as a case of 'what might have been'. His working habits might have been unusually disorderly, but his mind was organised to a remarkable degree. Furthermore, he was a man with a plan – an ambition, clearly inspired by the writings of Adam Smith, to consolidate Britain's growing prosperity through a network of trading agreements. To paraphrase Lord Palmerston, Pitt worked on the premise that Britain had no natural enemies or rivals, but only potential partners. His deal with France, in 1786, was a remarkable coup; and although his primary impulse was chiefly economic, from Pitt's liberal perspective it was not difficult to expect a foreign policy dividend as the two nations exchanged their historic antagonism for beneficial interdependence.

The revolution in France destroyed these hopes, along with Pitt's cherished vision of a debt-free future thanks to his sinking fund. While Fox, with typical impetuosity, welcomed the initial developments in Paris as a decisive blow in the struggle for human liberty, Pitt thought that the Revolution was likely to result in the establishment of a regime much like his own – led by earnest technocrats whose idea of glory was a budget surplus rather than territorial annexations. Contrary to legend, far from hankering after a 'war of reaction' Pitt was anxious to avoid continental conflict, and was forced to enter the war only when the French proved all too successful in mobilising their citizens, transforming a struggle for national survival into one of conquest. Pitt had to turn his economic ingenuity to the task of raising subsidies for the benefit of European powers who had already shown their limitations as allies through maladroit tactics which had made defence of the Revolution into a litmus test of French patriotism. Ironically, the challenge of recruiting and retaining allies in the years of war which stretched ahead had been made much harder by the success of Pitt's own father as an exponent of imperial expansion. To varying degrees, Austria, Prussia and Russia suspected British intentions, fearing that a knockout blow against France would alter the balance of power, in Europe and beyond, to their disadvantage.

In other words, what started off as a 'war of ideas' in which Pitt was reluctant to take a hand soon took on the more traditional lineaments of European conflict, in which calculations of national advantage were at least as important as principles. But while Pitt's approach to the war had initially been pragmatic, he became increasingly attentive to the possibility that the battle with France would inspire demands for radical changes in the British constitution – not least because before the war he had been convinced that the system should be rebalanced to take more account of public opinion. Whether or not Pitt recognised that the French Revolution had been fostered by the unavailing concessions of well-meaning reformers, he decided that the British system of limited monarchy could only be saved if the process of change was arrested for the duration of the war. His concern was sharpened by a fear that the popular discontent which invariably followed poor harvests could be turned to political advantage by British radicals; and that Thomas Paine, who had helped to stoke the fires of rebellion in the American colonies, was providing enemies of the British constitution with highly effective arguments.

Convinced that the 'war of ideas' was likely to spread from France to Britain, Pitt decided that it was not enough to put aside his own plans for limited reform; he would have to argue that certain rights and liberties which Britain's political classes had begun to take for granted should now be seen as provisional, liable to suspension by means of a parliamentary vote. The persistent idea that the government embarked on a 'Reign of Terror' cheapens the vocabulary of moral outrage, not just in the context of the crimes which were committed by the French in the name of Liberty, but also when one recollects that the contemporary British judicial system still considered death or deportation as fitting punishments for minor offences committed by the poor. Nevertheless, even if the attempt to crush political dissent by force was similar to the fairly recent judicial murder of Admiral Byng – an exercise in selective persecution *pour encourager les autres* – it exposed a very unsavoury vindictive streak which Pitt had already shown in his campaign to invalidate Fox's election as MP for Westminster.

While Pitt's repressive policies tarnished his reputation, prompting the charge of 'apostasy' from contemporary observers and repelling subsequent historians, it also allowed Fox to burnish his credentials as a 'man of the people'. Obviously we will never know what Fox would have done if he had been responsible for policy towards alleged 'subversives', but he would have come under overwhelming pressure from his alarmist allies – like Burke, as well as self-appointed vigilantes outside Parliament – to do *something*. Equally, it is hazardous to speculate about Fox's likely performance if he had been entrusted with ultimate responsibility for Britain's war effort. In his Ford Lectures of 1956 A. J. P. Taylor asserted that Fox would have been far more successful than Pitt, but the value of this accolade was reduced by his claims that the latter 'ranks with the worst War Ministers in our history' as well as being an all-round rotter.[5] In reality, Fox's brief spell as Foreign Secretary under the 'ministry of all the talents' demonstrated an approach to diplomacy which was broadly consistent with his outlook during the 1790s. His belief that Napoleon could be persuaded to make an honourable peace suggests that his sincere and highly creditable hatred of war encouraged him to indulge in a degree of wishful thinking which would not have been helpful to the fulfilment of British aims at any time after 1793. His misunderstanding of Napoleon's character is all the more telling since he had the advantage of having met the emperor during the temporary cessation of conflict in 1802–3. Pitt showed much greater insight in his observations from a distance. In itself this illuminates a telling contrast between the two men; Fox, with his desire to focus on positive human characteristics, clearly deserves an honoured place in the liberal tradition, while Pitt, hoping for the best but acutely aware that all human beings are influenced by mixed motives, is in many ways a better representative of conservative ideology than Burke himself. Pitt, of course, never considered himself to be a Tory, preferring, like his father, to be known as an 'independent Whig'. In practice, however, especially after his junction with the Portlandite Whigs in 1794, he was the effective leader of the Tory Party, and has been so recognised by the party ever since.

It might be argued that Fox could not have been a successful wartime prime minister unless he had entrusted diplomatic activity to a more pragmatic (if not pessimistic) colleague. In principle there is no reason to doubt that Fox would have adopted this approach if he found it necessary; although he obviously liked leadership, he could have worked happily with senior subordinates, as Pitt did (for the most part) with Dundas and Grenville. However, this consideration indicates another important difference between Fox and Pitt. The former believed that political cooperation should be based on friendship; he cultivated his closest allies because he liked their company. In their different ways, both Pitt and Fox mixed pleasure with business: but while Fox made his friends into political colleagues, Pitt made his colleagues into friends. For Fox, the enduring bonds of loyalty forged by personal friendship could lure him into damaging political situations, such as his initial idea that he could stay on amicable terms with Burke despite their insuperable political differences, and his willingness to be duped by the Prince of Wales (on the latter score, it is interesting that Whig historians have tended to forgive Fox for his dealings with that egregious individual while placing a sinister construction on Pitt's relations with George III, who, notwithstanding his limitations and prejudices, did at least try to uphold a certain idea of public service).

The difference, in short, is that while Fox could probably have organised the dream dinner party (provided that he was brave enough to exclude 'Prinny'), Pitt could be trusted to appoint the best possible government from the talent available to him. Despite his gauche manners, Pitt was also able to recruit talented individuals from the ranks of his opponents. Within unavoidable constraints, he usually managed to place his ministers in the appropriate positions. It is unlikely that Fox would have been equally skilled in Cabinet-building. He would have found it difficult to deny senior positions to his boon companions, whatever their aptitude for the relevant jobs; and patronage would have had to be extended to the special cronies of the 'illustrious personage' who Fox had chosen to make into the ultimate arbiter of his fortunes.

Since it was most unlikely that any prime minister, however gifted, could have led Britain to a conclusive victory over France by 1806, the country was probably fortunate to have found, in William Pitt, the best person to lead its unsuccessful efforts. His greatest weakness – a tendency to oscillate between over-optimism and exaggerated gloom – would have been more damaging if it had not been tempered by the advice of more cautious colleagues. At the time of his death, Pitt was understandably despondent about the prospects of a lasting peace settlement, but in his final term he had fleshed out a plan for collective security in Europe based on pre-Revolutionary boundaries, which provided the basis for the diplomacy of his devoted follower, Lord Castlereagh, at the Congress of Vienna.[6]

If Pitt really was the best-qualified pilot to weather the storm, it could be argued that George III's implacable opposition to Fox turned out to be an uncovenanted advantage to the country and even to humanity. With no expectation of an early ministerial appointment, Fox could turn the full power of his oratory to humanitarian causes, leaving a glorious legacy to the idealists of the future. Pitt the Elder and Henry Fox had dreamed that their favourite sons would surpass their own achievements, and it is unlikely that either would have been disappointed. Respectively, they bred the most remarkable prime minister and perhaps the greatest Opposition leader in British history. Together, they could be cited as evidence that the hereditary principle might have some value in politics after all – an ironic inference that would have evoked uneasy sensations in both Fox and the younger Pitt.

Although Fox and Pitt lived longer than near-contemporaries like Mozart, Keats and Byron, who also succumbed to diseases which would be treatable nowadays, it would be reasonable to say that they both wore themselves out in characteristic ways. Fox's demise was undoubtedly hastened by his epicurean lifestyle, while Pitt was driven to early death by his consuming passion for public service. Neither seemed to be remotely attracted by the prospect of prolonging their lives through a complete change of habits. Pitt was persuaded to visit Bath more than once, but while he was drinking the waters he was sure to be thinking of politics. Fox did slow down a bit in his final years, but this only enabled him to outlive Pitt by a few months. He died at the age of 57 – a decent enough span by contemporary standards, but a striking departure from recent family history (his grandfather Stephen was not merely alive at 78, but also capable of siring a son, Henry, who himself lived into his late sixties).

Since they lived in trigger-happy times, it is somewhat surprising that the political duel between Fox and Pitt never took a more physical form. If the two titans had ever levelled pistols at each other, their records suggest that they would have presented a greater danger to passing pigeons than to each other. But their lack of marksmanship was more than compensated by their mutual animosity – certainly Pitt went out of his way to provoke

Fox's deputy, George Tierney, into challenging him for what was in effect a proxy duel, and Fox's private correspondence is testimony to his personal dislike of Pitt. This was no synthetic quarrel; one might almost conclude that George III did them a favour by ensuring that they never had to serve in the same Cabinet. In their different ways Henry Fox and the elder Pitt imbued their political heirs with an identical aspiration – to emulate the achievement and rival the posthumous fame of the greatest classical orators. It is most unlikely that either would have fulfilled this ambition without the stimulus provided by the other. A biographical study of one which did not give equal attention to the other would be incomplete, like the story of Hamlet without the inspirational input of Shakespeare.

Notes

Preface

1   Erich Eyck, *Pitt versus Fox: Father and Son, 1735–1806*, trans. Eric Northcott (London, 1950).
2   John Campbell, *Pistols at Dawn: Two Hundred Years of Political Rivalry, from Pitt and Fox to Blair and Brown* (London, 2009), pp. 9–56.
3   Sir George Otto Trevelyan, *George the Third and Charles Fox: The Concluding Part of the American Revolution*, Vol. I (London, 1912), p. 13.
4   John Ehrman, *The Younger Pitt: Volume I, The Years of Acclaim* (London, 1969), p. 55.

1. The Parliamentary Cockpit

1   Dick Leonard, *The Great Rivalry: Gladstone and Disraeli* (London, 2013).
2   Stanley Ayling, *Fox: The Life of Charles James Fox* (London, 1991), p. 77.
3   Lewis Namier, *The Structure of Politics at the Accession of George III* (London, 1957), p. 75.
4   Chris Cook and John Stevenson, *British Historical Facts 1760–1830* (Basingstoke, 1980), pp. 53–9.
5   Ibid, p. 59.
6   Edward Gibbon, *Autobiography and Correspondence of Edward Gibbon* (London, 1869).
7   Namier, *The Structure of Politics*, p. 457.
8   Dick Leonard, *A History of British Prime Ministers: Walpole to Cameron* (London, 2015), pp. 2–3.
9   Cook and Stevenson, *British Historical Facts 1760–1830*, p. 49.
10 Namier, *The Structure of Politics*, p. xv.

2. Fathers and Sons

1   For the relationship between Hervey and Stephen Fox, see Lucy Moore, *Amphibious Thing: The Life of Lord Hervey* (London, 2000).

277

2 Erich Eyck, *Pitt versus Fox: Father and Son, 1735–1806*, trans. Eric Northcott (London, 1950), p. 42.
3 Ibid.
4 Ibid.
5 Ibid., p. 61.
6 The prestige of this property was signified in 1817, when it was bought by the government and bestowed on the Duke of Wellington in gratitude for his military exploits.
7 This figure has been multiplied by 138 to give the equivalent value in 2018. For the basis of the calculation of modern-day values, see inflation. stephenmorley.org.
8 Stanley Ayling, *The Elder Pitt: Earl of Chatham* (London, 1976), p. 22.
9 Eyck, *Pitt versus Fox*, p. 68.
10 Sixth Earl of Ilchester, Giles Stephen Holland Fox-Strangways, *Henry Fox, 1st Lord Holland, His Family and Relations*, Vol. II (London, 1920), p. 3.
11 Dick Leonard, *A History of British Prime Ministers: Walpole to Cameron* (London, 2015), p. 120.
12 Ayling, *The Elder Pitt*, p. 201.
13 Eyck, *Pitt versus Fox*, p. 79.
14 Quoted in Ayling, *The Elder Pitt*, p. 262.
15 Marie Peters, *The Elder Pitt* (London, 1998), p. 116.
16 Ilchester, *Henry Fox*, Vol. II, p. 135.
17 Stella Tillyard, *Aristocrats: Caroline, Emily, Louisa and Sarah Lennox 1740–1832* (London, 1994).
18 Eyck, *Pitt versus Fox*, p. 102.
19 W. J. Smith (ed.), *The Grenville Papers*, Vol. I (London, 1852), p. 452.
20 Horace Walpole, *Memoirs of the Reign of George II*, ed. John Brooke, Vol. I (New Haven, CT, 1985), p. 128.
21 Ayling, *The Elder Pitt*, p. 253.
22 This nickname is taken from Nikolai Tolstoy, *The Half-Mad Lord* (London: Jonathan Cape, 1978).
23 Leonard, *A History of British Prime Ministers*, p. 132.

3. Charles James Fox: Early Life, 1749–74

1 Linda Kelly, *Holland House: A History of London's Most Celebrated Salon* (London, 2013), p. xi.
2 Sixth Earl of Ilchester, Giles Stephen Holland Fox-Strangways, *Henry Fox, 1st Lord Holland, His Family and Relations*, Vol. II (London, 1920). There are also numerous references in L. G. Mitchell, *Charles James Fox* (Oxford, 1992), which has been a major source for this chapter.
3 Ilchester, *Henry Fox*, Vol. I, p. 174.

4   John W. Derry, *Charles James Fox* (London, 1972), p. 12.
5   Mitchell, *Charles James Fox*, p. 4.
6   Derry, *Charles James Fox*, pp. 11–12.
7   Mitchell, *Charles James Fox*, p. 3.
8   Michael J. Turner, *Pitt the Younger: A Life* (Hambledon and London, 2003), p. 6.
9   Mitchell, *Charles James Fox*, p. 7.
10 Ilchester, *Henry Fox*, Vol. II, p. 354.
11 Ibid.
12 Derry, *Charles James Fox*, p. 15.
13 Ibid., p. 17.
14 Ibid.
15 Mitchell, *Charles James Fox*, p. 12.
16 Ilchester, *Henry Fox*, Vol. II, p. 326.
17 Mitchell, *Charles James Fox*, pp. 19–20.
18 Ibid., p. 20.
19 Ilchester, *Henry Fox*, Vol. II, p. 347.
20 John Brooke, *King George III* (London, 1972), p. 273.
21 Mitchell, *Charles James Fox*, p. 22.
22 Derry, *Charles James Fox*, p. 52.
23 As previoulsy noted, these figures should be multiplied by 138 to give the equivalent value in 2018.
24 Derry, *Charles James Fox*, p. 50.

4. The Early Career of Pitt the Younger: A Chip off the Old Block?

1   'A letter to a noble lord', in *The Works of the Right Honourable Edmund Burke*, ed. F. and C. Rivington, Vol. VII (London, 1801), p. 397.
2   W. C. Sellar and R. J. Yeatman, *1066 And All That* (London, 1930), p. 82.
3   For John Pitt, see Jacqueline Reiter, *The Late Lord: The Life of John Pitt, 2nd Earl of Chatham* (Barnsley, 2017).
4   Stanley Ayling, *The Elder Pitt: Earl of Chatham* (London, 1976), p. 248.
5   John Ehrman, *The Younger Pitt: Volume I, The Years of Acclaim* (London, 1969), p. 5.
6   Ayling, *The Elder Pitt*, p. 249.
7   Ehrman, *The Younger Pitt: Volume I*, p. 6.
8   W. S. Taylor and J. H. Pringle (ed.), *Correspondence of William Pitt, Earl of Chatham*, Vol. II (London, 1838), p. 439.
9   Ian R. Christie (ed.), *The Correspondence of Jeremy Bentham, Vol. 3: January 1781 to October 1788* (London, 1971), pp. 69, 93–4.
10 Ehrman, *The Younger Pitt: Volume I*, p. 23.
11 Ibid.

12 Ibid., p. 22.
13 Hague, *William Pitt*, p. 68.
14 W. S. Hathaway (ed.), *The Speeches of the Right Honourable William Pitt, in the House of Commons*, Vol. I (3rd edn, London, 1817), pp. 1–7.
15 Nathaniel William Wraxall, *Historical Memoirs of My Own Times* (London, 1904), p. 377.
16 Ehrman, *The Younger Pitt: Volume I*, p. 107.
17 Hague, *William Pitt*, p. 69.
18 Ehrman, *The Younger Pitt: Volume I*, p. 55.
19 Wraxall, *Historical Memoirs of My Own Times*, p. 376.
20 Hague, *William Pitt*, p. 79.
21 Michael J. Turner, *Pitt the Younger: A Life* (Hambledon and London, 2003), pp. 38–9.

5. The Third Man: A Stubborn and Determined Monarch

1 The full text of this poem, written in 1855, was: 'George the First was always reckoned / Vile, but viler George the Second; / And what mortal ever heard / Any good of George the Third? / When from earth the Fourth descended / (God be praised!) the Georges ended.'
2 John Brooke, *King George III* (London, 1972), p. 48.
3 H.T. Dickinson, 'St John, Henry, styled first Viscount Bolingbroke (1678–1751)', in *Oxford Dictionary of National Biography* (Oxford, 2004) [online], http://www.oxforddnb.com/view/10.1093/ref:odnb/9780198614128.001.0001/odnb-9780198614128-e-1001252.
4 Erich Eyck, *Pitt versus Fox: Father and Son, 1735–1806*, trans. Eric Northcott (London, 1950), p. 94.
5 Richard Pares, *King George III and the Politicians* (London, 1953), p. 61.
6 Reed Browning, *The Duke of Newcastle* (New Haven, CT, 1975), p. 283.
7 Ibid., pp. 288–9.
8 John Cannon, *The Fox–North Coalition: Crisis of the Constitution, 1782–4* (Cambridge, 1969), p. 66.
9 Brooke, *King George III*, p. 100.
10 For an account of these six premierships, see Dick Leonard, *A History of British Prime Ministers: Walpole to Cameron* (London, 2015), chs 4, 6–10.
11 Charles Daniel Smith, *The Early Career of Lord North the Prime Minister*, pp. 25–67. See also Leonard, *A History of British Prime Ministers*, pp. 167–8.
12 Dermot Englefield, Janet Seaton and Isobel White, *Facts about the British Prime Ministers* (New York, 1995), p. 6.

6. From Tory to Whig

1   L. G. Mitchell, *Charles James Fox* (Oxford, 1992), p. 38.
2   Ibid., p. 33.
3   Ibid., p. 34.
4   Quoted in Erich Eyck, *Pitt versus Fox: Father and Son, 1735–1806*, trans. Eric Northcott (London, 1950), p. 199.
5   Ibid., p. 209.
6   Ibid., p. 214.
7   Stanley Ayling, *Fox: The Life of Charles James Fox* (London, 1991), p. 84.
8   Eyck, *Pitt versus Fox*, p. 216.
9   Ibid., p. 215.
10 Ayling, *Fox*, p. 71.
11 Mitchell, *Charles James Fox*, p. 29.
12 The 'King's Friends' – a group of some 40 peers and MPs who were unconditionally committed to the King. Most of them were former followers of the Earl of Bute. Two of the most prominent were Robinson and Charles Jenkinson, later First Earl of Liverpool, whose son was prime minister from 1812 to 1827.
13 Ayling, *Fox*, p. 27.
14 John W. Derry, *Charles James Fox* (London, 1972), p. 108.
15 Ibid., p. 74.
16 Ayling, *Fox*, p. 95.
17 Peter Whiteley, *Lord North: The Prime Minister Who Lost America* (London, 1996), p. 195.
18 Peter D. G. Thomas, *Lord North* (London, 1976), p. 132.

7. Peace with America: The Rockingham and Shelburne Governments

1   Peace with Holland was reached only in May 1784, under a fourth government, that of the younger Pitt.
2   L. G. Mitchell, *Charles James Fox* (Oxford, 1992), p. 47.
3   Ibid.
4   Stanley Ayling, *Fox: The Life of Charles James Fox* (London, 1991), p. 96.
5   Dick Leonard, *A History of British Prime Ministers: Walpole to Cameron* (London, 2015), p. 104.
6   Quoted in Dermot Englefield, Janet Seaton and Isobel White, *Facts about the British Prime Ministers* (New York, 1995), p. 43.
7   John Brooke, *King George III* (London, 1972), p. 122.
8   Charles Stuart, 'Lord Shelburne', in Hugh Lloyd-Jones, Valerie Pearl and Blair Worden (eds), *History and Imagination: Essays in Honour of H. R. Trevor-Roper* (London, 1981), p. 247.

9 Ibid.

10 Ayling, *Fox*, p. 102.

11 John Cannon, *The Fox–North Coalition: Crisis of the Constitution, 1782–4* (Cambridge, 1969), p. 18.

12 John Ehrman, *The Younger Pitt: Volume I, The Years of Acclaim* (London, 1969), p. 70.

13 Ehrman, *The Younger Pitt: Volume I*, p. 71, note.

14 Ibid., p. 72.

15 Cannon, *The Fox–North Coalition*, p. 18.

16 Ibid.

17 Ibid.

18 Erich Eyck, *Pitt versus Fox: Father and Son, 1735–1806*, trans. Eric Northcott (London, 1950), p. 234.

19 Ayling, *Fox*, p. 187.

20 I. M. Davis, *The Harlot and the Statesman: The Story of Elizabeth Armitstead and Charles James Fox* (Bourne End, 1986), pp. 63–4.

21 Katie Hickman, *Courtesans: Money, Sex and Fame in the Nineteenth Century* (London, 2003), p. 84.

22 Cannon, *The Fox–North Coalition*, p. 30.

23 Leonard, *A History of British Prime Ministers*, p. 175.

24 Ibid., p. 161. It was only several years later, in 1776, that he relented and reluctantly paid off the debt.

25 Ibid., p. 176.

26 Cannon, *The Fox–North Coalition*, p. 37.

27 Ibid., p. 49.

28 Ibid., p. 53.

29 Ibid., p. 54.

30 Ibid.

31 William Hague, *William Pitt the Younger* (London, 2004), pp. 110–11.

32 Ibid., p. 57.

33 W. S. Hathaway (ed.), *The Speeches of the Right Honourable William Pitt, in the House of Commons*, Vol. 1 (3rd edn, London, 1817), p. 31 (see Appendix 1 for full speech).

34 Ibid., pp. 24–38.

35 Cannon, *The Fox–North Coalition*.

36 Ibid., p. 66.

37 Ibid.

38 Ibid.

39 Ibid.

40 Hague, *William Pitt*, p. 118.

41 Cannon, *The Fox–North Coalition*, p. 67.

42 Ibid.

43 Ibid, p. 69.

44 Ibid, p. 71.
45 Mitchell, *Charles James Fox*, p. 60.
46 Cannon, *The Fox–North Coalition*, p. 66.
47 Ibid., pp. 80–1.

8. The Fox–North Coalition and the King's *'Coup d'État'*

1 Dick Leonard, *A History of British Prime Ministers: Walpole to Cameron* (London, 2015), pp. 44–5.
2 John W. Derry, *Charles James Fox* (London, 1972), pp. 119–20.
3 Leonard, *A History of British Prime Ministers*, p. 181.
4 John Cannon, *The Fox–North Coalition: Crisis of the Constitution, 1782–4* (Cambridge, 1969), p. 96.
5 Christopher Hibbert, 'George IV (1762–1830)', in *Oxford Dictionary of National Biography* (Oxford, 2004) [online], doi: https://doi.org/10.1093/ref:odnb/10541.
6 Stanley Ayling, *Fox: The Life of Charles James Fox* (London, 1991), p. 118.
7 Ibid., p. 120.
8 William Hague, *William Pitt the Younger* (London, 2004), p. 140. Emphasis in original letter.
9 Lord John Russell (ed.), *Life and Times of Charles James Fox*, Vol. II (London, 1853), pp. 218-20.
10 L. G. Mitchell, *Charles James Fox* (Oxford, 1992), p. 64.
11 Cannon, *The Fox–North Coalition*, p. 120.
12 Hague, *William Pitt*, p. 149.
13 John Campbell, *Pistols at Dawn: Two Hundred Years of Political Rivalry, from Pitt and Fox to Blair and Brown* (London, 2009), p. 28.
14 Cannon, *The Fox–North Coalition*, p. 122.
15 Ibid.
16 Hague, *William Pitt*, p. 144.
17 Cannon, *The Fox–North Coalition*, p. 138.
18 Ibid., p. 139.
19 Ayling, *Fox*, p. 123.
20 Cannon, *The Fox–North Coalition*, p. 141.
21 Ibid., p. 140.
22 Ibid., p. 144.
23 Erich Eyck, *Pitt versus Fox: Father and Son, 1735–1806*, trans. Eric Northcott (London, 1950), p. 256.
24 Cannon, *The Fox–North Coalition*, p. 151.
25 Campbell, *Pistols at Dawn*, p. 31.
26 I. M. Davis, *The Harlot and the Statesman: The Story of Elizabeth Armitstead and Charles James Fox* (Bourne End, 1986), p. 56.

9. The 'Mince-Pie' Government

1 Nathaniel Wraxall, *Historical Memoirs of My Own Times* (London, 1904), p. 616.
2 John Ehrman, *The Younger Pitt: Volume I, The Years of Acclaim* (London, 1969), p. 84.
3 Ibid, p. 145.
4 George Tomline, *Memoirs of the Life of the Right Honourable William Pitt*, Vol. I (London, 1821), pp. 273–4.
5 William Edward Hartpole Lecky, *A History of England in the Eighteenth Century*, Vol. V (London, 1892), pp. 247–8; Earl Stanhope, *Life of the Right Honourable William Pitt*, Vol. I (London, 1861–2), p. 176.
6 W. S. Hathaway (ed.), *The Speeches of the Right Honourable William Pitt, in the House of Commons*, Vol. I (3rd edn, London, 1817), p. 90.
7 Ehrman, *The Younger Pitt: Volume I*, p. 139.
8 Quoted ibid., p. 141.
9 Hathaway (ed.), *The Speeches of the Right Honourable William Pitt*, Vol. I, p. 107.
10 Lecky, *A History of England*, Vol. V, p. 255.
11 Ibid, p. 216.
12 John Cannon, *The Fox–North Coalition: Crisis of the Constitution, 1782–4* (Cambridge, 1969), pp. 206–27.
13 William Hague, *William Pitt the Younger* (London, 2004), p. 178.
14 I. M. Davis, *The Harlot and the Statesman: The Story of Elizabeth Armitstead and Charles James Fox* (Bourne End, 1986), p. 76.
15 Ibid.

10. The Young Reformer

1 Nathaniel Wraxall, *Historical Memoirs of My Own Times* (London, 1904), p. 627.
2 Earl Stanhope, *Life of the Right Honourable William Pitt*, Vol. I (London, 1861–2), p. 221.
3 Michael J. Turner, *Pitt the Younger: A Life* (Hambledon and London, 2003), p. 267.
4 See John Morrow, *British Flag Officers in the French Wars, 1793–1815: Admirals' Lives* (Bloomsbury Academic, 2018, 92–5)
5 John R. Breihan, 'William Pitt and the commission on fees, 1785–1801', *Historical Journal* 27/1 (1984), p. 81.
6 John Ehrman, *The Younger Pitt: Volume I, The Years of Acclaim* (London, 1969), p. 213.
7 Lord Rosebery, *Pitt* (London, 1891), pp. 74–5.

8 For changing historical interpretations of Pitt's attitude towards parliamentary reform, see Jennifer Mori, *William Pitt and the French Revolution 1785–1795* (Edinburgh, 1997), pp. 8–9.
9 Quoted in Ehrman, *The Younger Pitt: Volume I*, p. 234.
10 Quoted in William Hague, *William Pitt the Younger* (London, 2004), pp. 291–2.
11 Ehrman, *The Younger Pitt: Volume I*, pp. 391–3.
12 Ibid., p. 644.

11. The Regency Crisis

1 Stanley Ayling, *Fox: The Life of Charles James Fox* (London, 1991), p. 158.
2 Ibid, p. 151.
3 Ibid, p. 148.
4 L. G. Mitchell, *Charles James Fox* (Oxford, 1992), p. 78.
5 Ibid., p. 81.
6 Ida Macalpine and Richard Hunter, *George III and the Mad-Business* (London, 1991), p. 54.
7 Thomas Moore, *Memoirs of the Life of the Right Honourable Richard Brinsley Sheridan*, Vol. II (5th edn, London, 1827), pp. 37–8.
8 Ibid.
9 Ibid., p. 38.
10 Ibid., p. 42.
11 John Ehrman, *The Younger Pitt: Volume I, The Years of Acclaim* (London, 1969), p. 655.
12 Earl Stanhope, *Life of the Right Honourable William Pitt*, Vol. II (London, 1861–2), p. 6.
13 Ibid., p. 23.
14 William Hague, *William Pitt the Younger* (London, 2004), p. 266.

12. The French Revolution and Foreign Relations

1 W. S. Hathaway (ed.), *The Speeches of the Right Honourable William Pitt, in the House of Commons*, Vol. I (3rd edn, London, 1817), p. 31.
2 John Ehrman, *The Younger Pitt: Volume II, The Reluctant Transition* (London, 1983), pp. 43–5.
3 Ibid., p. 47.
4 Reilly, *Pitt the Younger* (London, 1978), p. 177.
5 Ibid., p. 181.
6 Ehrman, *The Younger Pitt: Volume II*, pp. 21–4.
7 Ibid., pp. 34-41.

8 The best available edition of *Reflections* was published as a Penguin Classic in 1968. It includes a brilliant introduction by Conor Cruise O'Brien.

9 L. G. Mitchell, *Charles James Fox* (Oxford, 1992), p. 113.

10 Ibid., pp. 294–5.

11 Ibid., p. 113.

12 Stanley Ayling, *Fox: The Life of Charles James Fox* (London, 1991), p. 171.

13 *The Journal and Correspondence of William, Lord Auckland*, Vol. III (London, 1861), p. 320.

14 Quoted in William Hague, *William Pitt the Younger* (London, 2004), p. 290.

15 Ehrman, *The Younger Pitt: Volume II*, p. 80, note.

16 Hague, *William Pitt*, p. 316.

17 Mitchell, *Charles James Fox*, p. 122. Italics in original.

18 Ibid.

19 John Keane, *Tom Paine: A Political Life* (London, 1995), pp. 334–414.

20 John Ehrman, *The Younger Pitt: Volume I, The Years of Acclaim* (London, 1969), p. 389, note.

21 Erich Eyck, *Pitt versus Fox: Father and Son, 1735–1806*, trans. Eric Northcott (London, 1950), p. 297.

22 William Doyle, *The Oxford History of the French Revolution* (Oxford, 1989), p. 19.

23 Eyck, *Pitt versus Fox*, p. 297.

24 Ayling, *Fox*, p. 179.

25 Hathaway, *The Speeches of the Right Honourable William Pitt*, Vol. I, p. 400.

26 Ibid., p. 435.

27 A. H. Millar, rev. G. M. Ditchfield, 'Palmer, Thomas Fyshe (1747–1802)', in *Oxford Dictionary of National Biography* (Oxford, 2004) [online], doi: https://doi.org/10.1093/ref:odnb/21220.

28 H. T. Dickinson, 'Muir, Thomas (1765–1799)', in *Oxford Dictionary of National Biography* (Oxford, 2004) [online], doi: https://doi.org/10.1093/ref:odnb/19498.

29 Ayling, *Fox*, p. 183.

30 John W. Derry, *Politics in the Age of Fox, Pitt and Liverpool* (Basingstoke, 1990), p. 97.

13. The Younger Pitt as War Leader

1 Lord Macaulay, *Miscellaneous Writings of Speeches* (London, 1900), p. 421.

2 Michael Duffy, *The Younger Pitt* (London, 2000), pp. 191–2.

3 Michael J. Turner, *Pitt the Younger: A Life* (Hambledon and London, 2003), p. 118.

4 Dick Leonard, *A History of British Prime Ministers: Walpole to Cameron* (London, 2015), p. 204.

5 L. G. Mitchell, *Charles James Fox* (Oxford, 1992), p. 132.
6 Henry Offley Wakeman, *Life of Charles James Fox* (London, 1890), p. 218.
7 John Ehrman, *The Younger Pitt: Volume II, The Reluctant Transition* (London, 1983), p. 645.
8 Lord Rosebery (ed.), *Orations on the French War, to the Peace of Amiens, by William Pitt* (London, 1906), pp. 203, 216.
9 Ibid., pp. 216, 217.
10 John Ehrman, *The Younger Pitt: Volume III, The Consuming Struggle* (London, 1996), p. 72.
11 Ibid., pp. 72–3.
12 Robin Reilly, *Pitt the Younger* (London, 1978), pp. 256–60.
13 William Hague, *William Pitt the Younger* (London, 2004), p. 394.
14 Ibid., p. 393.
15 Ibid., p. 394.
16 Ehrman, *The Younger Pitt: Volume III*, p. 32.
17 Ibid., pp. 47–9.
18 Hague, *William Pitt*, pp. 405–6.

14. Union and Resignation

1 Lord Rosebery (ed.), *Orations on the French War, to the Peace of Amiens, by William Pitt* (London, 1906), p. 253.
2 I. M. Davis, *The Harlot and the Statesman: The Story of Elizabeth Armitstead and Charles James Fox* (Bourne End, 1986), p. 117.
3 Details of this transaction are given in Stanley Ayling, *Fox: The Life of Charles James Fox* (London, 1991), pp. 186–7.
4 Ibid, p. 187.
5 John Ehrman, *The Younger Pitt: Volume III, The Consuming Struggle* (London, 1996), p. 116.
6 Ayling, *Fox*, p. 201.
7 Ehrman, *The Younger Pitt: Volume III*, pp. 117, 126.
8 Samuel Taylor Coleridge, 'Fears in Solitude' (composed April 1798).
9 Ehrman, *The Younger Pitt: Volume III*, p. 127.
10 Ibid., pp. 181–2.
11 Ibid., p. 499.
12 Piers Mackesy, *War without Victory: Downfall of Pitt, 1799–1802* (Oxford, 1994), p. 189.
13 Ehrman, *The Younger Pitt: Volume III*, p. 507.
14 Ibid., p. 508.
15 John Holland Rose, *Pitt and Napoleon: Essays and Letters* (London, 1912), p. 14.
16 Irene Cooper Willis (ed.), *Charles James Fox: Speeches During the French Revolutionary War Period* (London, n.d.).

17 Roger Wells, *Wretched Faces*, (Gloucester, 1988), p. 222.
18 Ehrman, *The Younger Pitt: Volume III*, p. 509.

15. The Addington Interlude

1   Philip Ziegler, *Addington* (London, 1965), p. 98.
2   Ibid., p. 93.
3   William Hague, *William Pitt the Younger* (London, 2004), p. 482.
4   Ziegler, *Addington*, p. 94.
5   Hague, *William Pitt*, p. 477.
6   L. G. Mitchell, *Charles James Fox* (Oxford, 1992), p. 195.
7   Stanley Ayling, *Fox: The Life of Charles James Fox* (London, 1991), p. 210.
8   Ibid., p. 213.
9   Ibid.
10 Mitchell, *Charles James Fox*, p. 174.
11 Ibid.
12 Ibid., p. 175.
13 Ibid, pp. 174–5.
14 Ibid, p. 175.
15 Ibid, p. 179.
16 Ibid, p. 173.
17 Ayling, *Fox*, pp. 198–9.
18 Hague, *William Pitt*, pp. 505–6.
19 Ibid.
20 Frank McLynn, *Napoleon: A Biography* (London, 1997), pp. 264–7.
21 Quoted ibid., p. 322.
22 This quote is taken from Alexander Pope's poem *Epistle to Dr. Arbuthnot* (1735).
23 Erich Eyck, *Pitt versus Fox: Father and Son, 1735–1806*, trans. Eric Northcott (London, 1950), p. 351.

16. Return and Death

1   John Ehrman, *The Younger Pitt: Volume III, The Consuming Struggle* (London, 1996), p. 572, note.
2   Earl Stanhope, *Life of the Right Honourable William Pitt*, Vol. IV (London, 1861–2), p. 177.
3   Ibid., p. 173.
4   Ibid., p. 190.
5   Ibid., p. 181.
6   Ibid.

7   Ibid., p. 174.
8   Roger Knight, *Britain against Napoleon: The Organization of Victory, 1793–1815* (London, 2014), p. 223.
9   Stanhope, *Life of the Right Honourable William Pitt*, Vol. IV, p. 296.
10 William Hague, *William Pitt the Younger* (London, 2004), p. 539.
11 Stanhope, *Life of the Right Honourable William Pitt*, Vol. IV, p. 225.
12 Knight, *Britain against Napoleon*, pp. 252, 276–7.
13 Quoted in Ehrman, *The Younger Pitt: Volume III*, p. 808.
14 Quoted in Michael J. Turner, *Pitt the Younger: A Life* (Hambledon and London, 2003), p. 270.
15 Ibid.
16 Hague, *William Pitt*, pp. 570–1.
17 Ibid., p. 576.

17. Fox's 'Last Hurrah' … and Final Disappointment

1   *Speeches of the Rt. Hon. Charles James Fox*, ed. J. Wright, Vol. VI (London, 1815), p. 625.
2   Stanley Ayling, *Fox: The Life of Charles James Fox* (London, 1991), p. 225.
3   Fox, *Speeches*, Vol. VI, p. 626.
4   Ibid, p. 627.
5   Ibid, p. 629.
6   John Brooke, *King George III* (London, 1972), p. 381.
7   Ibid.
8   L. G. Mitchell, *Charles James Fox* (Oxford, 1992), p. 221.
9   I. M. Davis, *The Harlot and the Statesman: The Story of Elizabeth Armitstead and Charles James Fox* (Bourne End, 1986), p. 163.
10 Erich Eyck, *Pitt versus Fox: Father and Son, 1735–1806*, trans. Eric Northcott (London, 1950), p. 370.
11 Ibid.
12 Ibid., p. 371.
13 Ibid.
14 John Wolffe, 'Wilberforce, William', in *Oxford Dictionary of National Biography* (Oxford, 2004) [online], doi: https://doi.org/10.1093/ref:odnb/29386.
15 Fox, *Speeches*, Vol. VI, p. 660.
16 Mitchell, *Charles James Fox*, pp. 248–9.
17 Fox quoted ibid., p. 659.
18 Ayling, *Fox*, p. 193.
19 William Hague, *William Pitt the Younger* (London, 2004), p. 589.
20 Fox, *Speeches*, Vol. 6, p. 643.
21 John W. Derry, *Charles James Fox* (London, 1972), p. 427.

22 Mitchell, *Charles James Fox*, p. 236.

23 Ayling, *Fox*, p. 227.

24 Davis, *The Harlot and the Statesman*, p. 171.

25 John Campbell, *Pistols at Dawn: Two Hundred Years of Political Rivalry, from Pitt and Fox to Blair and Brown* (London, 2009), p. 54.

18. The Long Aftermath

1 *The Diary of J. Farington*, ed. K. Garlick and A. Macintyre, Vol. VII (New Haven, CT, 1978–98), 25 June 1806.

2 L. G. Mitchell, *Charles James Fox* (Oxford, 1992), pp. 181–2.

3 John Cannon, *The Fox–North Coalition: Crisis of the Constitution, 1782–4* (Cambridge, 1969), pp. 231–2.

4 Earl Rosebery, 'Tomline's estimate of Pitt', *Monthly Review* 12 (July–September 1903), p. 3.

5 A. J. P. Taylor, *The Trouble Makers* (London, 1993), p. 23.

6 Sir Charles Webster, *The Foreign Policy of Castlereagh, 1812–1815: Britain and the Reconstruction of Europe* (London, 1950), pp. 56–63.

Select Bibliography

Ayling, Stanley, *The Elder Pitt: Earl of Chatham* (London, 1976).
—— *Fox: The Life of Charles James Fox* (London, 1991).
Bigham, Clive, *The Prime Ministers of Britain, 1721–1924* (London, 1924).
Black, Jeremy, *Walpole in Power* (Stroud, 2001).
Brooke, John, *King George III* (London, 1972).
Browning, Reed, *The Duke of Newcastle* (New Haven, CT, 1975).
Burke, Edmund, *Reflections on the Revolution in France* (London, 1790; repr. Harmondsworth, 1968).
Campbell, John, *Pistols at Dawn: Two Hundred Years of Political Rivalry, from Pitt and Fox to Blair and Brown* (London, 2009).
Cannon, John, *The Fox–North Coalition: Crisis of the Constitution, 1782–4* (Cambridge, 1969).
Christie, Ian (ed.), *The Correspondence of Jeremy Bentham, Vol. 3: January 1781 to October 1788* (London, 1971).
Clark, J. C. D., *The Dynamics of Change: The Crisis of the 1750s and English Party Systems* (Cambridge, 1982).
—— (ed.), *The Memoirs and Speeches of James, 2nd Earl Waldegrave, 1742–1763* (London, 1985).
Cook, Chris and John Stevenson, *British Historical Facts 1760–1830* (Basingstoke, 1980).
—— *British Historical Facts 1688–1760* (Basingstoke, 1988).
Davis, I. M., *The Harlot and the Statesman: The Story of Elizabeth Armitstead and Charles James Fox* (Bourne End, 1986).
Derry, John W., *Charles James Fox* (London, 1972).
—— *Politics in the Age of Fox, Pitt and Liverpool* (Basingstoke, 1990).
Doyle, William, *The Oxford History of the French Revolution* (Oxford, 1989).
Duffy, Michael, *The Younger Pitt* (Harlow, 2000).
Eccleshall, Robert and Graham Walker (eds), *Biographical Dictionary of British Prime Ministers* (London, 1998).
Ehrman, John, *The Younger Pitt: Volume I, The Years of Acclaim* (London, 1969).
—— *The Younger Pitt: Volume II, The Reluctant Transition* (London, 1983).
—— *The Younger Pitt: Volume III, The Consuming Struggle* (London, 1996).

Englefield, Dermot, Janet Seaton and Isobel White, *Facts about the British Prime Ministers*, (New York, 1995).

Eyck, Erich, *Pitt versus Fox: Father and Son, 1735–1806*, trans. Eric Northcott (London, 1950).

Farington, Joseph, *The Diary of J. Farington*, ed. K. Garlick and A. Macintyre, 7 vols (New Haven, CT, 1978–98).

Fox, Charles James, *A History of the Early Part of the Reign of James II* (London, 1808).

Grafton, Augustus Henry Fitzroy, Third Duke of, *Autobiography and Political Correspondence of Augustus Henry, Third Duke of Grafton*, ed. Sir William Anson (London, 1898).

Hague, William, *William Pitt the Younger* (London, 2004).

Hathaway, W. S. (ed.), *The Speeches of the Right Honourable William Pitt, in the House of Commons*, 3 vols (3rd edn, London, 1817).

Hickman, Katie, *Courtesans: Money, Sex and Fame in the Nineteenth Century* (London, 2003).

Hilton, Boyd, *A Mad, Bad, and Dangerous People? England 1783–1846* (Oxford, 2013).

Hoffman, Ross J. S., *The Marquis: A Study of Lord Rockingham, 1730–1782* (New York, 1973).

Holland Rose, John, *William Pitt and National Revival* (London, 1911).

—— *William Pitt and the Great War* (London, 1911).

—— *Pitt and Napoleon: Essays and Letters* (London, 1912).

Howat, G. M. D., 'The Duke of Devonshire', in Herbert Van Thal (ed.), *The Prime Ministers, Vol. I: From Sir Robert Walpole to Sir Robert Peel* (London, 1974).

Ilchester, Giles Stephen Holland Fox-Strangways, Sixth Earl of, *Henry Fox, 1st Lord Holland, His Family and Relations*, 2 vols (London, 1920).

Jupp, Peter, *Lord Grenville, 1759–1834* (Oxford, 1985).

Keane, John, *Tom Paine: A Political Life* (London, 1995).

Kelch, Ray A., *Newcastle, A Duke without Money: Thomas Pelham-Holles 1693–1768* (London, 1974).

Kelly, Linda, *Holland House: A History of London's Most Celebrated Salon* (London, 2013).

Knight, Roger, *Britain against Napoleon: The Organization of Victory, 1793–1815* (London, 2014).

Lawson, Philip, *George Grenville: A Political Life* (Oxford, 1984).

Lecky, William Edward Hartpole, *A History of England in the Eighteenth Century* (London, 1892).

Leonard, Dick, *Eighteenth-Century British Premiers: Walpole to the Younger Pitt* (Basingstoke, 2011).

—— *The Great Rivalry: Gladstone and Disraeli* (London, 2013).

—— *A History of British Prime Ministers: Walpole to Cameron* (London, 2015).

Levy, M. J., *The Mistresses of King George IV* (London, 1996).

Macalpine, Ida, and Richard Hunter, *George III and the Mad-Business* (London, 1991).

Macaulay, Lord, 'William Pitt', in *Miscellaneous Writings and Speeches* (London, 1900).

Martinet, J., *Vie politique, littéraire et privée de Charles James Fox* (Paris, 1807).

McKelvey, James Lee, *George III and Lord Bute: The Leicester House Years* (Durham, NC, 1973).

Mackesy, Piers, *War without Victory: Downfall of Pitt, 1799–1802* (Oxford, 1994).

McLynn, Frank, *Napoleon: A Biography* (London, 1997).

Mitchell, L. G., *Charles James Fox* (Oxford, 1992).

Moore, Lucy, *Amphibious Thing: The Life of Lord Hervey* (London, 2000).

Moore, Thomas, *Memoirs of the Life of the Right Honourable Richard Brinsley Sheridan*, 2 vols (5th edn, London, 1827).

Mori, Jennifer, *William Pitt and the French Revolution, 1785–1795* (Edinburgh, 1997).

Morrow, John, *British Flag Officers in the French Wars, 1793–1815: Admirals' Lives* (London, 2018).

Namier, Lewis, *The Structure of Politics at the Accession of George III* (London, 1957).

Norris, John, *Shelburne and Reform* (London, 1963).

O'Gorman, Frank, *The Long Eighteenth Century: British Political and Social History 1688–1832* (London, 1997).

Owen, John B., *The Rise of the Pelhams* (London, 1957).

Pares, Richard, *King George III and the Politicians* (London, 1953).

Pearce, Edward, *The Great Man: Sir Robert Walpole: Scoundrel, Genius and Britain's First Prime Minister* (London, 2007).

—— *Pitt the Elder: Man of War* (London, 2011).

Peters, Marie, *The Elder Pitt* (London, 1998).

Powell, David, *Charles James Fox: Man of the People* (London, 1998).

Reilly, Robin, *Pitt the Younger* (London, 1978).

Reiter, Jacqueline, *The Late Lord: The Life of John Pitt, 2nd Earl of Chatham* (Barnsley, 2017).

Rosebery, Lord, *Pitt* (London, 1891).

—— *Chatham: His Early Life and Connections* (London, 1910).

Rosebery, Lord (ed.), *Orations on the French War, to the Peace of Amiens, by William Pitt* (London, 1906).

Russell, Lord John, *Life and Times of Charles James Fox*, 3 vols (London, 1859–66).

Russell, Lord John (ed.), *Memorials and Correspondence of Charles James Fox*, 4 vols (London, 1853–7).

Schweizer, Karl, *Lord Bute: Essays in Re-Interpretation* (Leicester, 1998).

Sedgwick, Romney (ed.), *Lord Hervey's Memoirs* (London, 1952).

Sellar, W. C. and R. J. Yeatman, *1066 And All That* (London, 1930).

Simms, Brendan, *Three Victories and a Defeat: The Rise and Fall of the First British Empire* (London, 2007).

Smith, Charles Daniel, *The Early Career of Lord North the Prime Minister* (London, 1979).

Smith, W. J. (ed.), *The Grenville Papers*, 4 vols (London, 1852).

Stanhope, Earl, *Life of the Right Honourable William Pitt*, 4 vols (London, 1861–2).

Taylor, A. J. P., *The Trouble Makers: Dissent over Foreign Policy, 1792–1939* (London, 1993).

—— *British Prime Ministers and Other Essays* (London, 2000).

Taylor, W. S, and J. H. Pringle (ed.), *Correspondence of William Pitt, Earl of Chatham* (London, 1838).

Thomas, Peter D. G., *Lord North* (London, 1976).

Tillyard, Stella, *Aristocrats: Caroline, Emily, Louisa and Sarah Lennox 1740–1832* (London, 1994).

Tomline, George, *Memoirs of the Life of the Right Honourable William Pitt*, 2 vols (London, 1821).

Trevelyan, Sir George Otto, *The Early History of Charles James Fox* (London, 1899).

—— *George the Third and Charles Fox: The Concluding Part of the American Revolution*, Vol. I (London, 1912).

Turberville, A. S., *English Men and Manners in the 18th Century* (New York, 1964).

Turner, Michael J., *Pitt the Younger: A Life* (Hambledon and London, 2003).

Van Thal, Herbert (ed.), *The Prime Ministers, Vol. I: From Robert Walpole to Robert Peel* (London, 1974).

Wakeman, Henry Offley, *Life of Charles James Fox* (London, 1890).

Walpole, Horace, *Memoirs of the Reign of George II*, ed. John Brooke, 3 vols (New Haven, CT, 1985).

—— *Memoirs of the Reign of George III*, ed. Derek Jarrett, 4 vols (New Haven, CT, 2000).

Webster, Sir Charles, *The Foreign Policy of Castlereagh, 1812–1815: Britain and the Reconstruction of Europe* (London, 1950).

Whiteley, Peter, *Lord North: The Prime Minister Who Lost America* (London, 1996).

Wilkinson, David, *The Duke of Portland: Politics and Party in the Age of George III* (Basingstoke, 2003).

Willis, Irene Cooper (ed.), *Charles James Fox: Speeches during the Revolutionary War Period* (London, n.d.).

Wraxall, Nathaniel William, *Historical Memoirs of My Own Times* (London, 1904).

Wright, J. (ed.), *Speeches of the Rt. Hon. Charles James Fox*, 6 vols (London, 1815).

Ziegler, Philip, *Addington* (London, 1965).

Appendix I

Extract from Pitt's speech against the formation of the Fox–North coalition, 21 February 1783

S IR, Revering, as I do, the great abilities of the honourable gentleman who spoke last [Fox], I lament, in common with the house, when those abilities are misemployed, as on the present question, to inflame the imagination, and mislead the judgement. I am told, Sir, 'he does not envy me the triumph of my situation on this day': a sort of language which becomes the candour of the honourable gentleman as ill as his present principles. The triumphs of party, Sir with which this self-appointed minister seems so highly elated, shall never seduce me to any inconsistency which the busiest suspicion shall presume to glance at. I will never engage in political enmities without a public cause. [...] Sir, the steady triumphs of virtue over success itself shall be mine, not only in my present situation, but through every future condition of my life: triumphs which no length of time shall diminish; which no change of principles shall ever sully.

The fatal consequences of Tuesday's vote, which I then deprecated and foretold, is already manifest in this house, and it has been thought on all sides requisite, to give a new stability to the peace, which that vote had already shaken. But the proof which the present motion is about to establish, *that we are determined to abide by this peace*, is a declaration, that we have examined the terms, and have found them *inadequate*. Still less consistent is this extraordinary motion with the language of Tuesday. It was then urged, that no sufficient time had been allowed us to determine on the articles before us; and in the short space of two days, we are ready to pass a vote of censure on what we declare we have not had leisure to discuss. This, Sir, is the first monstrous product of that strange alliance, which threatens once more to plunge this devoted country into all the horrors of another war. [...]

Was this peace, Sir, concluded with the same indecent levity, that the honourable gentleman would proceed to its condemnation? Many days and nights were laboriously employed by his Majesty's ministers in such extensive negotiations; consultations were held with persons the best informed on the respective subjects; many doubts were well weighed, and removed; and weeks and months of solemn discussion gave birth to that peace, which we are required to destroy without examination: that peace, the positive ultimatum from France, and to which I solemnly assure the public there was no other alternative but a continuance of war.

Could the ministers, thus surrounded with scenes of ruin, affect to dictate the terms of peace? And are these articles seriously compared with the peace of Paris? There was, indeed, a time when Great Britain might have met her enemies on other conditions; and if an imagination, warmed with the power and glory of this country, could have diverted any member of his Majesty's councils from a painful inspection of the truth, I might, I hope, without presumption, have been entitled to that indulgence. I feel, Sir, at this instant, how much I had been animated in my childhood by a recital of England's victories:— I was taught, Sir, by one, whose memory I shall ever revere, that at the close of a war, far different indeed from this, she had dictated the terms of peace to submissive nations. This, in which I place something more than a common interest, was the memorable era of England's glory. But that era is past: she is under the awful and mortifying necessity of employing a language that corresponds with her true condition: the visions of her power and pre-eminence are passed away [...]

I repeat then, Sir that it is not this treaty, it is the Earl of Shelburne alone whom the movers of this question are desirous to wound. This is the object which has raised this storm of faction; this is the aim of the unnatural coalition to which I have alluded. If, however, the baneful alliance is not already formed, if this ill-omened marriage is not already solemnized, I know a just and lawful impediment, and, in the name of the public safety, *I here forbid the Banns.*

My own share in the censure, pointed by the motion before the house against his Majesty's ministers, I will bear with fortitude, because my own heart tells me I have not acted wrong. To this monitor, who never did, and, I trust, never will, deceive me, I will confidently repair, as an adequate asylum from all the clamour which interested faction can raise. I was not very eager to come in, and shall have no great reluctance to go out, whenever the public are disposed to dismiss me from their service. It has been the great object of my short official existence to do the duties of my station with all the ability and address in my power, and with a fidelity and honour which should bear me up, and give me confidence, under every possible contingency or disappointment. I can say with sincerity, I never had a wish which did not terminate in the dearest interests of the nation. I will at the same time imitate the honourable gentleman's candour, and confess, that I too have my ambition. High situation, and great influence, are desirable objects to most men, and objects which I am not ashamed to pursue, which I am even solicitous to possess, whenever they can be acquired with honour, and retained with dignity. On these respectable conditions, I am not less ambitious to be great and powerful than it is natural for a young man, with such brilliant examples before him, to be. But even these objects I am not beneath relinquishing, the moment my duty to my country, my character, and my friends, renders such a sacrifice indispensable. Then I hope to retire, not disappointed, but triumphant; triumphant in the conviction that my talents, humble as they are, have been earnestly, zealously, and strenuously, employed to the best of my apprehension, in promoting the truest welfare of my country; and that, however I may stand chargeable with weakness of understanding, or error of judgement, nothing can be imputed to my official capacity which bears the most distant connection with an interested, a corrupt, or a dishonest intention. But it is not any part of my plan, when the time shall come that I quit my present station, to threaten the repose of my country, and erect, like the honourable gentleman, a fortress and a refuge for disappointed ambition. The self-created and self-appointed successors to the present administration, have asserted with much confidence, that this is likely to be the case. I can assure them, however, when they come from that side of the house to this, I will for one most readily and cordially accept the exchange. The only desire I would indulge and cherish on the subject is, that the service of the public may be ably, disinterestedly, and faithfully performed. To those who feel for their country as I wish to do, and will strive to do, it matters little who are out or in; but it matters much that her affairs be conducted with wisdom, with firmness, with dignity, and with credit. Those entrusted to my care I will resign, let me hope, into hands much better qualified to do them justice than mine. But I will not mimic the parade of the honourable gentleman in avowing an indiscriminate opposition to whoever may be appointed to succeed. I will march out with no warlike, no hostile, no menacing protestations; but hoping the new administration will have no other object in view than the real and substantial welfare of the community at large; that they will bring with them into office those truly public and patriotic principles which they formerly held, but which they abandoned in opposition; that they will save the state, and promote the great purposes of public good, with as much steadiness, integrity, and solid advantage, as I am confident it must one day appear the Earl of Shelburne and his colleagues have done, I promise them, before-hand, my uniform and best support on every occasion, where I can honestly and conscientiously assist them.

In short, Sir, whatever appears dishonourable or inadequate in the peace on your table, is strictly chargeable to the noble lord in the blue ribbon [Lord North], whose profusion of the public's money, whose notorious temerity and obstinacy in prosecuting the war, which originated in his pernicious and oppressive policy, and whose utter incapacity to fill the station he occupied, rendered peace of any description indispensable to the preservation of the state. The small part which fell to my share in this ignominious transaction, was divided with a set of men, whom the dispassionate public must, on reflection, unite to honour. Unused as I am to the factious and jarring clamours of this day's debate, I look up to the independent part of the house, and to the public at large, if not for that impartial approbation which my conduct deserves, at least for that acquittal from blame to why my innocence entitles me. I have ever been most anxious to do my utmost for the interest of my country; it has been my sole concern to act an honest and upright part, and I am disposed to think every instance of my official department will bear a fair and honourable construction. With these intentions, I ventured forward on the public attention; and can appeal with some degree of confidence to both sides of the house, for the consistency of my political conduct. My earliest impressions were in favour of the noblest and most disinterested modes of serving the public; these impressions are still dear, and will, I hope, remain for ever dear to my heart; I will cherish them as a legacy infinitely more valuable than the greatest inheritance. On these principles alone I came into parliament, and into place; and I now take the whole house to witness, that I have not been under the necessity of contradicting one public declaration I have ever made.

I am, notwithstanding, at the disposal of this house, and with their decision, whatever it shall be, I will cheerfully comply. It is impossible to deprive me of those feelings which must always result from the sincerity of my best endeavours to fulfil with integrity every official engagement. You may take from me, Sir, the privileges and emoluments of place, but you cannot, and you shall not, take from me those habitual and warm regards for the prosperity of Great Britain, which constitute the honour, the happiness, the pride of my life; and which, I trust, death alone can extinguish. And, with this consolation, the loss of power, Sir, and the loss of fortune, though I affect not to despise them, I hope I soon shall be able to forget.

SOURCE: W. S. Hathaway (ed.), *The Speeches of the Right Honourable William Pitt, in the House of Commons*, Vol. I (3rd edn, London, 1817), pp. 24–38.

Appendix II

Speech of Charles James Fox on 10 June 1806

ABOLITION OF THE SLAVE TRADE
HC Deb 10 June 1806 vol 7 cc580–603

MR. SECRETARY FOX rose, in pursuance of the notice he had given, to submit to the house a Resolution on this subject, and spoke as follows:— Before, sir, I proceed to state the grounds on which I look with confidence for the almost unanimous countenance of the house in this measure, I feel myself called upon to say a few words by way of apology for being the person to come forward upon the present occasion. For the last sixteen or seventeen years of my life, I have been in the habit of uniformly and strenuously supporting the several motions made by a respectable gentleman [Mr. Wilberforce], who has so often, by his meritorious exertions on this subject, attracted the applause of this house, and claimed the admiration of the public. During the long period that I found it in such excellent hands, it was impossible for me to feel the slightest disposition to take it out of them. I am still of the same opinion; and cannot but think it would have been much better, if the same hon. member and his friends had retained it in their own hands, and they might certainly have depended upon me, and those with whom I have the honour to act, for the same ardent support which we have always uniformly given them. But, sir, the hon. member, and many of his friends, seem so strongly to entertain different sentiments in that respect, from me, that I submitted my own opinion to theirs, and now assume the task, reluctantly, on that account, but on every other, most gladly. So fully am I impressed with the vast importance and necessity of attaining what will be the object of my motion this day, that *if, during the almost forty years that I have now had the honour of a seat in parliament, I had been so fortunate as to accomplish that, and that only, I should think I had done enough, and could retire from public life with comfort, and conscious satisfaction, that I had done my duty.*

Having made these preliminary observations, I now come to the main question, but do not think it necessary to stop at present, for the sake of referring in detail to all the entries on your Journals, made at different periods since the year 1792, the different motions made by the hon. gent., the resolutions of the house, and the bills brought in to abolish the trade, particularly that which received the sanction of this house, though it was unfortunately negatived in another place. I have not lately had time, from other occupations, to prepare myself to refer minutely to dates and details; and must, therefore, content myself with a general reference, in which, should I fall into any mistake, I am sure there are gentlemen who will be certain to set me right. In the execution of this duty, I am happy to reflect, that whatever difference of opinion might have prevailed upon some points, of this subject, between a few members, and, at one time, unhappily, so as to defeat the measure, the opinion of this house upon the subject was, I will not say uniform, for in that I may be contradicted, but as nearly unanimous as any thing of the kind could be, 'That the Slave Trade is contrary to the principles of justice, policy, and humanity.' These, I believe, were the words of the resolution, adopted after long and serious deliberation; and they are those which I mean to submit for the resolution I shall propose this day. Surely, sir, it does not remain yet to be argued, that to carry men by violence away to slavery, in distant countries, to use the expression of an illustrious man, now no more [Mr. Burke], a man distinguished in every way, and in nothing more, than for his great humanity, 'is not a traffic in the labour of man, but in the man himself.' I will not now enter, for it would be unnecessary, into that exploded argument, that we did not make the negroes slaves, but found them already in that state, and condemned to it for crimes. The nature of the crimes themselves [witchcraft in general] is a manifest pretext, and a mockery of all human reason. But, supposing them even to be real crimes, and such as men should be condemned for, can there be any thing more degrading to sense, or disgusting to humanity, than to think it honourable or justifiable in Great Britain, to send out ships annually to assist in the purposes of African police? It has, I am told, been asserted by an authority in the other house of parliament, that the trade is in itself so good a one, that if it was not found already subsisting, it would be right to create it. I certainly will not compare the authority just alluded to with that of my hon. friend [Mr. Wilberforce], who, in the efforts he has used in order to abolish this dishonourable traffic, as well as in all his other pursuits, has always done himself so much honour. I will not compare that authority with that of a right hon. gent. now no more [Mr. Pitt], whose talents have always so justly been entitled to admiration, and whose eloquence was never more powerfully displayed on any occasion, than in opposition to this trade. I will not compare it with that of a noble lord [Sidmouth], one of your predecessors, but not your immediate one, in that chair, who though he opposed the manner in which we wished to obtain an abolition, yet as to the principle, no man ever enforced more strongly, or with more feeling, his utter detestation of it. Another noble lord also [lord Melville], who took a lead in constantly opposing our attempts at a total and immediate abolition; yet, in regard to the principle, when he prevailed in his measure of gradual abolition, recorded his opinion on the Journals, by moving, that the house considered the Slave Trade to be adverse to policy, humanity, and justice.

I do not, therefore, suppose, that there can be above one, or perhaps two members in the house, who can object to a condemnation of the nature of the trade, and shall now proceed to recall the attention of the house to what has been its uniform, consistent, and unchangeable opinion for the last 18 years, during which we should blush to have it stated, that not one step has yet been taken towards the Abolition of the Trade. If, then, we have never ceased to express our reprobation, surely the house must think itself bound by its character, and the consistency of its proceedings, to condemn it now. The first time this measure was proposed, on the motion of my hon. friend, which was in the year 1791, it was, after a long and warm discussion, rejected. In the following year,

1792, after the question had been, during the interval, better considered, there appeared to be a very strong disposition, generally, to adopt it to the full; but in the committee, the question for a gradual abolition was carried. On that occasion, wh [...] the most strenuous efforts were made to specify the time when the total abolition should take place, there were sev[eral divi]sions in the house about the number of years, and lord Melville, who was the leader and proposer of the gradual abolition, could not venture to push the period longer than eight years, or 1800, when it was to be totally abolished. Yet we are now in the year 1806, and while surrounding nations are reproaching us with neglect, not a single step has been taken towards this just, humane, and politic measure. When the question for a gradual abolition was carried, there was no one could suppose that the trade would last so long; and in the mean time we have suffered other nations to take the lead of us. Denmark, much to its honour, has abolished the trade; or, if it could not abolish it altogether, it has at least done all it could, for it has prohibited its being carried on in Danish ships, or by Danish sailors. I own, that when I began to con-sider the subject, early in the present session, my opinion was, that the total abolition of the whole might be carried this year; but subsequent business intervened, in the discussions of the military plan; besides which there was an abolition going forward in the foreign trade, from our colonies, and it was thought right to carry that measure through, before we proceeded to the other. That bill has now passed into a law, and so far we have already succeeded; but it was then too late to carry it through the other house. In this house, from a regard to the consistency of its own proceeding, we could indeed expect no great resistance; but the impediments that may be opposed to it in another, would not leave sufficient time to accomplish it. No alternative is therefore now left, but to let it pass over for the present session; and it is to afford no ground for a suspicion that we have abandoned it altogether, that we have recourse to the measure that I am now about to propose. The Motion will not mention any limitation, either as to the time or manner of abolishing the trade. There have been some hints indeed entertained, and thrown out in some quarters, that it would be a better measure, to adopt some-thing that must inevitably lead to an abolition; but after 18 years of close attention which I have paid to the subject, I cannot think any thing so effectual as a direct law for that purpose.

The next point is, as to the time when the abolition should take place; for the same reasons or objections which led to the gradual measure of 1792, may here occur again. That also I leave open; but I have no hesitation to state, that with respect to that, my opinion is the same as it is with regard to the manner, and that I think it ought to be abolished immediately. The motion, therefore, which I have to make, leaving to the house the time and manner of abolition, I cannot but confidently express my hopes and confident expectation, that it will be unanimously carried; and I implore gentlemen not to listen to that sort of flattery which they have sometimes heard [and particularly from one of the members for Liverpool], that they have abolished it already. When the regulations were adopted, for the space to be allowed for each negro in a slave ship, the same gentleman opposed it as being destructive, and exclaimed, 'Oh! if you do that, you may as well abolish it at once, for it cannot be done.' Yet, when we propose an abolition altogether, they use, as arguments against us, the great good already done, by regulating the slave ships, and bettering the condition of negroes in the colonies. In the same way, when we first proposed the abolition of the foreign trade, they told us it would have the effect of a general and total abolition; and I beg of them not to forget that declaration now; and having made it once, I must use to them a phrase in common life, 'sir, if that be the case, I must pray you to put your hand to it.' As to the stale argument of the ruin it would bring upon the West India islands, I would refer gentlemen to perhaps the most brilliant and convincing speech that ever was, I believe, delivered in this or any other place, by a consummate master of eloquence [Mr. Burke], and of which, I believe, there remains in some publications a report that will convey an inadequate idea of the substance, though it would be impossible to represent, the manner; the voice, the gesture, the manner, were not to be described.—'O! si illum vidisse, si illum audivisse!' If all the members of this house could but have seen and heard the great orator in the delivery of that speech, on that day, there would not now be one who could for a moment longer suppose that the abolition of the slave trade could injuriously affect the interests of the West India colonies. I am aware that a calculation was once made, and pretty generally circulated, by which it would appear, that were the importation of negroes into the islands put an end to, the stock of slaves could not be kept up; and if I recollect right, the calculation was made with reference to the island of Jamaica. Fortunately, however, for our argument, the experiment has been already tried in North America, where the trade was abolished; and the effect of it shewed, that the population of the negroes was nearly equal to that of the whites. As that is the part of the world where population proceeds more rapidly than in any other, and as we know that within the last 20 years, the population of whites has doubled, and that of negroes very nearly so, without importation; it affords, I will not say a damning, but a blessing proof, that our adopting a similar course would ultimately produce the happy effect of a gradual emancipation, of increasing population, of enabling negroes to acquire property as the reward of long servitude; and thus place these islands in a state of safety beyond any thing that could be done by fleets or armies.

Nothing now remains for me, sir, but to address a few words to those members opposite me, who are so fond of quoting the opinions of a right hon. gent. deceased [Mr. Pitt], and profess to entertain so profound a respect for his memory. They all know that there was no subject on which that right hon. gent. displayed his extraordinary eloquence with more ardour than in support of the Abolition of the Slave Trade. His speeches on that subject will not easily be forgotten; and, therefore, in supporting the present motion, they would not only have an opportunity of manifesting their private friendship for him, their admiration of his splendid talents, and the sincerity of their zeal and respect for his character and memory; but also the opportunity of quoting him with great advantage: added to which, they may now display all this for the public good, and on a subject upon which they cannot be suspected of making that respect and admiration, only a vehicle for party purposes.

Mr. Fox then moved the following resolution: 'That this house, conceiving the African Slave Trade to be contrary to the principles of justice, humanity, and sound policy, will, with all practicable expedition, proceed to take effectual measures for abolishing the said trade, in such manner, and at such period, as may be deemed advisable.'

The motion was opposed by General Tarleton, Mr. Gascoyne, Lord Castlereagh, Sir William Young, Mr. Rose, and Mr. Manning; and supported by Sir Ralph Milbanke, Mr. Francis, Sir Samuel Romilly, the Solicitor-General, Mr. Wilberforce, Lord Henry Petty, Mr. Barham, Sir John Newport, Mr. Canning, Mr. William Smith, and Mr. Windham.

The House divided on Mr. Fox's motion:*

	Tellers			Tellers	
YEAS	Sir S. Romilly / Mr. W. Smith	114	NOES	Sir Wm. Young / Gen. Tarleton	15

SOURCE: *The Speeches of the Right Honourable Charles James Fox in the House of Commons* (1815), vol. 6, pp. 658–64.

* This was the last motion made by Mr. Fox in the House of Commons. About the middle of June, he became so seriously indisposed, that he was forced to discontinue his attendance in parliament. Symptoms of both general and local dropsy declared themselves, and so rapid was the progress of his complaint, that after the middle of July, though informed of every step taken by his colleagues in the negociations [*sic*] with France, he could seldom be consulted by them on that or any other public measures till they had been carried into effect. It was at length thought necessary by his physicians to have recourse to the usual operation for his relief, which was accordingly performed for the first time on the 7th of August, and repeated on the 31st. After both operations, he fell into a state of languor and depression, but his medical attendants never absolutely despaired of his case till Monday, the 7th of September, when he sunk into an alarming state of lowness, in which he languished till the evening of Saturday, the 13th, when he expired in the arms of his nephew, Lord Holland, in the fifty-ninth year of his age. [D.L.: It was, in fact, his 58th year.]

Index

and George III 59, 84, 92, 95,
96, 97, 117, 121, 165, 211–13,
216, 219, 220, 230–1, 233, 234,
237–8, 240, 241, 245, 273
ill-health 45–6, 208, 229, 249–51
and Ireland 207–9
legacy of 264–75
MP for Appleby 3, 51–2, 145, 188
maiden speech 54–5
opposition to Addington 229–35
personal finances 50, 124, 135,
227, 252
personality of 53–4, 134–5, 195,
196–7
Regency crisis 149–60
'Reign of Terror' 174–6, 177–9,
181–4, 187, 198–9, 205, 271
resignation 217–220
returns to office 236–9
and slave trade 144, 302, 305
war leader 181–2, 186, 201, 214,
236–7, 246–50, 272
Portland, 3rd Duke of 80, 84, 97,
100, 101, 107, 108, 130, 152, 168,
175, 177, 191, 192, 210, 212, 219,
220, 221, 238, 253, 262, 267, 272
Pratt, John (1st Earl Camden) 117
Pratt, John (2nd Lord Camden) 49,
114, 205, 208
Pretyman, George (later Sir George
Pretyman Tomline) 49, 119,
168, 200, 244–5, 251, 269
Price, Dr Richard 99–100, 137, 138
Priestley, Joseph 187
Pulteney, William 10
Pye, Henry 204–5
Pynsent, Sir William 30

Reilly, Robin 165
Richmond, 2nd Duke of 10, 31–2
Richmond, 3rd Duke of 81, 87, 92,
118
Robinson, John 90, 108, 109, 221
Robinson, Mary ('Perdita') 88–9
Robinson, Sir Thomas 11, 19
Rockingham, 2nd Marquess 25, 56,
64, 68, 69, 70, 72, 73, 74, 76,
80, 81, 82–3, 84, 85, 86, 90, 99,
100, 118, 122, 201, 254
Rodney, Admiral 23, 77, 79, 129
Rose, George 139, 220, 229, 230
Rosebery, Lord 45, 141, 269
Russell, Lord John 266
Rutland, 4th Duke of 49, 51, 103, 117
Ryder, Dudley (later Lord
Harrowby) 207, 240, 248, 251

St Albans Tavern 123, 125
St Vincent, Lord 241
Sandwich, Earl of 57, 72, 100
Scott, Sir Walter 263
Selwyn, Sir George 204
Seven Years' War 20–3, 35, 62–3,
71, 78, 247
Shelburne, Lord 68, 72, 73, 76,
80–1, 83, 84–5, 86–7, 89, 90,
91, 92–3, 94–5, 96, 100, 102,
106, 107, 109, 114, 117, 118, 122,
136, 137, 162, 207, 296, 298
Sheridan, Richard Brinsley 7, 8, 88,
93–4, 150, 156, 171, 203, 221,
223, 254, 266
sinking fund 137–8, 140, 199
slave trade xiii, xiv, 143–4, 176, 226,
243, 255, 300–6